MICHAEL JACKSON'S
POCKET BEER BOOK

MITCHELL BEAZLEY

Key to symbols

This book attempts to review not only the principal names in each
important brewing region but also a selection of especially
interesting smaller houses. Star ratings are intended merely as a
guide, and assess beers against others from the same country.

    * Typical of its country and style
   ** Above average
 *** Worth seeking out
**** World Classic
  ☎ Telephone

Dedication

To my late father, Jack Jackson,
born Isaac Jakowitz, Yorkshire, 1909–84.

Acknowledgments

Brewers and importers of beer all over the world, and their trade
organizations, have gone to trouble and expense far beyond their
self-interest to help me research this book. My heartfelt thanks to all
of them. Many friends and professional colleagues have also helped,
and I owe a special debt of gratitude to Johannes Schulters, of
Bamberg, Germany; Antoine Denooze, of the Hopduvel, Ghent,
Belgium; Denis Palmer, of Anglo-Dutch Ales, and Henk Eggens, of
Café Gollem, Amsterdam, The Netherlands; Brian Glover and
Danny Blyth, of the Campaign for Real Ale, in Britain; Elisabeth
Baker, at The Grist; friends at CAMRA Canada and the Canadian
Amateur Brewers' Association; Alan Dikty, of The New Brewer;
Charlie Papazian and friends, at the American Homebrewers'
Association, in Boulder, Colorado; and – especially – Vince Cottone,
of Seattle; and to friends at Suntory, in Tokyo and Osaka, Japan.

Editor Alison Franks
Designer Jill Raphaeline
Proofreader and Indexer Rosamond Cocks
Research Assistant Sonia Abeliuk
Production Androulla Pavlou

Senior Editor Dian Taylor
Senior Executive Editor Chris Foulkes
Senior Executive Art Editor Roger Walton

Michael Jackson's Pocket Beer Book
Edited and designed by
Mitchell Beazley International Ltd., Artists House,
14–15 Manette Street, London W1V 5LB
Copyright © Mitchell Beazley Publishers 1986
Text copyright © Michael Jackson 1986
Maps and illustrations copyright
© Mitchell Beazley Publishers 1986
All rights reserved

ISBN 0 85533 556 4

Maps and Illustrations Jill Raphaeline
Photographs Ian Howes (top, page 27)
All other photographs Mima Richardson
Jacket photograph Jon Stewart

Filmsetting by Vantage Photosetting Co. Ltd., Eastleigh, England
Reproduction by Gilchrist Bros. Ltd., Leeds, England
Printed in Hong Kong by Mandarin Offset International (H.K.) Ltd

CONTENTS

INTRODUCTION

THE NEW APPRECIATION OF BEER

The *hauteur* that rightly attends wine has for too long overshadowed beer, but that is changing. It is increasingly being appreciated that the two are companions of honour as the principal types of fermented drink: part of the gastronomic heritage of the warm and cool climates that grow the grape and the grain respectively.

The spread in travel and leisure has made for a more universal interest in wine, and the same is true in respect of beer. There is an international wave of serious interest in beer, from Italy (where it is the most chic of drinks), through Germany and Belgium (where speciality styles are in ever-greater demand) to Britain (first came the "real ale" renaissance; now the surge of "foreign" lagers) and to the United States (where imported beers arrive in bewildering profusion). In all of these countries, there has also been in recent years a blessing of new, tiny *boutique* or *micro* breweries, often producing speciality styles of beer.

Most varieties of wine are understood outside their regions of production, but the stylistic diversity of beer is only now beginning to confront the consumer. From the Pilseners, Mucheners and Dortmunders to the different wheat beers of north and south Germany, to the spontaneously fermenting specialities and Trappist monastery ales of Belgium, to the ales of England and Scotland, the sweet and dry stouts of the British Isles, there are between 20 and 30 classic styles of beer, and yet more sub-categories.

Just as a Chablis or a champagne, a claret or a Zinfandel, each has a different purpose in life, so does each style of beer. An everyday, mass-market lager might do nothing more ambitious than quench the thirst, but some styles of beer are best served as aperitifs, others as digestifs; this with crustaceans, that with red meat; one as a restorative, another in a moment of reflection, a third as a nightcap.

An intensely dry aperitif beer will not necessarily quench the thirst. Nor will a big, warming brew. A tart, quenching beer may not be the one to sip in front of an open fire. The wrong beer for the occasion will at best disappoint and at worst confuse. The same is true if the beer is not served in the manner, or at the temperature, at which it best expresses its qualities of aroma, palate and character.

Whether the beer-fancier carries out his (or her)

explorations in the local pub or restaurant, or by trains and boats and planes, this Pocket Guide may be of assistance.

WHAT MAKES A GREAT BEER

Wine is more vulnerable to the mercies of soil and weather, but beer is the more complicated drink to make. The barley must first be malted and made into an infusion or decoction, the enigmatic (and none too hardy) hop added as a seasoning, and the whole brewed before it can be fermented, matured and conditioned.

In carrying out these procedures, the brewer is seeking to impart (in aroma, palate and finish) his own balance between the sweetness of the barley malt, the herby dryness of the hop, and the background fruitiness of the yeast used in fermentation. These characteristics are immediately evident in a fresh beer, especially one that has not been pasteurized (this process, unless it is carried out with the greatest of care, may merely deaden the beer to the ravages of travel and time).

The balance will be weighted differently according to the style of the beer, but it must always be achieved. A chef may intend one dish to be delicate, another to be robust, but each must have its own balance. After balance comes complexity. A winemaker knows that each style is expected to have certain features, but beyond those there should be the individuality of its own character. Each time the drinker raises a glass of fine wine, new dimensions of aroma and palate should become apparent. So it is with a fine beer.

Any fine food or drink is enjoyed with the eyes and nose as well as the palate. The more individualistic beers, especially of the darker styles, can have a great subtlety of colour; most styles will present a dense, uneven "rocky" head if they have been naturally carbonated in fermentation, rather than having been injected with carbon dioxide; a properly carbonated beer will leave "Brussels lace" down the sides of the glass after each swallow. A good beer should be poured gently down the side of a tilted glass. A final, upright, flourish may contribute to its appearance, but the formation of a good head should not rest on the beers being dumped violently into the glass.

Conventional beers are intended to be clear though excessive refrigeration can cause a "chill haze" in a good-quality, all-malt brew. The haze should subside once the beer reaches about 7°C (45°F). Conventional beers are also at risk of general deterioration (though they will not necessarily succumb to it) from the moment they leave the brewery. They are intended for immediate drinking, and not for keeping.

Brews indicated to be conditioned in the cask or bottle will contain living yeast. Unless the beer is poured carefully, the palate will have a "yeast bite", but the sediment is not harmful (in fact, its health benefits are quickly apparent). Very strong bottle-conditioned brews will improve with age.

Bottle-conditioned ales naturally have a very fruity aroma. In any beer, an unpleasant aroma reminiscent of damp paper or cardboard indicates oxidation (quite simply, the beer has gone stale). A cabbagey or skunky aroma means that the beer has been damaged by supermarket lighting or by being left in the sun. Beer is a natural product, and does not enjoy rough treatment.

Strength

This is not a measure of quality. The ideal strength for a beer depends upon the purpose for which it is intended. A beer that is meant to be quenching, and to be consumed in quantity, should not be high in alcohol. The classic example, the *Berliner Weisse* style, has around 3 percent alcohol by volume. A typical premium beer, whether in Germany, Britain or the United States, might have between 4 and 5 percent by volume. A strong "winter warmer" may typically have between 6 and 8 percent. Although there are specialities exceeding 13 percent, beers of this strength are hard to brew, and to drink in any quantity. At these levels, alcohol stuns beer yeasts to a point where they can no longer work, and the residual sugars make for heavy, cloying brews. There are, of course, wines of this strength, but they are not drunk by the half-pint.

Alcohol by volume is the system most commonly used to describe the strength of wine, and it is the simplest rating to understand. However, this system is rarely employed in respect of beer. The Canadians use it, but American brewers usually quote alcohol by weight. Since water is heavier than alcohol, this produces lower figures. In many countries, a measure of alcohol content is not required by law. In those countries, the authorities are more concerned to tax what goes into the beer: the malt, wheat or other fermentable sugars. This is variously described as density or original gravity. Each of the older brewing nations developed its own scale for measuring this, the German Plato and similar Czechoslovakian Balling systems being the most commonly used. In those countries, drinkers are inclined to be less familiar with alcohol content than with gravity.

The two do not have a direct relationship, since

alcohol content is also a function of the degree of fermentation. The more thorough the fermentation, the higher the level of alcohol produced from a given gravity. The less thorough the fermentation, the fuller the body. Alcohol content and body are quite different, and in this respect opposed, elements of a beer.

The Malts

As grapes are to wine, so barley malt is to beer the classic source of fermentable sugars. The barley is malted (steeped in water until it partially germinates, then dried in a kiln) to release the starches that are then turned into fermentable sugars by infusion or decoction in water in a mashing vessel. This process is parallel to that carried out in the first stages of production of malt whiskies.

In addition to deciding the proportion of malts to be used to achieve the desired density, the brewer is also concerned with their origin.

Certain varieties of barley are grown especially to be malted for the brewing industry. Among them, those that are grown in summer are held to produce cleaner-tasting, sweeter malts, though there is some debate on this. Some brewers also feel that inland, "continental" barleys produce better results than those grown in maritime climates. With varying harvests, there are differences in the quality and availability of barley, and the brewer has to account for this in the fine detail of his mashing procedure, its durations and temperatures. He will also adjust these according to the precise character he is seeking in his beer. They are among the hundreds of variables, and thousands of permutations, that contribute to the final character of every beer.

The traditional malting barleys are of varieties that have two rows of grain in each ear. Six-rowed barley is also used, though it produces a huskier, sharper character in the beer. Traditionalists stick to two-row barley but some brewers claim to seek the character they find in six-row varieties.

To the consumer, the more immediately obvious influence is the way in which the barley has been malted. There are many different standard malting specifications, each intended to produce a different result in terms of both colour and palate. As to colour, the more intense the kilning of the malt, the darker the beer. In palate, the character of the barley and the way in which it is malted can impart tones that are reminiscent, for example, of nuts, caramel, chocolate, espresso or licorice. These variations in malting differ in the moisture of the grains at the time of the kilning, as well as in the cycles of temperature and duration.

Depending upon the style of beer being produced, the brewer may use only one or two different types of malt, or as many as seven or eight. He may also use a proportion of unmalted barley, sometimes highly roasted, as in the case of dry stouts like Guinness. German and Belgian *Weisse* beers are made with a proportion of malted wheat. So, naturally enough, are *Weizen* beers (it means wheat, after all). Belgian *lambic* beers use a proportion of unmalted wheat. One or two highly specialized beers use a small quantity of oats. Less traditional grains include proportions of rice and corn, both used to lighten beers, and the latter especially for its low cost. Also for reasons of cost, and to boost alcohol in inexpensive strong beers like American malt liquors, cane sugar may be used. In Belgium, candy sugar is used in strong Trappist monastery beers. In Britain, milk sugars are used in sweet stouts.

In a cheap beer, barley malt may represent 60 percent of the mash, and corn or other adjuncts the rest. In Bavaria, barley malt and wheat are the only fermentable materials allowed. Elsewhere in West Germany, the same goes for domestic beers but not for exports. One or two other countries have similar laws, the closest being those of Norway and Greece.

The Hops

Early wine-makers lacked the knowledge to produce by fermentation alone products of the quality they sought, so they employed seasonings of herbs and spices, creating the forerunners of today's vermouths and of patent aperitifs like Campari. Distillers, faced with similar difficulties, used a spicing of juniper and coriander to dry the palate of their product, thus creating gin. Liqueurs like Chartreuse have a similar history of development. In the same tradition, early brewers used tree-barks, herbs and berries.

Juniper and coriander are still used in a handful of highly specialized beers, but the hop eventually became the normal choice. The hop is a climbing plant, a vine, that is a member of the same family as cannabis. In ancient times, its shoots were eaten as a salad, and in Belgium they still are. Its cone-like blossoms can have a sedative effect, and are used in hop pillows. The cones also produce tannins that help clarify and preserve beer, and resins and essential oils that are the principal sources of aroma and dryness.

Not to mince words, this is not so much a dryness as a bitterness, a quality that is greatly enjoyed by connoisseurs of good beer, but one that seems to frighten less devoted drinkers. Perhaps it is the negative connotations of the word "bitter". People who enjoy a Campari before dinner, or a coffee afterwards, complain that beer is too "bitter". Of course it is bitter; that is why the hops are there. That is why the British ask for "a pint of bitter". That is why some beers are such marvellous aperitifs; their bitterness arouses the gastric juices. Contrary to some opinions, there is also much more than bitterness to the hop; it has a tangle of fresh, earthy, arousing flavours that blossom like a herb garden. It is too adult a taste for people who have not yet grown out of doughnuts and Coca-Cola.

Since all hops contain elements of both bitterness and aroma, the same variety may be used for both purposes, but this is not generally done. Each variety of hop is usually identified as being ideal either for bitterness or aroma. A brewer may, indeed, use just one variety, but he is more likely to use two or three, occasionally even seven or eight. He may put hops into the kettle once, twice or three times. The early additions are to provide bitterness, the later ones to confer aroma. To heighten aroma, he may even add blossoms to the hop strainer, or to the conditioning vessel. This last technique is known as "dry hopping". At each addition, he may use only one variety, or a different blend of several. He may use hop oils or extracts, or the whole blossom, in its natural form or compacted into pellets.

There are many varieties of bittering hop, but few that enjoy special renown. Aroma hops are the aristocrats.

In continental Europe, the classic is the Saaz hop, grown in the area around the small town of Žatec, in Bohemia, Czechoslovakia. In Germany, considerable reputations are enjoyed by the Hallertau Mittelfrüh and Tettnang aroma hops, named after areas near Munich and Lake Constance respectively.

In Britain, the delightfully named Fuggles are often used for their gentle, rounded, bitterness, though they are also regarded as aroma hops. The counties of Hereford and Kent are known for their hops, and the latter especially for a slightly more bitter and hugely aromatic variety called Goldings. These are at their finest in east Kent, near Faversham, allegedly in a strip of countryside a mile wide.

In North America, the Cascade is the classic aroma hop, grown especially in the Yakima Valley of Washington State. There are hop-growing areas in British Columbia, Canada, too, and in not dissimilar latitudes of the southern hemisphere, in Tasmania.

The Yeast
Among wines, it might be argued – perhaps simplistically – that there is a central division along lines of colour, between the reds and the whites. Among beers

such a division concerns not colour but the type of yeast used.

For centuries, all brewing employed what we now know as top-fermenting, or "ale", yeasts. In those days yeast was barely understood, except as the foam which, when scooped from the top of one brew, acted as a "starter" for the fementation of the next. In this primitive method of brewing, the yeasts naturally rose to the top of the vessel, and were able to cross-breed with wild micro-organisms in the atmosphere. In the summer, they did so to a degree where beer spoilage made brewing impossible.

Brewers in the Bavarian Alps first discovered, empirically, that beer stabilized if it was stored (in German, *lagered*) in icy, mountain caves during the summer. Not only was it less vulnerable to cross-breeding; the yeast sank to the bottom of the vessel, out of harm's way. As scientists began to understand the behaviour of yeast in the 19th century, "bottom-fermenting" strains were methodically bred.

Today, all of the older brewing styles – ales, porters, stouts, German *Altbier* and *Kölsch* and all wheat beers – are (or should be) made with top-fermenting yeasts. All of the *lager* styles – Pilseners, Muncheners, Dortmunders, *Märzen*, Bock and double Bock and American malt liquors – are made with bottom-fermenting yeasts.

"Top" yeasts ferment at warm temperatures (classically 15–25°C/59–77°F), after which the beer may be matured for only a few days, or a couple of weeks, at warm temperatures. With modern means of temperature control, brewing in summer no longer poses a problem. A beer that has been "warm conditioned" will most fully express its palate if it is served at a natural cellar temperature, ideally not less than 12°C (55°F). This is why a well-run British pub will serve ales at such a temperature. British ale can be rendered worthless by refrigeration.

"Bottom" yeasts ferment at cooler temperatures (classically 5–12°C/41–54°F), and the beer is then matured by being stored (*lagered*) at around 0°C (32°F). Many mass-market beers are lagered for barely three weeks. Even in Germany, many brewers are content with four weeks, but traditionalists argue for three months. Bottom-fermenting beers taste best if they are chilled to between 7°C (45°F) and 10°C (50°F), the lighter their body, the lower the temperature and vice-versa.

In both techniques, very strong ales and lagers are matured for longer periods, sometimes for nine, or even 12, months. For whatever duration, this is a period in which the remaining yeast settles, harsh flavour compounds mellow out, and the beer gains its natural texture and carbonation (its "condition").

In top-fermenting ales that have a short period of maturation, the yeast may be settled with the aid of finings, usually isinglass. In Britain the classic ales are delivered to the pub with some working yeast still in the cask, so that they may reach the prime of condition in the cellar. This is known as *cask-conditioning*. Some speciality ales are bottled without filtration, or with an added dosage of yeast, as in the *méthode champenoise*. This is known as *bottle-conditioning*.

Because they pre-date the true understanding of yeasts, some top-fermenting strains are hybrids. Others have picked up some "house character" from the micro-organisms resident in the brewery. Some brewers of top-fermenting specialities intentionally use a blend of yeast, or employ different strains at different stages. Many, of course, use single-cell pure cultures, as do almost all brewers of bottom-fermenting beers. Bottom-fermentation has its origins in a more methodical, scientific, approach to brewing.

Beers made with top-fermenting yeasts are inclined to have more individualistic and expressive palates, often with elements of fruitiness and acidity. Bottom-fermenting beers tend to be cleaner and rounder but the trade-off is that they may be less individualistic.

The Water

Claims about the water used in brewing were probably the most common feature of beer advertizing in the Victorian and Edwardian periods, and they are still to be heard.

In the 18th and 19th centuries, sources of pure water were not always easy to find. That is why towns or cities with good sources — among them, Pilsen and Munich in continental Europe; Burton and Tadcaster in England — became centres of brewing.

Even today, a source of water that requires little or no treatment is an asset to a brewery. A great many breweries have their own springs or wells (this may not be the rule, but it is by no means the exception). In a good few instances, the town supply is adequate once the chlorine has been removed. Only in isolated cases is a water supply a problem. There is at least one island brewery that has to de-salinate sea water, and one in New Orleans has been known to truck in water, but they certainly are exceptions.

Even if the water does come from the brewery's own spring or well, natural salts may have to be added or removed for the production of different types of beer.

"It's the water!" boast some breweries. "It's the beer!" would be a more convincing claim.

THE LANGUAGE OF THE LABEL

Ale The English-language term for a brew made with a top-fermenting yeast, which should impart to it a distinctive fruitiness. Ales are produced to a wide variety of colours, palates and strengths (see also Bitter, Brown Ale, India Pale Ale, Light Ale, Mild, Old Ale, Scotch Ale, etc). Only in some American states is the term determined by law (wrongly) to indicate a brew of more than 4 percent weight (5 by volume).

Altbier A German term for a top-fermenting brew. The classic examples, copper in colour, mashed only from barley malt, fermented from a single-cell yeast and cold-conditioned, with an alcohol content of 4.5–4.7 by volume, are made in Düsseldorf.

Barley Wine An English term for an extra-strong ale (implied to be as potent as wine). Usually more than 6 percent by volume, and classically closer to 11. Most often bottled. Copper-coloured, tawny or dark brown.

"Beer" Often misunderstood by Americans to apply only to products that are, in fact, exclusively of the lager type. The British, on the other hand, are inclined to think that the only true beer is ale. Both lager and ale – as well as porter, stout, and all the Belgian and German specialities – are embraced by the general term "beer". It is all beer.

Berliner Weisse Berlin's classic "white" (cloudy), sedimented, top-fermenting wheat beer, with the quenching sourness of a lactic fermentation, the sparkle of a high carbonation, and a low alcohol content of around 3 percent by volume.

Bière de Garde French term originally applied to strong, copper-coloured, top-fermenting brews, bottle-conditioned for laying down. Today's examples have an alcohol content in the range of 5.5–6 by volume, and may be bottom-fermented and filtered.

Bitter English term for a well-hopped ale, most often on draught. Although examples vary widely, the name implies a depth of hop bitterness. There is usually some acidity in the finish, and colour varies from bronze to deep copper. Basic bitters usually have an alcohol content of around 3.75–4 percent by volume, "Best" or "Special" bitters come in at 4–4.75; the odd "Extra Special" at about 5.5.

Bo(c)k The German term for a strong beer. If unqualified, it indicates a bottom-fermenting brew from barley malt. In Germany, a bock beer has more than 6.25 percent alcohol by volume, and may be golden, tawny or dark brown. Outside Germany, strengths vary, and a bock is usually dark. Bock beers are served in autumn, late winter or spring, depending upon the country. (See also Maibock, Doppelbock, Weizenbier.)

Brown Ale In the south of England, a dark-brown ale, sweet in palate, low in alcohol (3–3.5 by volume). In the northeast, a reddish-brown ale, drier, of 4.4–5. The slightly sour, brown brews of Flanders are also ales, though they do not generally use the designation.

Cream Ale An American designation, implying a very pale, mild, light-bodied ale that may actually have been blended with a lager. Around 4.75 by volume.

"Dark beer" There are many, quite unrelated, styles of dark brew. If this vague term is used without qualification, it usually means a dark lager of the Munich type.

Diät Pils Nothing to do with slimming, but originally intended for diabetics. A German style so popular in Britain that many drinkers think there is no other kind of "Pils". Carbohydrates are diminished by a very thorough fermentation, creating a relatively high content of alcohol (about 6 percent by volume) and therefore lots of calories. In German law, the alcohol now has to be reduced back to a normal Pilsener level (5 percent).

Doppelbock "Double" bock. German extra-strong bottom-fermenting beer, tawny or dark brown. Around 7.5 by volume or stronger. Southern speciality, seasonal to March and April. Names usually end in *-ator*.

Dort Abbreviation used in Belgium and The Netherlands to indicate a beer in the Dortmunder Export style.

Dortmunder This indicates merely a beer brewed in Dortmund, but the city's classic style is Export (see separate entry).

Dunkel German word for "dark".

Eisbock An extra-strong (*Doppel*) bock beer in which potency has been heightened by a process of freezing. Because water freezes before alcohol, the removal of ice (*eis*) concentrates the beer.

Export In Germany, a pale, Dortmund-style bottom-fermenting beer that is bigger in body than a Pilsener, and less dry, but not as sweet as a Munich pale beer. It is stronger than either, at 5.25–5.5 by volume. Elsewhere, Export usually indicates a premium beer.

Faro Brussels' local style, a sweetened version of a *lambic*. 4.5–5.5 by volume.

Festbier In Germany, any beer made for a festival. Styles vary, but such beers are usually above average strength, often around 5.5–6 by volume.

Framboise A raspberry-macerated *lambic*. 5.5–6.

Gueuze A blend of old and young *lambic* beers. Around 5.5.

Hefe- The German word for yeast, indicating that a beer is bottle-conditioned and sedimented.

Hell German word for "pale", indicating an everyday beer that is golden in colour. Ordered as a *Helles* (*hell-es*).

Imperial Stout See **Stout**.

India Pale Ale A reminder of the days when the Indian Empire was supplied with ales (high in gravity, and well hopped, to stand the voyage) by the British. Today, the term implies a super-premium pale ale.

Kellerbier German term indicating an unfiltered lager, in which there is usually a high hop content and a low carbonation. Strengths vary according to the original style.

Kölsch Cologne's distinctive style of golden, top-fermenting brew. 4.3–5 by volume.

Kräusen In German custom, a traditional technique of carbonation is to add a small dosage of unfermented malt sugars (in English, wort) to the conditioning tank. In a normally *kräusened* beer, the wort ferments out and the beer is conventionally filtered. An unfiltered beer based on this technique is known as a *kräusenbier*.

Kriek A cherry-macerated *lambic*. 5.5–6.

Lager Any beer made by bottom-fermentation. In Britain, lagers are usually golden in colour, but in continental Europe they can also be dark. In Germany and The

Netherlands, the term may be used to indicate the most basic beer of the house, the *bière ordinaire*.

Lambic Spontaneously fermenting style of wheat beer unique to Belgium, notably the Senne Valley. About 4.4.

Light Ale English term describing the bottled counterpart of a basic bitter. In Scotland, "Light" indicates the lowest-gravity draught beer (usually dark in colour), neither term implies a low-calorie beer.

Light Beer American term, indicating a watery Pilsener-style beer. 2.75–4 by volume. Calories might better be saved by drinking fewer beers, eating fewer chips, or sticking to honest water.

Maibock A bock beer of super-premium quality. Usually pale. Made for the first of May to celebrate spring.

Malt Liquor Not especially malty, though they are usually low in hop character. Certainly not liquors, though they are usually the strongest beers in an American brewer's range. Malt liquor is the American term for a strong, pale lager, at anything from 5–7.5 by volume, often cheaply made. Regrettably, laws in some states encourage the term to be used on imported strong lagers of far greater character.

Märzen From "March" in German. Originally a beer brewed in March and laid down in caves before the summer weather rendered brewing impossible. Stocks would be drawn upon during the summer, and finally exhausted in October. In Germany, this tradition has come to be associated with one specific style. *Märzenbier* has a malty aroma, and is a medium-strong version (classically, more than 5.5 percent alcohol by volume) of the amber-red Vienna style. It is seasonal to the *Oktoberfest*, where it is offered as a traditional speciality alongside paler beers of a similar strength. Confusingly, in Austria the term refers not to style but to gravity.

Mild English term indicating an ale that is only lightly hopped. Some milds are copper in colour, but most are dark brown. These beers were devised to be drunk in large quantities by manual workers, and have in recent years suffered from their blue-collar image. Around 3 by volume, but often relatively full in body.

Munchener/Münchner Means "Munich-style". In international brewing terminology, this indicates a dark-brown lager, a style that was developed in Munich (although another Bavarian town, Kulmbach, also has a long tradition of – very – dark lagers). In Munich, such a brew is clearly identified by the word *Dunkel* ("dark"), and classic examples have an alcohol content of around, or just over, 5 percent by volume. The brewers of Munich, and Bavaria in general, also impart their own distinctively malty accent to their everyday, lower-gravity (alcohol content around 3.7) pale beers. These are sometimes identified as *Münchner Hell*, to distinguish them from the same brewers' Pilsener-style product.

Oktoberfest beers See **Märzen**.

Old (Ale) In Australia, "Old" simply means a dark ale. In Britain, it is most commonly used to indicate a medium-strong dark ale like Old Peculier, which has just under 6 percent by volume. However, by no means all ales describing themselves as "old" are in this style.

Pale Ale Pale in this instance means copper-coloured, as opposed to dark brown. Pale ale is a term used by some

English brewers to identify their premium bitters, especially in bottled form.

Pilsener/Pilsner/Pils Loosely, any golden-coloured, dry, bottom-fermenting beer of conventional strength might be described as being of this style (in its various spellings and abbreviations), though this most famous designation properly belongs only to a product of "super-premium" quality. Too many brewers take it lightly, in more senses than one. In their all-round interpretation, it is the German brewers who take the style most seriously, inspired by the *Urquell* (original) brew from the town of Pilsen, in the province of Bohemia, Czechoslovakia. A classic Pilsner has a gravity of around 12 Plato (4 percent alcohol by weight; 5 by volume) and is characterized by the hoppiness of its flowery aroma and dry finish.

Porter A London style that became extinct, though it has recently been revived. It was a lighter-bodied companion to stout, and the most accurate revivals are probably the porters made by American micro-brewers like Sierra Nevada. Around 5 percent by volume. In some countries, the porter tradition remains in roasty-tasting dark brews that are bottom-fermented, and often of a greater strength.

Rauchbier Smoked malts are used in the production of this dark, bottom-fermented speciality, principally made in and around Bamberg, Franconia. Produced at around 5 percent by volume and in *Märzen* and *Bock* versions. Serve with Bavarian smoked ham, or bagels and lox.

Saison Seasonal summer style in the French-speaking part of Belgium. A sharply refreshing, faintly sour, top-fermenting brew, often bottle-conditioned, 5.5–8 by volume.

Scotch Ale The ales of Scotland generally have a malt accent. In their home country, a single brewery's products may be identified in ascending order of gravity and strength as Light, Heavy, Export and Strong. Or by a system based on the old currency of shillings, probably once a reference to tax ratings: 60/-, 70/-, 80/-, 90/-. Alcohol content by volume might rise through 3, 4, 4.5 and 7–10. The term "Scotch ale" is sometimes used specifically to identify a very strong, often extremely dark, malt-accented speciality from that country.

Steam Beer A name trademarked by the Anchor Steam Beer brewery of San Francisco. This brewery's principal product is made by a distinctive method of bottom-fermentation at high temperatures and in unusually wide, shallow vessels. This technique, producing a beer with elements of both lager and ale in its character (though also distinctive in its own right), is said to have been common in California when, in the absence of supplies of ice, early brewers tried to make bottom-fermenting beers. Although there are more romantic explanations, the term "Steam" probably derives from the brewery's original source of power. In the days when it represented advanced technology, many breweries proclaimed "Steam" (in Germany, *Dampf-*) in their names, and some still do. In Germany, one brewery has trade-marked a product called *Dampfbier*, but this is not in the Californian style.

Stout An extra-dark, almost black, top-fermenting brew, made with highly roasted malts. *Sweet stout*, an English style, is typified by Mackeson, which has only about 3.75 percent alcohol by volume in its domestic market but more than 5 in the Americas. Sweet stout usually contains milk sugars (lactose), and is a soothing restorative. *Dry stout*, the Irish style, is typified by Guinness, which comes in at around 4 percent in the British Isles, a little more in North America and as much as 8 in tropical countries. Dry stouts sometimes contain roasted unmalted barley. *Imperial Stout*, originally brewed as a winter warmer for sale in the Tsarist Russian Empire, is medium dry and distinguished by its great strength: anything from 7 to more than 10.

Trappist This order of monks has five breweries in Belgium and one in The Netherlands. By law, only they are entitled to use the term Trappist in describing their products. Each of them produces strong (6–9 percent by volume), top-fermenting brews, all characteristically employing candy sugar in the kettle, and always bottle-conditioned. Colour varies from bronze to deep brown. In their daily life, the monks will drink their least-strong product, and may refer to their more potent variations (for religious holidays and commercial sale) as Double and Triple.

Ur-/Urquell "Original"/"-source of", in German. Justifiable when applied to, for example, Einbecker Ur-Bock or Pilsner Urquell, but often more loosely used.

Vienna Amber-red, or only medium-dark, lager. This was the style originally produced in Vienna. Brewers still talk of a "Vienna malt" to indicate a kilning to this amber-red colour, but the beer-style itself is no longer especially associated with the city. Examples include the aptly named Vienna All-Malt Lager, from Milwaukee; the amber Dos Equis, from Mexico; and the classic *Märzen* beers of Munich; among others. Strengths vary.

Weisse/Weissbier, Weizenbier German for "white" beer, implying a pale brew made from wheat. In the north, a special renown is enjoyed by *Berliner Weisse*, a style in its own right (see separate entry). A different style of *Weissbier* is made in the south, with a more conventional alcohol content (usually a little over 5 percent by volume), a higher proportion of wheat (at least 50 percent) and a yeast (again top-fermenting) that produces a tart, fruity, spicy palate, sometimes with notes of cooking apples and cloves. Often, instead of *Weissbier*, the southerners prefer the term *Weizen* (a similar-sounding word but it means, quite simply "wheat"). If the beer is sedimented with yeast, it may be prefixed *Hefe-*. Southern wheat beers are also produced in dark versions (these *Dunkel Weizen* brews have a delicious complex of fruitiness and maltiness), and in Export and Bock strengths. *Weizenbock* is sometimes served as a Christmas beer.

White A term once used in several parts of Europe to describe wheat beers. Apart from those of German-speaking countries, Belgium's Hoegaarden and Leuven white beers are of considerable interest.

Wiesen/Wies'n Among several words that are confusingly similar to the non-German speaker, this one means "meadow". It implies a beer brewed for a carnival or festival (an *Oktoberfest* beer may be described as a Wies'n Märzen) or a rustic speciality (such as Kuppers' unfiltered *Wiess*).

Zwickelbier German term for an unfiltered beer without the distinguishing features of either a *Kellerbier* or a *Kräusenbier*.

1

2

4

3

5

To sharpen the appetite . . . a dry beer. The dryness of the hop should be evident in any beer worthy of the designation Pilsener, not least the original, **1**, from Czechoslovakia. A hint of bitterness in the finish, too, to stimulate the gastric juices. A good Pilsener should be easy to find but more unusual brews add a touch of style. Drinkers who favour a Scotch before dinner might enjoy a German smoked beer, **3**, all the more teasing if it is based on wheat malt, kilned over beech logs **5**. Devotees of a pre-dinner *Kir Royale* should perhaps try a Belgian *kriek* beer, in which cherries are macerated during a third fermentation. There are *kriek* beers within the *lambic* ranges of Mort Subite, **2**, and Lindemans, **4**. Despite its threatening name, Mort Subite has a most enlivening effect.

WITH A MEAL

The London of Dickens and Disraeli knew the enigmatic pleasures of oysters (from the adjoining Thames-side counties of Essex and Kent) with porter or stout (in those days its predominant local brews). Today, the best English porter comes from a boutique brewery in Burton (a town better known for pale ales) **7**. The most famous stouts are the dry ones, from Dublin, **8**, or Cork, **3**, **7**, in Ireland. There is even a *château-* (to be pedantic, *Schloss-*) bottled example, Sir Henry's Stout, from Baron Henrik Bachofen von Echt, **I**, in Vienna. There are stouts, too, from Singapore, **5** (not to mention Sri Lanka and Japan), and from Australia, **2.** Africa, the Caribbean and North America all have stouts. They make a splendid accompaniment to crustaceans of all types, including crab and lobster. With gentler fish dishes, a pale, medium-dry, Export style beer from Dortmund, **10**, might be appropriate. Likewise with chicken or turkey. With pork, a sweeter pale beer, of the Munich *Helles* type. With spicy foods, a Vienna-style lager like Dos Equis (ideal with Mexican dishes). With noodle dishes, perhaps even a dark (*Dunkel*) lager. With red meats, a fruity ale from England (accompanying roast beef?) or Belgium (with a *carbonade Flamande*, or a French-speaking casserole), **4**, or from Canada, **9** (with a prairie steak or a Quebecois meat pie?).

And with dessert? There is a style of beer even for that occasion: a honeyish "white" wheat brew like the classic example, **6**, from the village of Hoegaarden, in Belgium.

AFTER A MEAL

In the Anglo-French custom of its being served after the main meal, the cheese might be of the same origin as the accompanying beer. The French-speaking Belgian monastery, **1**, of Chimay is just one of several that produce cheese, **5**, as well as beer. Chimay's three principal strong Trappist brews are crown-corked in red, white and blue, **3**, in ascending order of potency. Among these "burgundies of Belgium", the natural accompaniment to cheese is the vintage-dated *Capsule Bleue*, or "Chimay Blue", also available as Grande Reserve. Later still, the brandies of the beer world are those brews so strong that the warmth of alcohol comes through in the finish. The Belgian speciality Cuvée de l'Ermitage, **2**, is an Armagnac among beers. Rarer still, the German beer Abt's Trunk, **4**, from a secularized monastery brewery in Swabia, is reminiscent of an Alpine liqueur.

IN SPRING

Even before winter has retreated, but when its grip is being relaxed, the Germans strain at the leash, and reach daringly for the pleasures of outdoor drinking. It is still too cold, really, for such ventures, so a warming *Doppel* ("double") *bock* is proffered. The ritual begins in March or April – before Easter – with the ceremonial tapping of the first barrel of a new season's Paulaner Salvator Doppelbock, **3**, at the brewery's beer hall and garden in Munich. Echoing the original, *Doppelbock* beers usually affect names ending in *-ator*. A fine example is the brew known in Germany as Fortunator and in the United States as, appropriately, Celebrator, **2**. By May, spring can be greeted with more confidence, as it has been since pagan times. There are Maypoles in Bavaria, and there is the slightly less strong (though still potent) "single" *Bock* beer. Again in Munich, the Hofbräuhaus, **6**, the world's most famous beer garden and hall, taps its *Maibock*, **4**. There is also a *Maibock* from farther north, from Lower Saxony, from the town of Ein*beck*, **5**, where the style was conceived. Several continental European countries have *Bock* beers (though some are saved for autumn and winter, in an overlapping of traditions). In the United States, where *Bock* beers are enjoying something of a revival, they are usually served in late winter and early spring. The tradition is strongest in Wisconsin, but a fine newcomer, **1**, is from a boutique brewery in Montana.

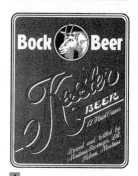

3

4

5

6

IN SUMMER

In some countries, most beers are thought of as summer refreshers, but continental Europe has its own specialities to quench warm-weather thirsts. The principal categories are the wheat beers, with their sharp, tart palates. The south German type, **1**, are served in a vase-shaped glass, often with a slice of lemon. They are produced in (from right to left), dark, clear and sedimented versions. Another good range is made by Weihenstephan, **2**, the world's oldest brewery. The north German type of wheat beer, **3**, **7**, is served in a glass resembling a large champagne saucer. It is laced with essence of woodruff or, more commonly, raspberry syrup. Wheat beers, too, are enjoying a revival in the United States, with examples from Hibernia, Kessler, Pyramid, Widmer and Anchor Steam. In addition to summer wheat beers, Belgium has intentionally sour, quenching, Flemish ales like Rodenbach, **4**, **6**, sometimes laced with grenadine. The seasonal theme is graphically portrayed when winter takes the beer it has been keeping in cold store, and presents it to summer, **5**. Sezoens is a proprietary brand in Flanders.

IN AUTUMN

Before September has passed, the October festivals are already beginning in the German-speaking world. This is the time when the idealized representation of the Bavarian barmaid is often exceeded in performance by the flesh and blood, **5**, **4**. She raises litre glasses, rather than consciousness, but such traditions endure. The beer she carries at *Oktoberfest* should, confusingly, be of the *Märzen* style. What was laid down in March is exhausted in October. The home of the style is Munich's Spaten brewery, which also defers to tradition with deliveries by horse and dray, **2**, **3**. American versions are produced in the Midwest by the revivalist brewers at Hibernia, **1**, and the old-established brewery of Hudepohl, **6**, **7**.

4

5

6

7

Special Oktoberfest Beer

Ludwig **Hudepohl** *Special* **Oktoberfest** *Beer*

...fest Beer is a rich, smooth beer our brewmaster... ...a salute to a great Germanic tradition. This special... ...roasted dark roasted barley malt and imported hops. PRO... ...filled by The Hudepohl Brewing Co., Cincinnati, OH...

IN WINTER

A wintry country like Scotland should know how to produce warming brews. In the best traditions of the Auld Alliance, Traquair House, **2**, offers a château-bottled Scotch ale. Such delights taste best from a thistle-shaped glass, even if the Gordon's marque, **3**, is perversely only available in Belgium. Lovers of Lorimer's Caledonian might recognize MacAndrew's, **4**, which is available only in the United States. These Scottish ales are not as smoky as their compatriot whiskies, but they are more malty than most blends. Furthermore, a bottle of a strong Scotch ale is more potent than a large whisky. The English have several seasonal ales with "winter" in their name. The most famous is Winter Warmer, from Young's of London (the same name is used in the United States by Hale's Ales, of Colville, Washington). Young's is a draught ale, but its stronger, bottled counterpart is Old Nick, a devilish brew to set among the various strong ales (or "barley wines") named after bishops, **1**. Although these examples are all produced by secular breweries, the allusion has its origins in the days of ecclesiastical brewing in England.

AT CHRISTMAS

"Yule" might sound coy, but *Jule*, **1**, is Norwegian for Christmas. This Norwegian seasonal brew is a lovely tawny, nutty beer. Brewers in several countries produce special beers for the season, whether the allusion is to the gift-giving time, as in the Swiss Samichlaus (Santa Claus), or the eve of Christ's birth, as in Mexico's dark Nochebuena, **2**. Samichlaus is the world's strongest beer, at 14 percent alcohol by volume. It is produced in both pale (amber) and dark (deep red) versions, with a vintage date, a feature of several Christmas brews. All of these beers are bottom-fermenting, but a number of British and American brewers produce ales for Christmas. In the US this practice is spreading. Those

from the Anchor Steam Brewery, of San Francisco, are greatly prized. With both bottom- and top-fermenting brews, there is no definitive style for Christmas, but most examples are strong and of some character and quality. Some brewers, especially in Denmark, also have Easter and Whitsun brews.

VINTAGE BEERS

THE STRONGEST BEER IN BRITAIN
This beer is one of very few British beers bottled with its natural yeast, and it will mature in the bottle. Its flavour will improve if stored at 12°C (55°F) and will last for at least 25 years. If the bottle is disturbed before drinking, stand for 48 hours to allow natural sediment to settle and then pour carefully.
**Eldridge Pope & Co. plc
Dorchester, Dorset**

Most beer should be consumed as soon as possible: time is its enemy, and no further excuse should be needed. However, a handful of specialities are brewed to improve with age. That was the original significance of the French term *bière de garde* and it remains the meaning of the Flemish term *provisie bier*.

An even clearer imprecation is that on the back label of Thomas Hardy's Ale, **1**, from England. This lays down conditions that not every beer-lover can keep. Bottles from the 1960s have been offered by collectors for sale in the US at $1,000. Though not vintage-dated, Feuerfest, **2**, from Germany, carries a limited-edition number.

The classic vintage-dated beer is Courage's Imperial Russian Stout, **1**. This brew is made in Britain, and was originally produced for export to Russia during the time of the Tsarist Empire. Several brewers and shippers, one with the memorable name of A. Le Coq, **2**, exported "imperial" stouts during the 16th and 17th centuries. The Courage product is the last direct descendant of this trade, and has in recent years been harder to find in Britain than in some continental European countries. Since it no longer

has a long maturation period at the brewery, it will benefit all the more from being laid down for a year or two, ideally at 12°C (55°F). Recently, another British brewer, Samuel Smith, has produced an imperial stout for export to the United States. This is not, however, intended for laying down. Neither is Koff Imperial Stout, **4**, from Finland. Another revivalist example, **3**, is produced by the Grant's boutique brewery, in Yakima, Washington. This is principally a draught beer.

CZECHOSLOVAKIA

The world's most widely known style of beer originates from the town of Pilsen, in Bohemia (the kingdom of Wenceslas in the Middle Ages and the province around which the modern state of Czechoslovakia was created).

The expression "Bohemian", meaning nonconformist, seems to have been inspired by gypsies from across the Hungarian border, which lies to the east. It is from the west, though, that this meeting point of Germanic and Slavic cultures has been seen as an incubator of brewing since the Dark Ages.

The international fixation with the term *Pilsener* can be dated, precisely, to 1842. Until that time, all of the world's beers had been dark, or at least reddish in colour, or murky. Dark malts can make for tasty beers but they were, in those days, also a way of covering up the haziness of yeasty instability.

In 1842, Pilsen's local brewery, which was then owned by the town, produced the world's first golden-coloured, clear, stable, beer by bottom-fermentation, thus "inventing" pale lager. This "invention" came at a time when opaque drinking vessels of stoneware or pewter were giving way to mass-produced glass.

At this time, the German-speaking Austrian Empire ruled Bohemia. "Pilsener-style" beer soon became chic throughout the German-speaking world and beyond. By the time steps were taken to protect the name, the drayhorse had bolted.

When the American brewer Adolphus Busch toured Europe in the late 19th century to study the lagering technique, he was particularly taken with the beers of a town called, in German, Budweis (in Czech, Ceské Budějovice), once the home of the Bohemian royal court brewery. He decided upon this allusion when he set about launching his "King of Beers" in the USA in 1876, but he had the sense to protect the name Budweiser. Busch's "super-premium" trademark Michelob (from a town now known as Michalovce) is also protected.

The Bohemians' devotion to brewing has no doubt been encouraged by the availability of fine raw materials. Although Bohemia first made wheat beers, it has excellent malting barley – sweet and clean, grown in a protected, temperate "continental" climate. The Bohemians have been famous for their hops since the earliest days, and still are. These are exclusively of the variety known as Bohemian Red, or as Saaz from the German-language name for Žatec, centre of the growing area. The fresh fragrance of these hops is said to be nurtured not only by the climate, with its gentle rainfall, but also by the soil, rich in clay and iron.

Most Czechoslovakian breweries have an everyday beer at 7–10 Plato (3–4 percent alcohol by volume); a premium product in the range of 11–12 Plato (4.5–5); sometimes a dark lager at 10 Plato and occasionally a speciality of 13–20 Plato (5.5–7.5).

Where to drink

Almost every town in Czechoslovakia offers its own beers locally. The capital, Prague, has 20-odd beer taverns. The most famous, U Fleků (11Křemencova) in the "New Town" (the city centre), has its own brewery, though for some years that has been undergoing a re-fit. U Fleků has a burlesque show. In the "Old Town", U Zlatého Tygra (17 Husova) is a sociable tavern selling Pilsner Urquell; while U Medvídků (7 Na Perštýně) is a somewhat basic home for Budweiser Budvar in Prague. In the "Lesser Town", U Svatého Tomáše (12 Letenská) serves beer from the small Braník brewery, of Prague; a lovely, firm, aromatic pale brew and a rather thin dark one. Prague's two larger breweries make the malty Staropramen and yeasty Prazanka beers.

Budweiser Budvar

Although it has a definite hop nose and finish, **Budweiser Budvar**★★★ → ★★★★ is sweet by Czechoslovakian standards, clean and rounded, with a hint of fruitiness. (Units of bitterness in the lower 30s; lagered for two or three months.) The Budvar brewery was not founded until 1895, so it must have been the similar beers from the older Samson brewery that inspired Busch. Even today, with all the changes in barley, hops, technology and market fashion, there seems to survive a vestigial resemblance between their beers and his.

Pilsner Urquell

The original. **Pilsner Urquell**★★★★ has a slightly fuller colour than some of its latter-day derivatives. The local water imparts a softness, and a faintly salty tang; the use exclusively of Žatec hops ensures a big, fresh bouquet (diminished by excessive pasteurization in export shipments) and a gentle bitterness (about 35 units); the huge, traditional, pitch-lined wooden barrels used for lagering add a touch of their own house character. An immensely complex beer. Pilsen also has the Gambrinus brewery, producing hop-accented beers which evince the cleanness of Bohemian malt.

EASTERN EUROPE

German/Prussian and Austrian/Bohemian influence left brewing traditions in bordering parts of Poland and Hungary, which both countries proudly retain. There is a Bohemian character to Poland's dry Żywiec/Krakus and the softer (but still hoppy) Okocim Pilsener-style beers, both sometimes found in the West. The creator of Vienna-style lager, Anton Dreher, founded the Kobánya Brewery, of Budapest, which proudly produces a full range of styles in Hungary. Budapest is also in the process of getting a new micro-brewery, to produce a pale lager. The Soviet Union has almost 400 breweries and is one of the world's biggest producers in volume. Quality and choice is variable.

AUSTRIA

When Austria had a European Empire it was an influential nation in many aspects of life, including beer, but its glories faded as quickly as the last waltz. The classic amber-red style of lager first brewed in Vienna is no longer even a speciality of the capital city. Even the term *Märzen*, which in other countries may suggest a Vienna-style beer, means something different in Austria. Here, by some perverted logic, it indicates simply a brewery's basic lager, albeit at a respectable Plato of 12-plus (5–5.25 alcohol by volume). *Spezial* indicates a beer of 13-plus (5.5–5.75). *Bock* suggests 16-plus (around 7).

Quite different speciality beers are, however, beginning to enjoy something of a revival. Baron Henrik Bachofen von Echt has his chocolatey-but-bitter **Sir Henry's Stout**★★★ (13.75; 6 by volume) and copper-coloured, ale-like **St Thomas Bräu**★★ →★★★ (12.25; 5.6) at his resuscitated brewery and restaurant (☎372652) in the Vienna suburb of Nussdorf. The Piesting brewery, south of Vienna, has an **Altbier**★★★. The Zwettle brewery, northwest of Vienna, has a **Zwickelbier**★★. These augment longer-established specialities like one or two *Weizenbiers* and the 23 Plato Ur-Bock of Eggenberg, between Salzburg and Linz. Salzburg has a brewery owned by Augustine monks but operated by a secular company. Schlägl, north of Linz, has a brewery run by Praemonstraten brothers.

Brau A.G.

This anonymous-sounding group owns the famous Schwechat brewery where Anton Dreher created the Vienna style of lager. That brewery has a premium **Hopfenperle**★ →★★, relatively light in body and dry in finish, and a super-premium **Steffl**★, with a light-to-medium body and a hoppy finish. The group, which has it headquarters in Linz, also has a number of breweries producing the fruity **Kaiser**★ beers, which are a national brand. Near Salzburg, Brau A.G. has a regional brewery known for its very pale **Zipfer Urtyp** ★ →★★, with a hoppy aroma and sherberty dryness.

Steirische (Styrian Breweries)

Second-biggest grouping, based in Graz, embracing the local Reininghaus-Puntigam brewery and a larger company that takes its name from its Styrian home-town of Leoben-Göss. The **Reininghaus-Puntigam**★ →★★ beers are generally malty and fruity. Gösser has a hearty **Spezial**★★, with a full, bronze colour, a smooth, malty palate and some hop bitterness in the finish. Its **Export**★★ is slightly fuller-bodied, with a cleaner palate. Its new **Gösser Gold**★ is lighter and relatively bland. **Gösser Stiftsbräu**★ →★★ is a dark, malty, sweet beer of 12.2 Plato but only 3.6 percent alcohol by volume. It is named after the brewery's founding monastery.

SWITZERLAND

The world's strongest beer, called **Samichlaus** ★★★★ ("Santa Claus"), is produced in Switzerland. This relatively new label has led lovers of individualistic brews to take a fresh look at Switzerland, which has more speciality beers than is suggested by a reputation for products that are well-made but not distinctive. Swiss beer-making tradition, at least in the German-speaking part of the country, is evidenced by monastic brewery ruins in St Gallen that date from the 9th century.

Samichlaus is brewed only once a year, on December 6, the day when the Swiss celebrate St Nicolas (Santa Claus). It is matured throughout the following year and released next December 6. Its starting gravity is 27.6 Plato (around 1110) and it emerges with 11.1–2 percent alcohol by weight; 13.7–14 by volume. Although it has a predictably malty nose and full body, its long maturation and high alcohol make for a surprising firmness and a brandyish finish. A *Hell* ("pale", but actually reddish) version is available in some markets, but Switzerland has only the dark original.

These beers are produced by Hürlimann, of Zürich. Hürlimann's more conventional beers tend to be clean, light and dry, with a spritzy finish. The company also has an interest in the city's Löwenbräu brewery (unconnected with the Munich namesake). Swiss Löwenbräu's beers are characteristically mild and dry. Among the other majors' products, those of Cardinal are perhaps more flowery, those of Haldengut slightly smoky, and those of Feldschlösschen have a fruity bitterness; these are, however, only slight shades of difference.

A Swiss brewery's range might embrace a basic lager (at more than 11.5; 1046; around 3.8; 4.75); a deluxe beer (12; 1048; 4.1; 5.12); a "special" (12.5–6; 1050; 4.3; 5.37); a dark special (13.5; 1054; 4; 5); a "festival" brew of similar strength; a "strong" beer of 16; 1064; 5.4; 6.75; and perhaps a dark strong beer of 19; 1076; 5.9; 7.3.

Cardinal and Warteck both have *Altbiers* in their ranges. *Weizenbiers* are produced by Calanda, Frauenfeld and the Ueli brewery at the Fischerstube "brewpub" (Rheingasse 45, Basel. ☎061-329495).

The strangest speciality from Switzerland's 30-odd breweries is a beer that is intended to taste of corn (maize) – and does. It is called **Maisgold**, contains 30 percent corn (which would hardly be unusual in the United States) and is produced by the Rosengarten brewery, of Einsiedeln.

GERMANY

As northern Europe is the home of brewing in the modern world, so Germany remains its hearth. Among Germany's many claims to this central position, the strongest is that it has far more breweries than any other country. Their number is astonishing, despite many closures in recent years. Almost 40 percent of the world's breweries are in Germany; 1,200-odd in the West and more than 200 in the East, a much smaller country. Although closures outnumber openings, about ten new boutique breweries have established themselves in recent years, not only in northern cities like Essen and Dortmund but also in the more conservative south, in Munich and Nürnberg. Even a nation as lavishly served as Germany, and as rich in small breweries, has fallen for the charms of the boutique.

Germany was never for long a single state, and its relatively recent, post-war, division encouraged local loyalties. With Berlin sliced through, the other great cities of Germany vie with each other, not least in their brewing traditions. In general, the north has the driest beers; the southwest, especially the state of Baden-Württemberg, has softer brews, allegedly to suit palates weaned on wine; and the southeast (Bavaria) has sweeter, fuller-bodied products.

What is yet more interesting for the beer-lover is that each region has its own specialities. Germany has a considerable range of beers. Berlin is known for its light, slightly sour, style of *Weisse* wheat beer, a summer quencher; Hamburg and the north in general are noted for extra-dry *Pilsener*-style beers; the Old Town restaurants of Bremen and Münster have several esoteric local specialities; Dortmund, which makes more beer than any other city in Germany, has its confusingly-named *Export* style, medium in both body and dryness; Düsseldorf drinks as its everyday brew a copper-coloured, top-fermenting *Altbier*. Cologne protects through *appellation contrôlée* its pale, top-fermenting *Kölschbier*. Einbeck and Munich share the strong *Bock* beer, especially in spring, though the latter city lays claim to winter's *Doppelbock*. Munich is the greatest of cities for stylistic variety. It also shares a tradition of dark or *dunkel* beers with Kulmbach and other Bavarian towns (though Bamberg specializes in smoked-malt *Rauchbier*). Munich has a special interest in amber *Märzenbier* and various types of *Weizen* wheat beers.

Few of these varieties are wholly restricted to their own area or season, though they are always freshest at the appropriate time and taste best in their native place. Some brewers specialize in just one variety of beer, but more produce a range. Some brewers with regional roots have cross-bred with others to form semi-national groupings. The biggest are formed by Dortmunder Union, with Schultheiss of Berlin; Dortmunder Actien, with Binding of Frankfurt and Kindl of Berlin; and Bavaria St Pauli of Hamburg, with Hannen of Rhineland-Westphalia, Henninger of Frankfurt, and Tücher of Nürnberg.

Links between breweries in the north and south are less evident, though some of the bigger companies, while still quite separate, have investment from the same major banks. The biggest output of any brewery in Germany is that of Binding, which sells about 2.5 million hectolitres a year. A medium-sized brewery might produce half a million hectolitres; some small local firms have an output of less than 10,000hl; in Bavaria, there are inns producing a few hundred.

The north has the greater number of very large

breweries, often extremely modern. This may stem from its being mainly Protestant and therefore having a long tradition of secular, commercial brewing. A northern city but a Catholic one, Cologne, has the greatest number of breweries: a baker's dozen within its boundaries and the same number again in its hinterland. The Catholic south, with a surviving tradition of monastic brewing (albeit interrupted by Napoleon), has more village beers. Two-thirds of all the breweries in the Federal Republic are in the single state of Bavaria. Many of these are around Munich, but several smaller towns have a greater number of breweries, especially in the region of Franconia.

Within any varietal style, German breweries – especially the larger ones – are apt to make similar products. This is in part because clear standards are laid down by law. There is also the separate question of the *Reinheitsgebot*, the German Pure Beer Law of 1516. In 1985 one or two brewers were found to be in breach of this law and there was a scandal. They were also felt to have embarrassed Germany, since the Purity Law was at the time being challenged in the European Community as a restriction on free trade. The Purity Law has its origins in Bavaria, where it is observed even in the case of products made for export. Equally, Germany has always been willing to accept imports that conform to its laws. (The *Reinheitsgebot* is not applied in East Germany.) Irrespective of the law, the national standard of housekeeping in breweries in Germany is impeccable, whether they be stainless steel factories or copper classics.

The nation as a whole always features among the top two or three countries in the world's annual league table of beer consumption per head. The north, though, drinks less than the south, and does so in smaller glasses, of 20 or 30cl. In the relationship between average consumption and customary size of serving, it is not clear which is cause and which effect. Apart from the differences in size, there are also customary shapes of glass for each style of beer, in both north and south. Most German beers are served cool – at around 9°C (48°F), though there are slight variations of local habit. If the beer is to remain cool on a warm day, it had better not linger, in which case a small glass makes more sense. Nonetheless, it is in the south, where the summers can be warm, that 50cl and litre glasses are normally used. At festivals, the litre glass is often the only serving available. It is known as a *Mass* ("measure") and, whether of glass or stoneware, it qualifies as a stein only if it has a lid.

Weather, again, plays its part in the regional styles of drinking place. The northerner may well take his pleasures indoors, and there is an element of Protestant opprobium to some of the names he gives to drinking places: *Pinte*, *Kneipe* and *Wirtshaus*. *Gastwirthschaft*, *Gasthaus* or *Gasthof* sound more innocent. The southerner may drink at a similar place, or at a beer hall, but his greatest joy is when the weather permits him to go outside to the beer garden. At village festivals, there will also be a tent big enough to accommodate the entire population. The celebrations and seasons of village life in Bavaria are accompanied by religious blessings in the morning and beer in the afternoon, from the saint's day at the local church through Easter, Ascension Day, Whitsun, the harvest festival and Christmas.

HAMBURG

Around the world, imported beer from Germany often means Holsten, Beck's or St Pauli Girl. The first comes from Hamburg, the latter two from Bremen. These two cities remain the principal ports in Germany, a largely landlocked country, and they have been exporters of beer for more than 600 years. Their great importance in the brewing industry dates back to one of the early attempts at organized trade in Europe, the 15th century Hanseatic League.

The extra-dry speciality Pilseners produced in this part of Germany owe their character to the same circumstance. In the days when transport by water was easier than travel across land, Hamburg was twice blessed. Not only did it, as a seaport, have Europe's greatest sales of beer, its requirement for hops was met by trade down the river Elbe from Bohemia, the classic area of cultivation. The dryness of these Pilseners echoes Hamburg's role as a great hop market. The hops were used not only for flavour but also as a natural preservative in beer that was destined for long sea journeys.

Holsten is the best-known of Hamburg's three breweries. Next comes the confusingly named Bavaria St Pauli (nothing to do with St Pauli Girl of Bremen), then Elbschloss. All three produce generally dry beers, though with differences of emphasis. The Holsten products have an assertive dryness. Those from Bavaria St Pauli are perhaps a little fruitier. The Elbschloss beers are very clean-tasting, reserving their dryness for a long, lingering finish.

Many visitors to Hamburg, in their meanderings along the Reeperbahn, perhaps with a stop in the picaresque bars of David Street, notice the Bavaria St Pauli brewery. It stands at the top of David Street, where the St Pauli district falls away to dockland. In the next neighbourhood out of the city, the once-separate township of Altona, is the Holsten brewery. On the far edge of Altona, in the unlikely location of a stockbroker suburb, is Elbschloss, the most attractive and traditional of Hamburg's breweries, with its own maltings in its cellars.

Where to drink

Despite its brewing history, Hamburg has no traditional beer taverns. Local beers are, though, a ready accompaniment to the dubious pleasures of a seaport *Labskaus* (beef hash) or countless more appetizing eel dishes, at The Old

Commercial Room, opposite St Michael's Church, or in the waterside restaurants of Deich Strasse. There is a good selection of northern brews at the beer bar of the Intercontinental Hotel. A number of new, mock-rustic places serve beers from other parts of Germany. The biggest range is at the youthful, disco-like Posemuckel, on Bleichen Brücke.

Bavaria St Pauli

Names like "Bavaria" were adopted in the late 19th century by brewers who were following the south's lead in lager-brewing. The Bavaria brewery of Hamburg and the more locally named St Pauli merged in 1922. As if its name were not confusing enough, the brewery markets its products under the Astra label. The company's basic lager, **Astra Urtyp**★, has a pleasant, light hop aroma and palate. The premium **Astra Pilsener**★ has a very aromatic bouquet and palate. Astra also has a beer called **Exclusiv**★, in the style the Germans call Export (like the Dortmund variety) and a dark **Urbock**★ (again a confusing name, since this is a doppelbock). In addition to that fairly standard range, there is a light-bodied but very dry Pilsener called **Grenzquell**★ which was for some time heavily promoted in the USA. The company is best known for one outstanding product from its subsidiary Jever brewery, in the northern town of the same name in German Friesland.

Jever Pilsener★★★★, which is regarded as something of a Friesian speciality, is the most bitter beer in Germany, despite a slight mellowing in recent years. Jever has a big bouquet (the aroma hops are of the Tettnang variety), a yeasty palate (the brewery has had its own strain since 1936) and an intense aperitif bitterness in the finish. A smooth **Jever Export**★★ and a firm-bodied **Maibock**★★ are hard to find outside Friesland.

A Friesian nation once straddled what are now the borders of The Netherlands, Germany and Denmark, and its traditional drinks suggest a liking for intense and bitter flavours. In its handsome resort town, Jever is a proud and prosperous brewery, with a very modern plant.

Elbschloss

This brewery takes its name from the river Elbe which flows parallel to the road on which the brewery stands. Masked by rowan trees, hawthorns and sycamores, the brewery is in its original, 1881 brick building. The *Schloss* is in the woods behind. Elbschloss is partly owned by DUB-Schultheiss. It has a full range of products, including the very pleasant and splendidly dry **Ratsherrn Pils**★★★. There is also a good, malty Doppelbock called simply **Ratsherrn Bock**★★. None of the Elbschloss beers are pasteurized.

Holsten

In the days when the nobility controlled such matters as licences to brew beer, the Duchy of Schleswig-Holstein held sway over Hamburg. The Duke of Holstein who granted the city the right to brew is remembered in the name of this company, and on its labels. The company's basic local beer is the firm-bodied **Holsten-Edel**★. It also has a German-style **Export**★, with a satisfying, wholesome texture, and a soft, dry **Pilsener**★. Holsten is the biggest German exporter to

Britain, where one of its products has to the uninformed drinker become synonymous with the term "Pils". Ironically, the beer thus dubbed is not a regular Pilsener. It is the product that the company would prefer to be known by its full name of **Holsten Diät Pils★★ → ★★★**. This very dry low-carbohydrate beer was originally produced for diabetics. Since it has a relatively high alcohol content, at 5.8 percent by volume, its calorie count does not suit weight-watchers. Its real virtue is that it is a genuine import, with plenty of hop character. Holsten has also recently begun to export its **Maibock★★**, labelled in Britain as Urbock. This strong beer has a malty dryness, with a hint of apricot. Holsten's beers are kräusened.

Like its principal local rival, Holsten also has a super-premium product from a subsidiary brewery. In this case, the brewery is in Lüneburg, a spa town of stepped-gable houses, their styles evolving from the 14th–18th centuries. A group of them form the old brewery and guest-house, now converted into a beautifully-arranged beer museum and a restaurant serving local dishes. The new brewery is very modern, and its dry, hoppy beer is called **Moravia Pils★★**. The name Moravia must have come down the Elbe at some time. The beer is notable for its big bouquet, and has a rather light body. In addition to Moravia, which enjoys some prestige, there are a number of minor products, some under the Bergedorf name, and associated breweries in Kiel, Neumünster and Brunswick.

BREMEN

Churches and monasteries dedicated to St Paul have given their name to a good few breweries in Germany, including one in Bremen, long destroyed. This does not altogether explain how one of the city's famous export beers came to be known as St Pauli *Girl*, and the people who might know claim they can't remember. Another noted export is Beck's, while the local brewing company is called Haake-Beck. Recently there has also been a tentative export called Roland Light. Roland is the legendary knight (celebrated in *chanson*) whose statue stands in the main square of Bremen (and other north German cities) as a symbol of civic, secular independence.

Bremen had the first Brewer's Guild in Germany, in 1489, and such is its beery history that it still has a large number of brewery names. Most of these names are of brewing companies that were once independent and which are still separate but linked in a complicated corporate structure. Other labels to be taken into consideration are Hemelinger (nothing to do with a British brand of a similar name) and Remmer. Hemelinger produces a *Spezial*, a rather perfumy but sweetish beer. Remmer produces an interestingly malty *Altbier*. All of the linked breweries in Bremen share a single complex of modern buildings, with two brewhouses, in the town centre, close to the river Weser. Outside of this group is Dressler, which no longer has a brewery but survives as a beer brand owned by Holsten.

Where to drink

The Old Town area of Bremen, known as the Snoor, is a delight, and has some lovely taverns. Especially recommended for its local speciality beers is the narrow, wedge-shaped Kleiner Ratskeller, in an alley called Hinter dem Schütting. This is not to be confused with the Ratskeller itself, which is famous for the hearty consumption of wines from the Rhine and Mosel.

Beck's

The single product brewed by Beck's carries no description beyond a straightforward **Beck's Bier★→★★**. It is broadly within the Pilsener style, with a fresh aroma, a faintly fruity, firm, crisp palate and a clean, dry finish. It is light by German but heavy by international standards, and difficult to place in context. A very pale malt is used, and the hopping leans heavily toward the Hallertau aroma variety. Within the Beck's brand is a dark version, available in some markets. Beck's Bier is fermented with its own house yeast, at fairly low temperatures, and kräusened.

Haake-Beck

A traditional copper brewhouse is used to produce a full range of beers for Bremen and its hinterland, and also local specialities. Both its regular **Edel-Hell★** and its **Pils★→★★** have a floral bouquet and a light, clean palate. While its cosmopolitan cousins do not make specific claims to the style, this Pils does, and properly has a little more bitterness than either in the finish. It is kräusened, and – unusually – is available locally (in the Old Town, for example) in unfiltered form. This version is identified as **Kräusen Pils★★★**, and has living yeast in suspension. As if to emphasize the resultant cloudiness, it is served in cracked-pattern glasses. Even by the standards of a German Pilsener, it has a mountainous head, followed by a soft palate, with just a suggestion of chewy, yeast bitterness.

Haake-Beck also produces, as a summer speciality, a Bremen interpretation of a northern wheat beer. **Bremer Weisse★★★** is served in a bowl-shaped glass similar to those used in Berlin, and is a wonderful summer refresher. In its natural state, it has a palate reminiscent of under-ripe plums, though it is usually served sweetened with a dash of raspberry juice. It has a gravity of 7.5 Plato, producing 2.2 percent alcohol by weight (2.75 by volume). In addition to a top yeast, there is a controlled, pure-culture lactic fermentation.

Yet a third speciality, **Seefahrt Malz**, cannot strictly be rated as a beer, since it is not fermented. It is a heavily hopped malt extract, of a daunting 55 Plato, with a syrupy viscosity but a surprisingly pleasant taste. Seefahrt Malz was for a time on sale, but is now available only to eminent citizens who are invited to the House of Seafarers' annual dinner in Bremen. It is ceremonially served in silver or pewter chalices. Despite its size, the company itself has a taste for traditions. From among its towering buildings each morning emerges a line of drays drawn by Oldenburg horses to deliver beer to the people of the inner city area.

St Pauli Girl

This is produced in the older of Bremen's two brewhouses. Like Beck's, it has a lot of aroma hopping, though it emerges with a slightly lesser bouquet. **St Pauli Girl★→★★** has floral tones in its bouquet and palate, and is very clean. It has marginally less bitterness than Beck's, and is not kräusened. Although each of the two beers is made to its own specification, each with a different yeast background, the distinctions between them are less striking than the similarities. St Pauli Girl, too, is available in a dark version.

HANOVER AND LOWER SAXONY

Famous extra-dry Pilseners like Jever and Moravia (both becoming better known outside Germany) are brewed in the state of Lower Saxony. Neither name, though, is readily associated with the state, which sprawls for many miles across the north of Germany. Jever has its own, more localized regionality, and both beers have to a great extent been appropriated by the city-state of Hamburg.

The most important city in Lower Saxony is Hanover, noted not only for its huge spring industrial fair but also since the 16th century as a brewing centre. Its local speciality is Broyhan *Ältbier*, from Lindener Gilde, one of three brewing companies in the city. Hanover's other breweries are the smaller Wülfel and the medium-sized Herrenhauser. Of the three, Herrenhauser is the best known outside Germany. This part of Germany is also well known for grain schnapps, including the gins of Steinhägen. A local trick is to hold a glass of beer and a schnapps in the same hand and drink from them simultaneously.

To the southeast, the town of Brunswick (known in German as Braunschweig) is appreciated for its rich architectural heritage and for the Nettelback brewery, which makes an esoteric speciality called *Braunschweiger Mumme*. This is a malt extract beer similar to that of Bremen. It is served in the Ratskeller and several other restaurants, either neat as a tonic or in a shandy with one of the more conventional local beers, of which there are a number. Mumme, which is named after its first brewer, was originally produced for seafarers, and was launched in the year that Columbus discovered America (1492). Between the 16th and 18th centuries "Brunswick Mumm" seems to have been well-known in England. The poet Alexander Pope referred to "mugs of mum" and the diarist Samuel Pepys to a "mum-house". A treatize of the time suggests that Brunswick Mumm should be produced in Stratford-upon-Avon, in what would presumably have been the brewing world's first licensing arrangement. Even today, a similar product, Mather's *Black Beer*, is produced in Leeds, Yorkshire (associated with the county's great seafarer Captain Cook). At this point, the story blends with those concerning beers made from molasses and flavoured with spruce or birch twigs. A similar *Schwarzbier* is produced across the East German border in Bad Köstritz.

A much more important speciality is brewed to the south in the small town of Einbeck. The last syllable of Einbeck is believed to have been corrupted into *Bock*, and a good example of this style is produced in the town. The bock tradition seems to date from the local nobility having at a very early stage given the citizens licence to brew. As a result, Einbeck became one of Germany's most productive brewing towns during the 14th century, making beers of a high gravity so that they could be transported far and wide while fermenting-out on their journey. A high-gravity brew thus came to be known in the German-speaking world as a "bock" beer. Martin Luther is said to have been fortified with Einbecker bock beer during the Diet of Worms in the 16th century. In the 17th century, a northern Duke took several casks with him when he went to Munich to marry a southern noblewoman. Ever since, Munich has claimed bock as one of its own styles. The first bocks were probably strong, dark wheat beers, produced by top fermentation. Today, the term indicates a strong beer made with barley malt and a bottom-fermenting yeast.

Where to drink

Worthy of special attention, because such establishments are few in the north, is the Felsenkeller Brewery Gasthof in Lauenau southwest of Hanover. The tiny brewery, owned by the Rupp family, is noted for its dark bock beers. The adjoining inn has five rooms (☎05043-2275). This brewery has no connection with the several other Felsenkellers. The name means simply "rock cellar".

Einbecker Brauhaus

The only remaining brewery in Einbeck, controlled through Elbschloss of Hamburg by DUB-Schultheiss. Einbecker Brauhaus produces three types of Bock. These include the pale **Ur-Bock Hell**★→★★, the dark **Ur-Bock Dunkel**★★★ →★★★★ and, between the two in colour, a **Mai-Bock**. All three have a gravity of 16.7 Plato, a profound, smooth maltiness and a gentle Hallertau hop character. The Mai-Bock is available from the beginning of March to the end of May.

Herrenhäusen

Herrenhauser Pilsener★★ is the speciality of this company. It is a smooth beer with a sweetish palate and a very dry, but not bitter, finish. Because it has just over 4 percent alcohol by weight, it is labelled in some American states as a "malt liquor". While Herrenhauser has every right to feel insulted about that, it compounds the felony by labelling its beer Horsy in some markets. A sillier name is hard to imagine, even if the company's trademark is a rearing horse.

Lindener Gilde

The company takes its name from its origins as a civic brewery, operated by a guild. Today it produces a range of very well-made beers. Its speciality **Broyhan Alt**★★★ is named after a great Hanover brewer of the 16th century. This is a top-fermenting *Altbier* in a similar style to those of Düsseldorf but a little stronger (12.4 Plato; 4.2 percent alcohol by weight; 5.25 by volume), slightly darker, relatively light-bodied, malt-accented, with a delicate hop character and a low bitterness. The brewery also has a regular **Gilde Pilsener**★→★★ and a premium **Ratskeller Edel-Pils**★★, both with a complex hop character and some Saaz delicacy, as well as a German-style **Edel-Export**★.

MUNSTER

The university city of Münster, rich in history as the capital of Westphalia, is regarded with affection by knowledgeable

beer-lovers all over Germany for the specialities produced at
its Pinkus Müller brewery and restaurant. Pinkus Müller is
an institution, despite it being nothing larger than a
Hausbrauerei (small private brewery), producing fewer than
10,000hl a year. It makes some extraordinary beers and has
the impudence to export to the USA.

It also has the impudence to survive. When Pinkus Müller
was founded in 1816, as a shop and restaurant embracing its
own brewery, bakery and chocolate factory, it was not alone;
there were 40 breweries in town. The last of its rivals, a
500,000hl brewery, closed in 1984.

Pinkus Müller's premises in the Old Town (what people in
Münster call the "cow quarter", *Kuhviertel*) were originally
nine houses. Over the years they have been integrated, with
considerable rebuilding in the 1920s and some more recently.
There are four dining rooms; in the main one the centrepiece
is a Westphalian oven, set among Dutch tiles illustrating
Bible stories. The fireplace hangs with Westphalian hams, a
good indication of the style of food.

Behind the restaurant is a simple, two-vessel brewhouse,
surprisingly modern in design. The brewery uses both barley
and wheat malt, and exclusively the aromatic variety of
Hallertau hops, in blossom form. It has its own well, uses
open fermenters, and has a warren of lagering cellars. It is
operated by Hans Müller, who is in his fifties and the head of
the founding family. Half a dozen members of the family
work in the brewery and restaurant. In the mid 1980s, a
teenage daughter departed for the famous brewing institute
at Weihenstephan, so that the succession would be ensured.

Where to drink

Pinkus Müller, where else? It's hard to escape, but there are
other small breweries in Westphalia, and there is a brewery
Gasthof (nine bedrooms, ☎02522–2209), at Oelde, southeast of Münster. This is called the Oelder Brauhaus, and two
beers are produced and splendidly served by the Pott-
Feldmann family.

Pinkus Müller

The brewery produces no fewer than four beers and is best
known for what it describes as **Pinkus Münster Alt★★★ →
★★★★**. In this instance, the term *alt* indicates simply an old
style, without suggesting anything on the lines of the
Düsseldorf classics. Pinkus Münster Alt is a very pale, top-
fermenting beer made from an unusual specification of 40
percent wheat and 60 percent barley malt, to a gravity of
11.3 Plato. It has a long (six months) maturation, including
a kräusening. The maturation takes place at natural cellar
temperature, but in conventional lagering tanks in which
there is a resident lactic culture. The result is a very crisp
beer indeed, dry, with a faint, quenching acidity in the
finish. In several respects, not least its higher gravity,
relative clarity and restrained acidity, this is a different
product from the Bremer or Berliner Weisse. It is wheatier
than any Kölsch, yet it does not qualify as a weizen; it is a
unique speciality. In fact, the brewery does produce a
Pinkus Weizen★★ →★★★, which is worthy of special attention if only for its unusual lightness, though it is characteristically low on hop bitterness, and has a fruity finish. It is a
rather northern-tasting *Weizen*, though it has a thoroughly

southern ratio of 60–40 (wheat has the majority).

There are also two bottom-fermenting beers: **Pinkus Pils★→★★**, with a light but firm body and a hoppy dryness; and **Pinkus Spezial★★★**, a pale beer of 12.66 Plato, brewed with organically grown barley malt and hops. This clean, malty, dry beer, with a medium body, is sold in wholefood shops. Despite Pinkus Müller having all of these unusual brews, the house speciality is not a beer alone. The Müllers steep diced fresh fruit in sweetened water so that it forms its own syrup. They then add a tablespoon of the fruit and syrup to a glass of Pinkus Alt, so that its fresh flavours suffuse the beer and marry with the acidity of the wheat. The availability and contents of this confection depend upon which fruit is in season. Fruits with stones are not used, since they impart an incongruous, almondy bitterness. In summer, strawberries or peaches are favoured; in winter, oranges may be used. The fruit is steeped for a day in a pickling jar, with a kilo of sugar. When it is added to the beer, using a cylindrical glass, the result is known as an Altbier Bowl. It is a Pinkus Müller speciality and a Westphalian favourite.

DORTMUND

The word "Dortmunder" features in the names of seven brewing companies, thus providing great confusion for beer-lovers who are not familiar with Germany. Some of these companies share facilities, but there are no fewer than five sizeable breweries in the city of Dortmund, plus a new *Hausbrauerei*. Since each of the seven brewing companies has its own range of products in various styles, there are about 30 beers with Dortmunder names. In this respect, "Dortmunder" is an *appellation contrôlée*, since no beer brewed outside the city may, in Germany, bear the designation. In other countries, however, brewers have over the years produced beers that they have identified as being in the Dortmunder style. There was a vogue in The Netherlands and Belgium for a beer style described as "Dort".

There is, indeed, a Dortmunder style. In the days when the great brewing cities of Europe vied for ascendency by promoting their own styles, that of Dortmund was a pale, medium-dry beer, very slightly bigger in body and higher in alcohol than its rivals from Munich or Pilsen. It was drier than a Munich pale beer, but less dry than a Pilsener.

As Dortmund's efforts were repaid with sales in other parts of Germany, and in adjoining countries, the local brewers began to refer to their characteristic beer as *Export*. That is how *Export* became a classic German style. Today a good Dortmunder Export beer has a gravity of 13 Plato, producing 4.4 percent alcohol by weight and 5.5 by volume, and with about 25 units of bitterness.

Unfortunately, the Dortmunder brewers' exposition of their classic style can be hard to find outside their city and hinterland. Although it made for a bigger local market, the industrial growth of Dortmund and the Ruhr was a mixed blessing for the city's image as a centre of fine brewing. In recent years especially, Dortmund brewers went through a phase of self-doubt: did a Dortmunder beer sound like a product for cloth-capped miners and steelworkers? In Britain, such a testimonial would be valued, but more egalitarian countries like Germany and the USA have an infantile snobbism. Such a self-defeating insecurity afflicted the Dortmund brewers.

Although they have continued to make Dortmunder Export, the local brewers have in recent years neglected to promote it, preferring to concentrate on other products within their ranges, especially the Pilseners. This policy has not been a conspicuous success, nor does it deserve to be. Dortmund is Germany's largest brewing city, and should be proud of its name. Dortmund-inspired Export beers are, after all, included in the portfolios of brewers all over Germany. There are now, finally, signs that Dortmund is beginning to remember its traditions, with the opening of the Hövels Hausbrauerei and the Dortmunder Kronen Brewery Museum.

Where to drink

For years, Dortmund was content to offer its beers to visitors at uninspiring bars (each representing a different brewery) set around the market square and church. Having been damaged in the war and quickly rebuilt during the recovery years of the 1950s, this area is a little lacking in romance. Now, one of the city's brewers, Dortmunder Thier (output 700,000hl) has decided to soften its own forbidding facade by adding a separate boutique brewery (5,000hl), restaurant, bar and beer garden. This new establishment Hövels Hausbrauerei (Hoher Walls 5–7; ☎0231-141044) is named after Freiherr von Hövel, one of the founders, in 1854, of the parent company.

The tiny new brewhouse can be seen by drinkers and diners as they go about their pleasures. An excellent kitchen provides snacks, full meals or desserts.

DAB (Dortmunder Actien Brauerei)

The middle name merely indicates a joint-stock company. Perhaps that is where the phrase "a piece of the action" originated. This very large brewing company is now part of a national grouping, with Binding, Berliner Kindl and others. In its modern brewery on the edge of Dortmund it produces beers that generally have a light, malty, dryness. Its **Export**★→★★ has a slight malt accent, while remaining dry, and is on the light side for the style. The brewery's **Meister Pils**★ (marketed in the USA under the dismissive, lower-case name of dab beer), has a hint of malt in the nose but goes on to be dry, with some hop character in the palate and a fairly low bitterness. There is more hop aroma, with a very clean and light palate, in the brewery's **Original Premium**★, marketed in the USA as Special Reserve. DAB also has an **Altbier**★, again with a dry maltiness and a light body. This is marketed in the USA under the unflatteringly vague name of DAB Dark. In its local market, DAB has a pleasant **Maibock**★→★★ and **Tremanator Doppelbock**★→★★. DAB is a very marketing-orientated company, distributing its products widely in the north of Germany.

Dortmunder Hansa

This is part of the same group as DAB, and the two share the one brewery. In Germany, Hansa has been very active in the supermarket trade. Its **Export**★★ has a good malt aroma, a soft, full body, and a dry finish. Its **Pils**★ is light and crisp, with some hoppy acidity.

Dortmunder Kronen

Among their home-town beers, the people of Dortmund favour those from the Kronen brewery, one of two privately owned breweries in the city. Its beers are, in general, big and malty, with a clean, delicate sweetness. These characteristics are evident especially in its **Export★★★★**, and to a lesser degree in its super-premium **Classic★★ → ★★★**. **Pilskrone★★** has a flowery hoppiness. The brewery also has an **Alt★** with a relatively full body and a dense, rocky, head. And there is a dark bock, called **Steinbock★★**, with an intense crystal-malt dryness. It is a shame that only the Classic, and not the whole range, is available in the bar at the brewery's museum (open Tuesday–Sunday, closed Monday; entrance free, through the main gates in Märkische Strasse).

It is fitting that a great brewing city should have such a museum, and this gesture is no doubt intended also to focus attention on the fact that Kronen dates back to 1430, and has been in the same family since 1729. Something of the brewer's devotion to his art remains in Kronen's painstaking procedures, with three hopping stages (using only aroma varieties), very cold fermentation, and kräusening, for example – all of this taking place, however, in a plant and building that are uncomprisingly modern.

Dortmunder Ritter

Partly owned by DUB-Schultheiss but having its own brewery, this company produces firm-bodied, fruity-dry beers that generally have a long finish. These robust, matter-of-fact Dortmunder brews are popular in the industrial Ruhr Valley. The fruitiness is perhaps most evident in the **Export★ → ★★**. The **Pils★** has a malty start and a dry finish.

Dortmunder Stifts

The Stifts brewery no longer operates, but its beers are produced, to its own specification, under contract by Thier. Its beers have a very local following on the south side of the city, and are not very evident even in the centre of Dortmund. Stifts promotes only its **Stiftsherren Pils★**, which has a good, "herbal" hoppy aroma, a dry start and not much finish. Stifts is owned by the Stern brewery, of Essen, which is in turn part of Watney's in Britain.

Dortmunder Thier

This is a privately owned brewery and its **Export★★★ → ★★★★** is malty, smooth and full-bodied. It also has a well-made, dry, hoppy **Pils★★**. Although its beers sell well, they could benefit from a wider exposure. In its marketing, the Dortmunder Thier company kept something of a low profile until its opening of the adjoining Hövels Hausbrauerei in 1984 (see Where to Drink; facing page).

DUB (Dortmunder Union Brauerei)

The "Union" refers to the merger of ten or a dozen breweries more than 100 years ago. That union sufficed until 1973, when DUB linked with Schultheiss, of Berlin. The massive "U" of the "Union" logo, illuminated at night, is a Dortmund landmark atop the imposing brewery building which, looking rather like a 1920s power station, broods over the centre of the city. The DUB beers (all kräusened) have some malty sweetness and are generally mild in palate –

perhaps on the bland side – and smooth. The **Export★★★** is malt-accented, and medium-bodied. The **Siegel Pils★** has an agreeably hoppy palate but not much finish. The super-premium **Brinckhoff's No 1★**, named after a founder-brewer, has a character somewhere between the two.

Hövels Hausbrauerei

The first beer made by this new brewery was a big, malty German export called **Hövels Urtyp★★★**, produced at the end of 1984. It has gone on to make as its regular product a "house" beer of bronze colour, notably full body and a smooth, malty palate. This product is misleadingly called **Bitterbier★★★**, a name used in the late 19th century. It has a gravity of 13.5 Plato but an alcohol content of only 3.5 percent by weight, 4.37 by volume. A very big **Maibock★★ →★★★** has been produced in spring, and there are plans for other seasonal beers. Three malts are used in Bitterbier, with blossom hops. The brewery, gleaming in copper, with brass trim, has an open fermenter and its own lagering cellars. As is the custom of some house-breweries, spent grain is used in the making of bread. Bitterbier is available only at the house-brewery bar, restaurant and beer garden, though small barrels can be bought there. Hövels has plans to market other beers in the free trade.

DUSSELDORF

Where a city is lucky, or sensible, enough to have retained a distinctive style of brewing, it often reserves a special beer for particular occasions or moods. Düsseldorf takes a different view and is one of those cities (like its neighbour and rival Cologne – or Dublin) that likes to serve its speciality as its daily beer.

Düsseldorf's prized beer is more instantly distinctive than that of its neighbour. It has a dark copper colour, is top-fermenting and is superficially similar to a British ale. The Düsseldorf beer has, though, a much cleaner palate, with a complex blend of malty body and hop bitterness and has little of the yeasty fruitiness and acidity of the classic British ales. Since the Düsseldorf beer is a significant style in its own right, a German might resent its being compared to British ale. Internationally, however, the Düsseldorf style is little known, although it has been taken up by a couple of brewers on the West Coast of the USA. In this context, its character can perhaps best be summed up by comparing it with ale.

The differences in the Düsseldorf product derive not only from the typically German barley malts and hops used, but also from the use of single cell, pure culture yeasts and – perhaps most significant – a period of cold conditioning in tanks, usually for several weeks. A German would no doubt argue that the Düsseldorf beer is cleaner and smoother than a British ale. The British would argue that their ales have more individuality. As always, this is to compare apples with oranges, neither is better; they are different.

A typical Düsseldorf beer has a gravity of 12 Plato, or a fraction more. It may be made with two or three malts. Some Düsseldorf brewers favour an infusion mash, but the decoction system is also widely used. Two or three hop varieties may be employed; Düsseldorf brewers have traditionally favoured Spalt. Open fermenters are sometimes used, especially in the smaller breweries. The warmer fermentation temperatures are reflected in slightly less intense cold conditioning, at between 0°C (32°F) and 8°C (47°C), for anything from three to eight weeks. Alcohol content is typically 3.6–3.8 by weight; 4–4.7 by volume. Units of bitterness vary from the lower 30s to the 50s; colour around 35 EBC.

After its period of cold-conditioning, Düsseldorf beer is often dispensed in local taverns from a barrel, by gravity, with no carbon dioxide pressure, blanket or otherwise. Although this method is practiced in several taverns and restaurants, notably in the Old Town, it is especially associated with the city's home-brew houses. Such is the joy of this city for the beer-lover: not only does it have its own style, of some character and complexity, it has no fewer than four home-brew taverns. In these establishments, the stubby, cylindrical glasses favoured in Düsseldorf are charged as quickly as they are exhausted.

The home-brew taverns are the shrines of the Düsseldorf brewing style, and as such their beers must be regarded as German classics. The beer-loving visitor to Düsseldorf will want to visit all of them – and also to sample the beers made in the local style by the city's four other breweries, and several others in neighbouring smaller towns.

Düsseldorf's brewers may well wish that a less imitable name had emerged for their style; they call their brews nothing more memorable than *Düsseldorfer Altbier*. No other city has such devotion either to the production or serving of beer in this style, but brewers in several other towns have in their portfolio something which they call *Altbier*. In most instances, though not all, it bears a great similarity to the Düsseldorf style. "*Alt*" simply means "old", and indicates a style that was produced before the widespread introduction of bottom-fermentation.

"*Altbier*" is the style of Düsseldorf and its brewers produce little else, except stronger brews variously called "*Latzenbier*" ("beer from the wood") or "*Sticke*" ("secret" beer) that appear very briefly in some places in winter and autumn. Of the Düsseldorf home-brew houses, three are in the Old Town (Altstadt seems especially appropriate in this instance). The fourth, Schumacher, is in the more modern part of the city centre. Among the bigger brewers' *Altbiers*, the popular Diebels is firm-bodied; Hannen is soft, rounded and well-balanced; Frankenheim is hoppy and light-bodied; Schlosser malty, but dry; Düssel the fruitiest; and Rhenania can be slightly thick-tasting.

Where to drink

None of the home-brew houses should be missed, and Zum Uerige is mandatory. Its beer can also be sampled on draught in the chic food hall of the Carsch Haus department store. South of Düsseldorf at Langenfeld, half way to Cologne, the café-restaurant Brennpunkt International has more than 20 beers on draught and even more in bottle. This is unusual in Germany – especially in that the beers are, as the name suggest, international.

Im Füchschen

"The Fox" is noted not only for its beer but also its food. This home-brew house, in Ratinger Strasse, produces a very good *Altbier*, simply called **Im Fuchschen★★★ →★★★★**. It is a complex and beautifully-balanced beer, its firm, fairly full body at first evincing malty notes, then yielding to lots of hop flavour from Spalt and Saaz varieties. In the end, its hoppiness is its predominant characteristic.

The tavern's big main dining room serves hearty *Eisbein* and *Schweinhaxe*, at scrubbed tables. It can be very busy, but it is a friendly place and diners are usually happy to share tables.

Zum Schlüssel

"The Key" is not to be confused with the larger Schlösser ("Locksmith") brewery, however easy that may be. Zum Schlüssel, in Bolker Strasse, is a home-brew house. The brewery is visible from its main room. **Zum Schlüssel Altbier★★ →★★★** begins with an aromatic hoppiness of palate, but its predominant characteristic is a light maltiness, with a touch of "British" acidity in the finish. It has a fairly light body and a bright clarity. The restaurant is quite light and airy, too, with something of a "coffee shop" atmosphere. It was founded in 1936 (a little late for Heinrich Heine (1797–1856), who was born in this street: the site of his home is now a roast-chicken restaurant). In 1963, the company opened a second, free-standing brewery, whose **Gatzweiler Altbier★★** is widely available in Düsseldorf.

Ferdinand Schumacher

Despite being in a modern part of the city, this home-brew house in Ost Strasse, has the polite atmosphere of times past and is a quiet place at which to relax after shopping or a day at the office. Its **Schumacher Altbier★★★** is the lightest in palate and body, and the maltiest, very clean, with a lovely delicacy of aromatic hop character. The beer is also available at the Goldene Kessel, in Bolker Strasse.

Zum Uerige

This rambling tavern in Berger Strasse is named after a cranky proprietor. Cranky he may well have been, but it is a friendly enough place today – and produces the classic **Düsseldorfer Altbier**, an aromatic, tawny brew, deep in colour and flavour, with a slowly unrolling hop bitterness in its big and sustained finish. **Zum Uerige★★★★** beer is the most assertive, complex and characterful of the Alts. It is also the most bitter. Like all of the Düsseldorfer "house" beer, it is produced in traditional copper kettles, but this is the most beautiful brewery of them all. It also has a traditional copper cool-ship, and a Baudelot cooler, both still in use, and it is impeccably maintained and polished. The brewhouse can be seen from the most picaresque of the many bars. Every few minutes, barrels are rolled through Zum Uerige on their way to the various dispense points, while drinkers jink out of the way. Meals are not served, but Zum Uerige has its own sausage kitchen on the premises. Here, sausages of pork and liver, *Blutwurst* and brawn, are produced, with spiced dripping left over to serve with malodorous Mainzer cheese that has been marinated in beer. If those flavours are not sufficiently intense, robust gastronomes are encouraged to look for the "secret" *Sticke* beer that mysteriously appears for one brew only in January-February, and again in September-October. This is an

Altbier of 14 Plato, with an extra dash of roasted malt – and it is dry-hopped in the maturation tanks.

COLOGNE

German beer-lovers greatly admire the speciality brewing style of Cologne, even if the rest of the world has not so far noticed it. It would be widely imitated, too, if it were not protected by its appellation *Kölschbier* (the beer of Cologne). Except in cases of lengthy precedent, a beer may not label itself *Kölsch* unless it is made in the Cologne metropolitan area. Imitations are thus pointless: they cannot identify their aspirations.

Happily, there are a baker's dozen breweries in Cologne and as many again in its hinterland. All of them produce *Kölschbier*, and some do nothing else. At least one has dropped other, more conventional, styles from its portfolio. *Kölschbier* dominates Cologne: it is possible to go into an ordinary bar in the city and be unable to find a Pilsener – even though it may be advertized outside. In the city's "home-brew" houses, of course, *Kölsch* is the only beer available.

Cologne has more breweries than any other city in Germany (indeed, in the world). Being so blessed, it naturally has a great many bars and taverns, including its home-brew houses. For most of the year, it is an engrossing place in which to sample beers, except during its pre-Lenten carnival, when the drinking becomes less considered. Whether its wealth of drinking places results from, or serves to attract, the tourists is a matter for conjecture. Some people apparently go to Cologne to study its history, see its huge Cathedral, or take trips down the Rhine. They should not be distracted from the city's distinctive beer by such diversions, though it is comfortably possible to enjoy both.

For all the envy it attracts, *Kölschbier* is not at first sight especially distinctive. It is a pale beer, much the same colour as a Pilsener, but – as its lightly fruity aroma and palate should reveal – it is made by top-fermentation.

A classic *Kölsch* has that fruitiness in the beginning, a notably soft palate (influenced by the local water) and a very delicate finish. Although *Kölschbier* brewers pay a lot of attention to hop character (two or three varieties are used, often with a Hallertau accent), their aim is to achieve a light dryness in the finish and nothing too assertive.

The very subtle character of this style is no doubt influenced also by the background palate imparted by the typical Cologne yeasts. These generally create a very vigorous fermentation, which is followed by two, three or four weeks of cold conditioning at $0°-5°C$ ($32°-41°F$). The gravity range of *Kölsch* beers is from just over 11 to just under 12 Plato. A typical example has 11.5 Plato and emerges at between 3.5 and 4 percent alcohol by weight. Most often, it is 4 (5 by volume). Bittering units are typically at the top end of the 20s.

To the outsider, the two dozen *Kölsch* beers are very similar, but locals have their own firm favourites. Those produced in the home-brew houses are especially enjoyed. Drinkers in the *Schwemme* (standing area) of P.J. Früh's Kölner Hofbräu see beer being served at a world-record pace. A dumb-waiter elevates barrels every ten minutes or so, they are tapped, served by gravity, and exhausted. The tall, cylindrical glasses favoured in Cologne are loaded into a specially designed tray so that they look like cartridges in a gun, and dispensed by waiters nicknamed *Köbe* (believed to be derived from *Jakob*), uniformed in blue pullovers and leather aprons. As the drinker finishes one glass, another is put in its place.

Kölschbier is a lovely aperitif (not a bad digestif, either) and it is often consumed as an accompaniment to snacks. On its home ground, this may mean "half a hen" (Rhineland whimsy for a wedge of cheese with a roll) or "Cologne caviare" (blood sausage). Or *Mettwurst* of the tartare type. "With music" means garnished with onions.

Among the home-brew beers, P.J. Früh's is especially clean-tasting, that of Päffgen the hoppiest and Malzmühle, appropriately, the maltiest. Each has its own support as a local classic, though none of the three has a clear claim to be the definitive *Kölsch*. Nor among the rest of the *Kölschbiers* does one stand out, though a good claim is staked by Garde. This is a pronouncedly fruity *Kölschbier*, produced by an old-established private company at Dormagen-bei-Köln. Garde is one of the several companies in Germany with a woman brewer.

Differences between the more widely available *Kölschbiers* are so subtle as to be very open to the influence of freshness (of the beer or the taster). Gaffel is perhaps the driest; Sion flowery and hoppy; Gereons fruitier, with a dry finish; Sester fruity and dry; Gilden fruity, with a rather heavy texture; Zunft creamy; Reissdorf light, soft and delicious; Küppers soft and sweetish; Kurfürsten and Dom sweet at the front, with a drier finish. Küppers is part of the same company as Wicküler Pils; Gereons is associated with the same group; Dom belongs to Stern, of the Watney group; and Gilden to DUB-Schultheiss.

Where to drink

Visitors who go to Cologne to see the Roman museum or the Cathedral will find P.J. Früh's Kölner Hofbräu conveniently opposite, in Am Hof. Behind Früh is the Old Town, lined with bars and restaurants, especially on the *Heumarkt* (Haymarket). At the near end of the Heumarkt, the Päffgen Kölsch brewery family has a restaurant, a couple of doors from which is the Zlata Praha bar, serving draught Urquell Pilsner and Budweis Budweiser. At the far end of the Heumarkt is the Malzmühle home-brew cafe. Beside the Rhine, a pleasant ride on tram number 15 or 16 to the stop at Schönhauser Strasse leads to the Küppers Kölsch brewery, where there is a restaurant serving local dishes and *Wiess* beer, and a very worthwhile museum of brewing.

P.J. Früh's Kölner Hofbräu

An institution: a home-brew tavern and restaurant dating from the turn of the century, in the heart of Cologne. It is a favourite meeting place for lunch or an early evening drink, and it sells between one and two thousand litres of its home-brewed draught *Kölschbier* every day. Like some home-brew taverns elsewhere, Früh also sells beer by the barrel to private individuals and does a lively local trade in this way. The brewery's small, 20-litre, barrels are also on draught in some other taverns, and the beer can be found in the bottle.

Früh Echt Kölsch★★★ is a soft beer, delicate in both its fruitiness of entrance and its hoppy dryness of finish. It is made with only barley malt – no wheat – and hopped with the Hallertau and Tettnang varieties.

Küppers

By far the biggest producer and exporter of Kölschbier despite being a newcomer. Küppers was established 20-odd years ago in Cologne to meet the rules of appellation, so that a *Kölschbier* could be added to the portfolio of the large Wicküler Pils company of Wuppertal. This move followed a court case over the appellation. Sales since, supported by hefty marketing efforts, have justified the determination behind Küppers establishment, but tradition is harder to build. No doubt this was in mind when Küppers established their excellent restaurant and museum. The soft and sweetish **Küppers Kölsch★→★★** is unexceptional, but the brewery wins bonus points for another gesture to tradition, its confusingly-named *Wiess* beer. Although *Wiess* is the Rhineland dialect pronunciation of *Weiss* ("white"), the designation perhaps has less to do with the cloudy tone of this beer than its rustic style; Bavarians talk in the same vein about a *Wies'n* beer when they mean something that is to be served at a country fair. **Küppers Wiess★★★** is an unfiltered version of the normal Kölsch. It still has yeast in suspension, imparting the cloudiness and an astringent, refreshing, bitter-fruit quality. The name is not intended to suggest a wheat beer. Although some wheat is used, it is present only in the small proportion typical of Kölschbier.

Malzmühle

This is a home-brew cafe and restaurant with a pleasantly insouciant, relaxing atmosphere. Being at the far end of the Heumarkt, it is easily missed, but shouldn't be. Its **Mühlen Kölsch★★★→★★★★** is mild and rounded, with a warm, spicy aroma and palate, reminiscent almost of marshmallow. It is a distinctive and delicious beer, lightly hopped with Hallertau blossoms and fermented in open vessels.

Päffgen

A beautifully-kept home-brew restaurant in Friesen Strasse which has a small beer garden. Its **Päffgen Kolsch★★★→★★★★** has a soft palate with a big, hoppy bouquet. By the standards of Kölschbier, it has a very hoppy finish, too.

Sion

Originally a home-brew, too. Its tavern, in Unter Taschenmacher, in the Old Town, offers brisk service and a very fresh glass of its pleasantly flowery beer. Since **Sion Kölsch★★→★★★** is now produced under contract by the brewers of Gereons Kölsch, knowing drinkers whisper that the two beers are one and the same. This is not true; each is produced to its own specification. The flowery bouquet and dry finish of Sion Kölsch derives in part from Hersbrucker hops. **Gereons★★** is hopped exclusively with Hallertau.

RHINELAND'S PILSENERS

Apart from those cities that are islands of their own style, the whole of the Rhine and its hinterland is dotted with well

regarded breweries. The towns without a speciality style of
their own have in several cases put their best efforts behind a
Pilsener beer, developing, as Madison Avenue might term it,
a super-premium product and in several instances producing
nothing else.

Several of these products were among a selection dubbed
"The Premium Beers" in an article some years ago in the
influential newspaper *Die Welt*. The writer, Hans Baumann,
is a journalist who frequently comments on both the
business and social aspects of the brewing industry. His
intention was not to say that these "premium" beers were
the best, but that they were labels that seemed capable of
commanding a high price. His "premium" tag was grate-
fully seized by the breweries and he now has mixed feelings
about its continued use. There are, he points out, many other
good beers, not all of them as intensively marketed.

The German consumer has, however, come to believe in
recent years that a brewery concentrating on one style is
likely to do a better job than those with a whole portfolio of
products. This is a questionable proposition. If a chef
prepares the same dish every lunchtime, he is unlikely to
undercook or burn it, but are his skills necessarily those
of an Escoffier?

While the Pilseners of the far north are generally the
driest, the same leaning is evident in Rhineland, perhaps
with a softness and lightness emerging as the brewers enter
wine country. Even in the far north, the extra-dry Pilseners
represent a local accent rather than a varietal style, and it is
again a broad regionality – even looser, but still noticed by
the drinker – that groups these examples along and around
the Rhine: products from as far north as Duisburg (König-
Pilsener) and Essen (Stauder Pils), east into the Sauerland
(Warsteiner; Veltins; Krombacher) and as far south as the
Rheinpfalz (Bitburger). The north and south represent
extremes of the style, too. In the north, König-Pilsener is
unusually full-bodied and in the south, Bitburger is almost
as light as a German Pilsener can be.

Among the products that were not included in the
"premium" listing, but might have been, Herforder Pils
(taking its name from its home town) and Königsbacher
(from Koblenz) are conspicuous examples. No doubt Wicküler (from Wuppertal) would like to be included, too. Among
smaller, local brewers, Irle (of Siegen) is a Pilsener specialist
in the Sauerland. Although its emergence as a Pilsener-
brewing area owes less to history than coincidence, the
Sauerland has come to be especially associated with this
style. With its broad, green valleys, lakes and woods,
Sauerland is a pleasant place for a leisurely beer tour.

The foreign visitor who is unfamiliar with Germany had
better sort out the geography before starting to drink. It is
not only some of the beers but also the places that have
similar names. Sauerland is far from the river with which it
shares a name, for example. Oddly enough, the river Sauer is
closer to Saarland, which is a different place altogether.
What they all share is a selection of interesting beers, in
Pilsener and other styles.

Where to drink

In Stauder's home town of Essen, one of the company's
shareholders established a "house brewery" in 1984. The

Borbecker Dampfbier brewery, bar and restaurant is in Heinrich Brauns Strasse. The term *dampf* refers to the fact that the premises were a steam-powered brewery in the 1880s and not to the style of beer. An Export-gravity, medium-dark Salonbier is available, with or without filtration (in the latter case, it is called a *Zwickelbier*). It's a long way from the Pilseners of the region – and a delightful contrast.

At the opposite end of Premium Pilsner country, across the border and into Saarland, another *Zwickelbier* can be found, also in a "house brewery". This is the brewery guesthouse Zum Stiefel, run by the Bruch family, in the town of Saarbrücken. Another Saarland speciality, though not from a house brewery, is Bier Eiche (Oak Beer). This was originally produced for a festival concerning oak trees, but is now available all year round. It is a pale, top-fermenting beer of everyday gravity, with a delicate hop aroma and dryness. It is produced in Merzig, by Saarfurst, a local subsidiary of the region's Karlsberg brewery.

Karlsberg, in the Saarland town of Homburg, has – of course – nothing to do with the Danish brewery of a similar name but different spelling.

Bitburger

Taking its name from its home town of Bitburg, this is a specialist "Premium" Pilsener brewery. It is a very modern place indeed, producing a Pilsener with a low original gravity by German standards: 11.3 Plato. This is thoroughly attenuated, to produce an alcohol content of 3.9 by weight; 4.8/9 by volume. Bitburger Pils★→★★ is very pale, extremely light, and dry. It has a pronounced hop flavour but not much bitterness.

Beer-lovers who enjoy this very light interpretation of a Pilsener might also appreciate Bernkasteler Pils★→★★, which has an even lower gravity (11.2, producing 3.8; 4.7) but fractionally more bitterness. This is produced not far away by the Bürger brewery, of Bernkastel.

Herforder

Principally a Pilsener brewery though it does also produce beers in other styles. Herforder Pils★★→★★★ is full-bodied, with a clean, mild palate. Its gravity is 12.1 and its alcohol content 3.9; 4.8/9. Herforder also produces a malty but dry Export★→★★; a pale Mai-Bock★→★★ and a dark Doppelbock★→★★, both very malty. Herford is on the northern borders of Rhineland-Westphalia.

Irle

Another specialist Pilsener brewery its Irle Edel-Pils★→★★ having the classic combination of a 12 Plato gravity and an alcohol content of 4; 5. It has a clean palate and is very mild.

König

Known as a "Premium" Pilsener brewery but also produces other styles. Its Pilsener is very full-bodied but also clean and notably dry. König Pilsener★★★ has a rich aroma, a sustained, very smooth, bitterness and a perfumy finish. It has an original gravity of 12.1 but this is fermented down to an alcohol content of only 3.8; 4.6. The company also has a

König-Alt★ that is fractionally less full-bodied, and much milder in hop character.

König-Alt has a rival in its home town of Duisburg. A beer called **Rheingold-Alt★→★★** is the speciality of a smaller brewery in the town.

Königsbacher

A Coblenz brewery which produces several styles. It also has a number of subsidiaries, whose products include Richmodis Kölsch and Düssel Alt. The enjoyable **Königsbacher Pils ★★→★★★** is complex and satisfying medium-bodied with a fresh, hoppy bouquet and a well-sustained bitterness in the finish.

Krombacher

Taking its name from its location in Kreutzal-Krombach, this house is a specialist "Premium" Pilsener brewery, proud to announce that its water comes from a rocky spring. **Krombacher Pils★★** is medium-bodied, with a slight malt accent in the nose, a clean palate, and a pleasing hop bitterness in its late finish. In the American market, the beer has been promoted as having a crispness, a "hop taste", and "a noticeable lack of bitterness". It is hard to say whether the copywriter was being intentionally dishonest. or cloth-tongued.

Stauder

This is known as a "Premium" Pilsener brewery although Stauder does have other products. **Stauder Pils★★** is marketed especially to expensive hotels and restaurants. Its advertizing in Germany emphasizes cold maturation, making a play on the verb to rest. Brewers sometimes describe their beer as "resting" in maturation, and Stauder is promoted as a product to enjoy in tranquillity. Since a long maturation also "cleans" beer, there is an implication that Stauder-drinkers are strangers to the hangover. Stauder Pils does not, however, have an unusually clean nose or palate, and there is a hint of fruitiness in its character.

Veltins

This brewery led the movement to speciality Pilsener brewing in Germany and is owed a debt of fashionability by its fellow "Premium" producers, especially its neighbours in Sauerland. It is a relatively small brewery, and its **Veltins Pilsener★★★** still has something of a cult following. It is a clean beer, with an elegant hop bitterness in the finish.

Warsteiner

Although it does have other styles this concern is known as a "Premium" Pilsener producer. It is a very up-to-date brewery, aggressively marketing and exporting its premium-priced product. **Warsteiner Pilsener★→★★** has a light hop bouquet, a dry palate, and a moderately bitter finish.

Wicküler

Wicküler Pilsener★★ has a delicate hop bouquet and a light but firm body, with quite a bitter finish. A well-made Pilsener by the standards of mass-market products (which, in the Rhineland, it is). The brewery has a full range of styles, and owns Küppers in Cologne.

FRANKFURT AND HESSE

In the Old Town of Frankfurt, the *Sachsenhausen*, the bars and restaurants serve *Apfelwein*, a cloudy, medium-dry alcoholic cider. If Frankfurt has a speciality for the drinker, then this is it. There is a theory that Europe once had a cider belt, separating the wine-growing and beer-brewing areas. It is a tenuous theory, but in this instance the argument could, indeed, be put that Frankfurt has wine to its south and west; beer to its north and east.

In this pivotal position, Frankfurt has no beery leaning of its own, no varietal style. Nor has the surrounding state of Hesse. In so far as a country the shape of West Germany can have a middle, Frankfurt is the city that stands there. If its beers are middle-of-the-road, that is only to be expected.

What Frankfurt lacks in style, it makes up in scale. With an output in the region of 2.5 million hectolitres, the Frankfurt brewery company of Binding is the biggest in Germany. Binding belongs to the group that also includes Dortmund's DAB and Berlin's Kindl breweries.

Frankfurt's other brewing company, Henninger, is better known internationally. It has an output in the region of 1.75 million hectolitres, and is in the same group as Hannen and Bavaria St Pauli.

Just as it is an important state in the matter of large breweries, so Hesse has some significance for small – or, at least, independent – ones. A nationwide organization of privately-owned breweries, the Bräu Ring, has its headquarters in Hesse, at Wetzlar, which is also the home of one of its members, the Euler company. Several other member-breweries are in Hesse, including Alsfeld, the Andreas Kloster brewery, Busch, Marburger and the Unionbrauerei of Fulda.

Visitors are known to escape the post-war modernity of Frankfurt by heading for the 19th-century charm of the surrounding spa towns, but drinkers do not have to take the waters. The small breweries of Hesse, especially to the north, offer an interesting alternative. Then, if the breweries of Hesse prove insufficient, there is always the Bavarian Steigerwald not far east. Or, south in Mannheim across the "state line", Eichbaum brewery offers a smoked wheat beer (12.5 Plato) called **Rauch-Weizen★★★**.

Where to drink

Less than 32km (20 miles) south of Frankfurt, in the artists' and philosphers' town of Darmstadt, is a shop stocking more than 1,000 beers, from 250 countries. The shop is named B. Maruhn, "Der Groesste Biermarkt Der Welt", and is at Pfumgstaete Strasse 174, in the district of Eberstadt, in Darmstadt (☎06151-54876). Owner Bruno Maruhn is a jolly, enthusiastic chap, and his claim to have the world's biggest beer shop is probably safe, despite earnest competition from the USA.

Binding

Germany's biggest brewing company producing a full range of beers and perhaps most noteworthy for its premium version of a German-style Export called **Export Privat★★**. It has a fresh, light hoppiness in the nose; a clean, malt-accented palate; and a faintly fruity dryness in the finish. A very similar beer, but fractionally less dry, marginally fuller bodied, and slightly paler, is brewed for the American market under the name **Steinhauser Bier★★**. This has a little extra maturation, and is micro-filtered, to retain its freshness. It is an enjoyable beer, and did not deserve to be polluted by half-truth when it was launched in the USA, where a spokesman for Binding was quoted as saying: "Steinhauser tastes the same here as it does in Germany". Binding also produce a hearty double bock **Carolus★★**.

Busch

A famous name in brewing. Southwest of Frankfurt is Mainz, from which Adolphus Busch emigrated to the USA to start the world's biggest brewing company. Northwest of Frankfurt is Limburg, where a family called Busch run a rather smaller brewery. American Busch make 50 million hectolitres of beer in the time it takes their German counterparts to brew 15,000hl. The two families are not related and neither, of course, has anything to do with a product called Bush Beer (no "c"), made in Belgium. There are, on the other hand, historical connections, though distant, between the German town of Limburg and the Belgian and Dutch provinces of the same name. As to Limburger cheese, it originated in Belgium and is still made there and in The Netherlands, but its principal centre of production is Germany. The three Limburgs also share an interest in beer. The German one produces a pleasant, very mild **Golden Busch Pils★→★★** and a **Limburger Export★★**.

Euler

The cathedral in Wetzlar gives its name to Euler's **Dom Pilsener★★**, which is medium-dry. The brewery is also known for its slightly fuller-bodied **Euler Landpils★★**. Other products include a deep amber, malty **Alt Wetzlar★★** (*alt* in this instance refers to tradition, not style. This is not an *Altbier* but a bottom-fermenting "dark" beer). Its basic **Euler Hell★→★★**, a pale, malty beer, has an export counterpart called **Kloster Bier**. The Landpils is served unfiltered at the Wetzlarer Braustuben, adjoining the brewery.

Henninger

This may be the smaller of the two principal breweries in Frankfurt, but it is still a sizeable concern and the better known internationally. Its principal products, within a considerable range, include **Kaiser Pilsner★** and the drier **Christian Henninger Pilsener★→★★**. The latter has not only more hops but also a second "e". Henninger exports widely and for a time promoted its beer in the USA by emphasizing the colour of its bottles. The argument was that the beer is kept fresh because the bottles are made from brown glass. Beer bottled in green glass is more vulnerable to being harmed by supermarket lighting (and therefore more likely to contain additives to maintain "shelf-life"). The claim was intended to steal a march on those well-established imports in the American market that bottled in green. Although the argument is valid, a more impressive claim would have been to prove that Henninger's beer itself is more interesting than its rivals. There was for some years a Henninger brewery in Canada, and the label survives there despite the sale of the plant to Heineken.

STUTTGART AND BADEN-WÜRTTEMBERG

This is the place for the eclectic drinker. Here, wine and fruit brandies oblige wine to share the table, even though the state of Baden-Württemberg still contrives to have more than 180 breweries.

In the Black Forest – or, at least, its greener valleys – village brewers produce tasty, sometimes slightly fruity, beers that reveal the softness of the local water. On the west side of the forest, the Jehle family brewery of Biberach is an example, with its aromatic Privat Pils and its dry *Dunkel*. In another part of the forest, the *Schloss* brewery Zöhrlaut has a soft Edel-Pils and a fruity, coffee-ish *Dunkel*. Stuttgart has three breweries, all taking their water from Lake Constance (the Bodensee) and producing typically light and soft "wine country" beers. East of Stuttgart, towards the Swabian mountains, one or two maltier beers emerge. (The term "Swabian" is widely used in Germany to indicate the culture and kitchen of an imprecise region that might be considered to stretch from Stuttgart to Augsburg.) The Olpp brewery, in Urach, has some well-made beers, including a clean, light Grafen-Pils. In that direction, more southern styles are to be found, notably wheat beers.

Where to drink

Stuttgart, the principal city of Baden-Württemberg, is more of a wine-drinkers' than a beer-drinkers' city, but beer-lovers will want to have a nostalgic glass at the former Sanwald Brewery *Gasthof* in Silberburg Strasse. There is also a small beer garden round the corner in Rotebühl Strasse. The old Sanwald brewery's wheat beers are now made by Dinkelacker, in Tübinger Strasse. In front of the Dinkelacker brewery is a pleasant restaurant serving the company's beers and offering Swabian dishes like *Fladlesuppe* (clear soup with strips of pancake); *Maultaschen* (Swabia's salty retort to ravioli); and *Spätzle* (egg noodles). No one ever went to Germany to lose weight and the Swabians clearly subscribe to this view.

At the end of September and for the first two weeks in October this businesslike city lets its hair down for its annual fair on the Cannstatt meadows. This *Cannstatter Volksfest* is Stuttgart's counterpart to Munich's *Oktoberfest*. Beer is supplied by all three of the local breweries (three more than some cities have, though it is only half the number mustered by Munich). Special *Volksfest* beers are produced, in the *Märzen* style, and there are very similar *Weihnachts* brews at Christmas.

About half way between Heidelberg and Stuttgart, at the salt-water spa of Bad Rappenau, the Haffner brewery has its own resort hotel (33 rooms, ☎07264-1061). Its house beer is called *Kur* ("Cure") Pils.

South of Stuttgart, on the way to Lake Constance, is a brewery called Löwen (there are about 30 such, unrelated, "Lion" breweries in Germany). This Löwen brewery, at Tuttlingen, serves a *Kellerpils* in its restaurant. Drinkers who enjoy this excessively should be warned that there are no bedrooms. Between Tuttlingen and Ulm, at Bingen, the Lamm brewery serves a *dunkles Hefeweizenbier* and, yet more exotic, *Bierhefebrannt*, a clear spirit distilled from beer.

Closer to Ulm, at Trochtelfingen, the Albquell brewery (five rooms, ☎07124-733) serves a *Kellerbier*.

Where to drink in Swabian Bavaria

South of Ulm, there are four breweries with restaurants, three with bedrooms. At Roggenburg-Biberach the Schmid brewery restaurant specializes in *Dunkel* and *Märzen* beers, but has no bedrooms. Hotel Löwenbrau (20 rooms, ☎08247-5056), at Bad Wörishofen, has a *Kurpils*, and is proud of its *Doppelbock*. The Hirsch brewery, at Ottobeuren, has several interesting specialities including a house liqueur made by Benedictine brothers in the local monastery. The brewery's kettles are visible to guests who soak away their hangover in the indoor pool at the adjoining hotel (80 rooms, ☎08332-552/3). Nearby at Irsee, a secularized monastery brewery produces some beers of outstanding interest, as well as having a very good kitchen. The Irseer Klosterbrauerei (26 rooms, ☎08341-8331) specializes in unfiltered beers, some matured for more than six months. A speciality called Abt's Trunk, conditioned and sold in hand-made clay flasks, has been reported to have reached a record-shattering 15 percent alcohol by weight. This sounds unlikely and the owner reckons that 12 percent by volume is more realistic. This brewery also has a *Bierbrannt*. There is also a colourful range of home-produced beers and schnapps at the Post Brewery Hotel (22 rooms, ☎08361-238/9) in the mountain resort of Nesselwang. The hotel has a small museum of beer and holds seminars on the subject.

Fürstenberg

The "Premium" ratings were perhaps something of a northern notion and Fürstenberg is the only southern brewery to have been dubbed in this way. It is also a house of some nobility, controlled by the aristocratic Fürstenbergs, who have been brewing for more than 500 years. The family are patrons of the arts and there is an impressive collection of German masters in the Fürstenberg museum, at the palace of Donauschingen, in the Black Forest. In the palace grounds, the Danube emerges from its underground source. Donauschingen is also the home of what is now a very modern brewery. A full range of styles is produced, but the brewery is especially well known for its **Fürstenberg Pilsener**★★ → ★★★. This has quite a full body, a sustained, lasting bead, and a nicely hoppy taste in its dry finish.

Dinkelacker

The biggest brewery in the southwest; it might just achieve this ascendancy on the basis of local sales, but exports are the decider. The brewery is best known for its **CD-Pils**★★. Although this is marketed as a prestige beer, the name stands not for *corps diplomatique* but for Carl Dinkelacker, who founded the brewery in Stuttgart in 1888. The Dinkelacker family, brewers since the mid 1700s, still control the company. The brewery, not far from the city centre, is a blend of the traditional and the modern. Copper kettles are used, and the CD-Pils is hopped four times with half a dozen varieties (the final addition being Brewers' Gold, in the lauter tun). The CD-Pils is also fermented in the classic square type of vessel and kräusened during lagering; other products go into an ugly forest of unitanks.

Dinkelacker produces a range of bottom-fermenting beers that adopt a middle stance between those of its local rivals Stuttgarter Hofbräu and Schwaben Bräu. In general, Hofbräu's are the sweetest, Dinkel's medium, Schwaben's the driest, but these are ·fine distinctions since all three breweries produce typically soft southwestern beers. In addition to its pale beers, Dinkelacker has a dark single bock, **Cluss Bock Dunkel**★★, from its affiliate Cluss brewery in nearby Heilbronn – very malty in aroma and palate, but rather weak in finish. At its Stuttgart headquarters Dinkelacker also produces a number of specialities inherited when the local Sanwald brewery was absorbed. These include a rather thin **Stamm Alt**★ and two wheat beers, each made to the same specification: the sparkling **Weizen Krone**★★ and the **Sanwald Hefe Weiss**★★.

Schwaben Bräu

The smallest of Stuttgart's three breweries, in the pleasant suburban township of Vaihingen. It has a large, traditional copper brewhouse and splendidly cavernous lagering cellars. The relative dryness of its beers is best exemplified by its **Meister Pils**★★→★★★. The parent company, Rob Leicht, also owns the Kloster brewery at Pfullingen-Reutlingen. Its **Kloster Pilsner**★→★★ is available not only in the local market but travels as far as the USA. It has a lightly hoppy aroma and finish, a quite full, soft, texture, and a hint of sharpness in the finish. Another subsidiary, Bräuchle, in Metzingen, produces a pale **Bock**★★ for the whole group. The company plans a small museum of brewing, perhaps as a gesture to beer as a parent product – in the local market, it is almost as well known for its soft drinks.

Stuttgarter Hofbräu

The Hofbräu rivals, and may surpass, Dinkelacker in local sales. Its brewery is not far beyond that of Dinkelacker, on the edge of Stuttgart. It's a curiously rural fold of the city, and Hofbräu's turn-of-the-century buildings have flourishes that could be Scottish baronial. Inside, however, the brewery is uncompromisingly modern. The name Hofbräu derives from a former royal brewery, but the present company is publicly held, with most of the stock in the hands of one person. The notion that drinkers of German wines have a soft, sweetish palate is emphatically accepted by Hofbräu, and the brewery also takes pride in its beers' not being pasteurized. Its premium product is called **Herren Pils**★→★★.

BAVARIA: MUNICH AND THE SOUTH

Beer-lovers in other countries may be jealous of Germany in general but the focus of envy must be the state of Bavaria. No entire nation, nor even Germany's other states put together, can rival Bavaria's tally of breweries, which still exceeds 800. Between them, they produce about 5,000 beers. Only nine or ten of Bavaria's breweries are, by any standard, large (each producing more than half a million hectolitres a year). More than 500 are very small – 10,000hl or less and of those, about half are tiny, producing less than 2,000hl.

Almost every village has a brewery and some have two or

three. The very small breweries almost always have their own inn, and often their beer is available nowhere else. There are breweries in monasteries – and convents – and in castles. The castles and baroque-rococo churches are a reminder that Bavaria was a nation of extrovert pride in the 17th and 18th centuries and when in 1919 it joined the German Republic, one of the conditions was that its Pure Beer Law be retained.

Bavaria is the home of more beer styles than any other part of Germany. Its everyday beers are not especially potent, but its specialities include the strongest beer in Germany. It grows good malting barley and virtually all of Germany's hops (and exports them all over the world), it has water in the Alps and the icy caves where the usefulness of cold maturation – lagering – first came to be understood.

The mountain and forest isolation of village Bavaria has helped its culture to survive, not only in costume, everyday dress, worship, music and dance, but also in its sense of being a beer land. Isolation was favoured by the founders of monasteries, too, in the days when they were the sanctuaries of all knowledge, including the art of brewing. If there was communication in these matters, it was across the mountains and within the forests. From the Dark Ages, the cradle of modern brewing has been slung from St Gallen in Switzerland to Munich, to Vienna, to Pilsen in Bohemia. That cradle is filled to bursting point with hearty, thirsty, Bavaria, crying *ein prosit!* at every opportunity.

While the Federal Republic as a whole drinks 140-odd litres of beer per head each year, this figure is greatly exceeded in Bavaria where the figure is closer to 240.

No other state has such a defined calendar of drinking dates and styles. It may not matter much which beer you drink in the madness of the pre-Lenten *Fasching* (an answer in southern cities like Munich and northern ones like Cologne to the *Mardi Gras* of Nice and New Orleans, or the *Carnival* of Rio). However, in March and April, the appropriate beer is *Doppelbock*; in May, single *Bock*; in June, July and August Export-type beers at village festivals and *Weissbier* or *Weizenbier* in the beer gardens; at the end of September, and for the weeks that follow, *Märzenbier* for the *Oktoberfest*; by November, it is time to think of *Weihnachts* (Christmas) beer, which may be a variation on the festival speciality, or could be a *Weizenbock*.

Even the beer's accompaniments have a timetable. With the mid-morning beer, the appropriate snack is *Weisswurst*, a pair of succulent veal sausages coddled in a tureen of warm water. The veal is tempered with small proportions of beef and coarse bacon, and there is a seasoning of parsley (occasionally chives) and sometimes onion or lemon. *Weisswurst* is so important that purists argue over its proper contents. For lunch, the beer might be accompanied by *Leberkäse*, which is neither liver nor cheese but a beef and pork loaf, served hot. For an early evening snack, the ubiquitous large radish of the region, which has a black skin and white flesh. The flesh is sculpted into a spiral and assaulted with salt. If the salt on the radish doesn't make you thirsty, the granules on the big, fresh, soft pretzels will do the trick.

To the foreigner, not least the beer-lover, the state of Bavaria may be synonymous with its capital city, Munich. Within Bavaria, while its claims are universally recognized,

Munich and its hinterland have competition from other cities and regions where yet more breweries are to be found.

Munich's claims are that it has some of the biggest and most famous breweries, and that it has nurtured more styles of beer than any other city. Within its hinterland, stretching through the regions known as Upper and Lower Bavaria, into the Alps and to the Austrian frontier, are hundreds of breweries. The city itself is ringed by small breweries making excellent beers. The Maisach and Schloss Mariabrunn breweries are just two examples. To the southwest, it is only 32km (20 miles) to the lakes and the beginning of the mountains, with more local breweries to serve the terraces and beer gardens.

South of Herrsching, on the lake called Ammersee, is the monastic brewery of Andechs, whose immensely malty *Dunkel* and *Bock* beers were the extremely distant inspiration for the American Andeker brand. The brothers also have their own bitter liqueurs and fruit brandies, and there is a *Stube* and terrace. Farther into the Alps, near the ski resort of Garmisch-Partenkirchen, is another famous monastery brewery, Ettal, producing well-made and typically Bavarian beers but better known for its fruit brandy. Northeast of Munich near Landshut is the Klosterbrauerei Furth and also the celebrated convent brewery of Mallersdorf, just off the road to Regensburg. Another convent brewery, St Josef's, is at Ursberg, west of Augsburg, near Krumbach, on the road to Ulm.

A monastery brewery founded in 1040 at Weihenstephan, near Freising, less than 32km (20 miles) northeast of Munich, was to have great historical significance. Although the evidence for continuous production is hazy, the brewery survived long enough to be secularized by Napoleon and continues today under the ownership of the State of Bavaria. The Bayerische Staatsbrauerei Weihenstephan thus claims to be the oldest brewery in the world. It may be a cobwebbed claim, but there is none better. Although there are vestiges of the monastery from the 12th century, and today's buildings are set in a restored cloister from the 17th century, the brewery is modern. It also offers some training facilities to the adjoining brewing institute.

There are only a handful of Faculties of Brewing in the world, and Weihenstephan – part of the Technical University of Munich – is the most famous. In recent years it has had difficulties, arising originally from its efforts to deal with brewers who do not work in *Reinheitsgebot* countries, but its name remains a by-word in the industry. The Weihenstephan brewery produces a full range of beers but is perhaps best known for its Kristal Export Weizenbier (very fruity, with hints of blackcurrant, and extremely dry in the finish) and its Hefeweissbier (light for the style, and refreshing).

Wheat-beer brewing is especially associated with the area to the east of Munich. About 32km (20 miles) out of the city is the Erding wheat-beer brewery, perhaps the best-known of the specialists and certainly the fastest-growing. Farther east, in Mühldorf, the Jägerhof house brewery of Wolfgang Unerti produces a wonderfully turbid wheat beer.

To the south of Munich another tiny brewery specializes in wheat beers: Gmeineder, at Deisenhofen near Oberhaching. Much farther south, at Murnau, off the road to

Garmisch, another notable example of the turbid style of wheat beer is made by the Karg brewery.

Where to drink

Each of the principal Munich breweries has several of its own special outlets in the form of gardens, beer halls and restaurants. The best or most famous are detailed with their entries below. To the west of Munich and closer to Augsburg, the *Schloss* brewery at Odelzhausen specializes in a double bock called Operator (nothing sinister about the name – it is dedicated to the Munich opera). As is often the case, the *Schloss* (nine bedrooms, ☎08134-6606) is more like a country house, but it has a restaurant. To the north of Munich, the brewery guest-house Goldener Hahn (☎08461-419) is at Beilngries, about half way to Nürnberg. Farther north, at Lengenfeld-Velburg, the Winkler brewery guest-house (☎09182-326) is widely known for its Kupfer Spezial beer. This much-loved brew is a dark copper colour, with gravity of 14 Plato, bottom-fermented in open vessels and matured for between ten and 16 weeks. A remarkable feature of this family concern is that it grows and malts its own barley. Its beer is hopped with both Bavarian and Bohemian varieties. There are also brewery guest-houses to the northeast of Munich at Adlersberg (Prösslbrau; ☎09404-1822); Böbrach (Brauereigasthof Eck; ☎09923-685); Zwiesel (Deutscher Rhein; ☎09922-1651); and Zenting (Kamm; ☎09907-315).

Altenmünster

The name Altenmünster has become well-known among beer-buffs in the USA thanks to the export of one of its beers in large, 2-litre flagons. These flagons, with a sprung, porcelain "swing top" and pewter handle, are much in demand. In the American market, the brew is identified simply as **Altenmünster★★**, sometimes with the after-thought "Brauer Bier", but no indication of style. In fact, in its full golden colour and big palate, it is a good example of the German style known as Export. It has a firm body, with a leaning toward maltiness that is typically Bavarian.

Altenmünster is a village near Augsburg, but exports of this beer have been so successful that some are now handled from a sister brewery in Weissenbrunn, northern Bavaria. Both breweries belong to a group embracing several other companies. These include Sailer (it rhymes with "miler") producing a range of soft, easily drinkable but unexceptional beers in Marktoberdorf, south of Augsburg. There are also companies at Kulmbach and at Neustadt, near Coburg.

Augustiner

The favourite brews among serious beer-drinkers in Munich are those from Augustiner. The beers are generally the maltiest among those produced by the city's major brewers and in that sense are closest to the palate traditionally associated with Munich. This is especially true of August-iner's pale beers. The everyday **Augustiner Hell★★★★** qualifies as the classic pale beer of Munich, with its malty aroma and palate, soft entrance and firm, smooth finish. The brewery's interpretation of the German Export type has the brand name **Edelstoff★★★** in Germany and, con-fusingly, is described as "Augustiner Munich Light" in the

American market. "Light" refers, of course, to its colour and not to its body. This is hardly the lightest of German beers and even the slenderest of those is big by American standards. In recent years Augustiner has been emphasizing its pale beers, perhaps to the detriment of its dark styles. The basic dark beer is called **Dunkel Vollbier★★★**. There is also a **Dunkel Export★★ →★★★**, which has occasionally appeared in Germanic areas of the USA. The company has a number of other styles; its **Maximator Doppelbock★★★** is marketed in the USA under the unexciting description "Munich Dark".

The maltiness of Augustiner's beers has sources close to home. No fewer than three of Munich's brewers have their own maltings and Augustiner is one. Its malt is produced in cellars that stretch like the tunnels of a mine underneath the brewery, which itself belongs to industrial archaeology. Constructed in 1885 and a magnificent example of the proud brewery edifices of the time, it is now a protected building. In the brewhouse only one in three vessels is made from copper; the other two are of stainless steel. The dark beers have the benefit of a triple decoction; the pale a double. Only aroma hops are used, in five varieties, from both Bavaria and Bohemia. Fermentation is in unusual vessels, open but with a lid that can be brought down, without pressure, to collect carbon dioxide. Fermentation is at very cold temperatures and lagering is in traditional vessels, with kräusening. The brewery uses wooden casks to supply beer gardens and some inns in the Munich area. The casks are pitched at the brewery, adding another traditional aroma to that of the malty air.

Augustiner has as its near neighbours Hacker-Pschorr, Spaten and Löwenbräu; all four are in the traditional "brewery quarter" behind Munich's central railway station. Across the river are Paulaner and the Hofbräuhaus brewery. In the heart of the brewery quarter, on Arnulf Strasse, is the Augustiner Keller, relatively small and much loved by the people of Munich. In the centre of the city on Neuhauser Strasse, Augustiner has its elegant, somewhat eccentric, 1890s restaurant and brewery tap, with a small, Italianate garden. This building was originally constructed in 1829 to house the brewery after secularization. As its name suggests, Augustiner was originally a monastic brewery, and its first site was close to Munich's landmark cathedral, the Frauenkirche. The brewery dates at least from the 15th century, though there is some uncertainty about the claimed foundation date of 1328. It is without doubt an institution in Munich, favoured by yet a third famous outlet, the beer garden at the Hirschgarten, a public park near Nymphenburg Castle. This popular picnic spot is said to accommodate as many as 8,000 drinkers, while Löwenbräu's beer garden in Munich's huge central park holds a mere 6,000. How carefully this has been counted is open to dispute.

Ayinger

In Munich, the best-known country brewery is Ayinger. The position it enjoys in the city is evident: its beers are served in the restaurant and cabaret called the Platzl, on the square of the same name, directly opposite the Hofbräuhaus. The restaurant is owned by Ayinger and a special Platzl brew is produced – a miniature barrel of the beer is customarily set in the centre of the table, to accompany the evening's burlesque. After dinner, there might also be a clear fruit brandy, made from apples and pears and served in pot vessels shaped like tobacco pipes.

The Platzl beer is pleasant enough but a half-hour journey out of Munich to the village of Aying will provide just that freshness to make it taste delicious. In Aying (and in the USA) this brew is known as Jahrhundert. The name dates from the brewery's centenary in 1978. **Jahrhundert**★★ is a German Export-type beer. It has some herbal hoppiness in the nose and a big, malty palate that dries in a crisp finish.

Ayinger has a full range of styles, among which several are noteworthy. **Altbairisch Dunkel**★★ →★★★ is a splendid example of the Bavarian dark style, with a warm, sweetly fruity aroma and coffee-ish finish. **Fest-Märzen**★ →★★ is a little pale for the style but has a lovely malt bouquet, carrying through in the soft palate. **Maibock**★ →★★, too, is a classically malty Bavarian beer, with spicy, apricot notes. Most characterful of all is the double bock, labelled in Germany as Fortunator and in the USA as Celebrator. By whichever name, **Fortunator/Celebrator**★★★ is an outstanding example of double bock style and a beautifully balanced beer, its richness mellowing out in a long, dryish finish. When strong brews are served at the end of winter, Germans talk about taking the "springtime beer cure". Ayinger goes further: it dubs its home village a "beer spa".

Where the Munich basin, with its crops of malting barley, gives way to the foothills of the Alps the village of Aying provides for gentle exploration. Ayinger, with its own elderly maltings and modern brewhouse, stands on one side of the road, facing its guest-house on the other. A small beer garden, little more than a terrace, and an early baroque church complete the village square. In the square, the typical Bavarian maypole is set into a wooden tun that was once a maturation vessel in the brewery. The brewmaster at Ayinger also looks after the local museum.

Ayinger also owns Höll wheat-beer brewery in Traunstein, further up the road. This imposing brewery was built in the late 19th century and has not changed markedly since. It leans sleepily into a hillside in the valley of the river Traun. Four wheat beers are produced at Traunstein. **Export Weissbier**★ →★★ is filtered and has a full, relatively sweet, fruitiness (ripe plums, perhaps?). The unfiltered **Hefe-Weissbier**★ →★★ is much more tart. The **Ur-Weizen** ★★ →★★★ has a fuller, amber-red colour and bursts with fruitiness. It is also unfiltered and has the classic apples-and-cloves spiciness of a traditional wheat beer. A **Weizenbock**★★, 17 Plato, pale and filtered, is available in the local market at Christmas.

Forschungs

A secret well kept by the beer-lovers of Munich is the existence of a house-brewery in the city, in the market-gardening suburb of Perlach. The place does have the qualities of a mirage. For one thing, it operates only in summer (and even then closes on Mondays). For another, it looks like a cross between a seaside ice-cream parlour and the control tower at a small and dubious airport. It also happens to make the highest-gravity brew in Munich. Its speciality is a 19 Plato beer called **St Jacobus Blonder Bock**★★★. This potent product is soft and sweet but very clean with a big, malty finish. The supporting potion is curiously called **Pilsissimus**★★ → ★★★. It has both hops and malt in its big aroma and contrives to be both dry and soft in palate. The Forschungs brewery and its small, pebbled beer garden are at Unterhachinger Strasse 76, Perlach (☎089-6701169).

Hacker-Pschorr

There is a resonance about the names of Munich's principal breweries. Not so long ago, Hacker and Pschorr were two of them. They merged, and much more recently have been taken over by Paulaner. Despite that, the brewery continues to operate, with its own range of beers. They are on the dry side and perhaps not as smooth as some Munich brews. However, by the standards of some other regions and countries, they still have a fair degree of character. Hacker-Pschorr has never been identified with any single speciality, though it has recently been concentrating on its **Pils**★. Its *Oktoberfest* **Märzen**★ → ★★ and **Animator**★★ double bock are both pleasant. The company's beers can be tasted at Zum Pschorr-Bräu, in Neuhauser Strasse, and in summer on a terrace in the Marienplatz.

Hofbräuhaus

Perhaps the label "HB" is felt in Germany to speak for itself, but elsewhere in the world the allusion is not instantly clear. It stands for "Hofbräu" ("court brew"), and is the label of brews produced for the world's most famous beer hall. The Hofbräuhaus in Munich was originally the beer hall and garden of the Bavarian Royal Court Brewery. Lesser Hofbräus remain elsewhere in Germany, having passed from minor royalty into commercial hands, but the most important one still belongs to Bavaria, albeit to the state government. The garden is pleasant, though the rambling beer hall smells of stale cigarettes and the detritus of tourism. The beers are excellent, the conventional brews being malt-accented with a spritzy finish. Although the everyday beer is a fresh-tasting, malty **Export**★★ → ★★★, the Hofbräuhaus (founded in 1589) is credited with having, in its early days, introduced *Bock* beer to Munich. Its smooth, malty **Maibock**★★★★ is the classic example of the style. When the first cask is tapped at the Hofbräuhaus on May Day, the Prime Minister of Bavaria usually takes part in the ceremony. Maibock tastes especially good accompanied by a couple of *Weisswurst*. Since its earliest days the Hofbräuhaus has also had a tradition of wheat beers. Its **Edel Weizen**★★ → ★★★ has long been enjoyed, but **Dunkel-Weizen**★★ → ★★★ is not to be ignored: a complex beer with dense head, lavish lacework, a sweet start, toasty maltiness, and a lemony tartness in the finish.

Kaltenberg

Although by no means the only brewery owned by an aristocrat, Kaltenberg is perhaps the best known, not least because it is in a classic Bavarian castle. The castle dates from the 13th century, but the present structure was built in the 17th century based on designs by the architect who created Neuschwanstein for "Mad" King Ludwig II of Bavaria. The third King Ludwig was the last and his great-grandson, Prince Luitpold, runs the Kaltenberg brewery. In export markets Kaltenberg is known for a well-made **Diat-Pils★★**, but in its local market it is noted for a rich, malty, dark beer, with a coffee-ish finish, **König Ludwig Dunkel ★★ → ★★★**, which has a gravity of 13.3 Plato.

Kaltenberg Castle is near Geltendorf, less than 50km (30 miles) west of Munich. It has a beer garden and restaurant, and in June holds a beer festival and costumed jousting between "medieval" knights (for information, ☎08193-209). At these festivals, a **Dunkel Ritter Bock★★★** of 23 Plato is made available ("Ritter" means "rider" or "knight"). Because it is outside Munich, the Kaltenberg brewery is not permitted to offer its beer at the city's *Oktoberfest* so Prince Luitpold decided in 1985 to open a *Hausbräuerei* in Munich, producing a *Dunkelweizen*.

Löwenbräu

Internationally, the best-known name among the Munich breweries is Löwenbräu. About a quarter of its output is exported and it licenses its name to be used on products in other countries, including the USA and Japan. Despite international sales it is not the biggest brewer in Munich, though it comes a good second to Paulaner, which exports far less. In local preference, Löwenbräu's beers are somewhere in the middle of the league table. In general, the beers are malt-accented but well-balanced, with a late hint of hoppiness in the finish. Löwenbräu is not especially associated with any one style, but promotes its **Pils★★**, which is unusually hoppy by Munich standards. The brewery owns the biggest beer hall, the 5,000-seat Mathäser, in Bayern Strasse, near the central railway station. The Mathäser has the look of a railway station itself, with its cafeteria entrance, but its 15 or so inner halls are worth exploring. The cellar restaurant features wheat beer. Löwenbräu also has one of the biggest beer gardens in the huge central park called the English Garden. Löwenbräu's encircles the park's famous pagoda, the "Chinese Tower".

Paulaner

The biggest brewery in Munich is especially associated with its classic **Salvator★★★★** double bock. This extra-strong, very dark beer, with deep amber highlights, has a gravity of 18.5 Plato and is made with three malts. Only Hallertau hops are used, though of both bittering and aroma varieties. The beer has a very rich start, drying out in a long finish. Its alcohol content is around 6 percent by weight, 7.5 by volume. The brewery has its origins in the early 17th century with a community of monks of St Paul, who became well known throughout the city for the strong beer they brewed, called Salvator (Saviour) to sustain themselves during Lent. Being a very strong beer, it came to be known as a "double" bock and gave rise to that style. Most other double bock beers echo the Saviour's brew by bearing names ending in *-ator*. Double bock beers are drunk to warm the soul as winter gives way to spring and the beer gardens think about reopening. This happens a week before Easter, and the first new barrel of Salvator is ceremonially tapped by the Mayor of Munich or Prime Minister of Bavaria at the brewery's 3,500-seat beer hall and garden on the hill called Nockherberg. There are also Salvator celebrations on March 19, the saint's day of Paulaner.

The brewery was secularized in the early 19th century and has since had several owners, but it still stands on the same site, though it has grown to straddle the hill. From the modern office block, a tunnel through the hillside leads to the maltings and the brewhouse, which is still in traditional copper. The brewery uses classic fermenters and traditional lagering cellars, maturing its everyday beers (which are kräusened) for five or six weeks and its stronger specialities for three to eight months. Paulaner has one of Germany's first refrigeration machines, made for the brewery by Carl von Linde, and an early water turbine powered by a stream that runs down the hill. Paulaner's beers are firm-bodied and dry for Munich, often with an assertive finish. The dark **Alt-Münchner Dunkel**★★ → ★★★ has a fine colour, a smooth, full body and a maltiness in that dry finish. The export-style **Urtyp 1634**★★ has, again, a full, smooth body but a slightly tannic finish. The pale **Original Münchner Hell**★★★ is similar but milder. The brewery produces a full range of styles – with about ten principal beers – including a dry, rounded **Altbayerische Weissbier**★★ that has helped popularize wheat beers in the USA.

Schneider

The specialist wheat-beer brewery of George Schneider and Son has been a feature of the Munich scene for more than a century, and has a restaurant on Tal Strasse. However, after World War II the company moved production out of the city, northeast to Kelheim, near Regensburg. Since Munich and the area to the east have such a long and thriving tradition of wheat beers, **Schneider-Weisse**★★★ → ★★★★ might be regarded as the classic example of the style. For flavour, though, it is exceeded by the brewery's *Weizenbock*, **Aventinus**★★★★ which, with its huge head and insistent sparkle, adds its own flourish to beer drinking in Munich.

Spaten

This is one of the world's most important brewing companies because of its influence on the beers most nations drink today. All lager beers, whether dark, amber or pale, owe much to the work of the Spaten brewery in the 19th century. The influence of this company should be far more widely recognized internationally, but perhaps its reputation has been subsumed, with those of its neighbours, into that of Munich itself. Although it still takes great pride in earlier styles such as wheat beers (notably the dry, spicy, full-bodied and fluffy **Franziskaner Hefe-Weissbier**★★ → ★★★ and its cleaner, sparkling **Club-Weisse**★★), Spaten's greatest contributions are in the development of bottom-fermenting beers: in the perfecting of the Bavarian dark style, as typified by its own **Dunkel Export**★★★ → ★★★★; in the popularization of the amber type, as represented by its world classic **Ur-Märzen**★★★★; and in the perfecting of the Munich pale variety, as exemplified by its **Münchner Hell**★★★. From an historical viewpoint, all these beers are classics, and they are still produced in a manner that blends tradition with modern technology. Spaten has its own maltings, uses traditional kettles and lauter tuns (copper in the old brewhouse, stainless steel in a new one), closed classic fermenters and horizontal lagering tanks.

An especially interesting feature of Spaten's methods is

that three different yeasts are used in the production of bottom-fermenting beers. The pale beers of conventional gravities (including a very dry **Spaten Pils**★★ →★★★ have one yeast; the **Franziskus Heller Bock**★★ another; the darker brews a third. Most breweries would use only one strain for all those types, but Spaten feels that yeasts should be chosen according to their suitability to ferment the different worts and their contribution to background palate.

The company traces its origins to a brewery of 1397, and its name (meaning "spade") is a jocular corruption of Spaeth, an early owner. The royal court brewmaster Gabriel Sedlmayr took over the company in 1807 and his son, Gabriel the Younger, became the father of modern lager-brewing. Studies carried out by Gabriel in the 1830s introduced Bavaria to more scientific methods, notably the use of the saccharometer in the control of fermentation. Sedlmayr gathered disciples who spread the reputation of Bavarian bottom-fermenting techniques, and Sedlmayr's friend and rival Anton Dreher went on to introduce the amber style of lager in Vienna in 1840/41. A year later, the Pilsen brewery produced the first pale lager. In 1873, Sedlmayr worked with von Linde on his first refrigerator, at the instigation of Dreher (Paulaner's Linde machine came later) and in 1876 he introduced the world's first steam-heated brewhouse (companies that followed liked to call themselves "steam breweries"). The present company was constituted originally from Gabriel's business and his brother Joseph's Franziskaner brewery.

Spaten is still predominantly owned by the Sedlmayr family. It is proud of its family ownership and of its traditions, and still delivers beer in Munich by horse and dray. Regrettably, the building from which they emerge looks less like a brewery than a fair-sized airport.

NORTHERN BAVARIA: FRANCONIA

For the beer-drinker, Munich and southern Bavaria might seem like the pearly gates, but heaven is further north. Up there Bavaria has a region that is almost a state within a state: Franconia (Franken), with Nürnberg as its largest city and Bamberg (with no fewer than ten) and Amberg (a mere nine) as its most heavily-breweried towns.

There are more small breweries in Franconia than any-where in the world. It remains a centre of production for dark Bavarian lagers. It has more unfiltered beers than anywhere else and a greater number of eccentric specialities.

From south to north, the region stretches from Regens-burg to Bayreuth, Kulmbach and Coburg, on the frontier with East Germany. Due east the Bohemian Forest forms the frontier with Czechoslovakia, with Česke Budějovice (Budweis) and Pilsen nearby. To the west the small-brewery country of the Steigerwald reaches to Würzburg and wine territory.

Bamberg is the centre for a highly unusual speciality, the smoky *Rauchbier*. Kulmbach is the traditional centre for dark beers and produces some especially strong *Doppelbock* brews. Coburg has its unique, revivalist *Steinbier*, brewed with hot rocks. Bayreuth has a proprietary speciality, the Maisel brewery's *Dampfbier*.

Even in towns not specifically associated with a single style, many breweries have their own minor specialities. Sometimes these are dark beers. Often they are unfiltered. While an unfiltered *Kräusenbier* is cause for comment elsewhere in the country, such brews are not uncommon in Franconia. As its name suggests, this type of beer is kräusened. Then, before the kräusen has worked out, the maturation vessel is tapped, revealing intentionally cloudy beer. Another type of unfiltered beer is not kräusened. This is *Kellerbier*, which is allowed to settle in the maturation tanks before being tapped. As might be expected it has a notably low carbonation. Traditionally, this type of beer has been heavily hopped to guard against infection. A well-known example is made by St Georgenbräu, of Buttenheim, just south of Bamberg. Another excellent *Kellerbier* comes from Maisel of Bamberg (there are four Maisel breweries in Bavaria, each quite separate but linked by family).

Bamberg is a town of only 70,000 people but it is a remarkable centre of brewing. High on the hill that overlooks the town is the 17th-century Romanesque church of St Michael, part of a former monastery which had a brewery (the monks' brewhouse has now been converted into a Franconian Beer Museum). The town itself is a living museum, not only for its German Renaissance buildings but also for its selection of breweries. There is plenty of half-timbering and gilding about the breweries and their guesthouses, too, but their principal contribution is in terms not of architecture but of social and economic history. Two even have their own maltings so that they can do the kilning necessary to produce *Rauchbier* (made by kilning the malt over beech logs). There are also two free-standing maltings.

By no means do all of Bamberg's ten breweries regularly feature *Rauchbier* and, though the town is the centre for production, companies elsewhere have been known to produce a beer in this style. In Bamberg, the Heller brewery has Aecht Schlenkerla Rauchbier as its principal product; the family Merz's Hausbrauerei Spezial produces nothing else; Greifenklau's beer has only a faint hint of smokiness; and Kaiserdom Rauchbier is produced in Eltmann for Burgerbrau-Bamberg; Maisel's Rauchbier is made by another Eltmann brewery.

Among other Bamberg breweries, Fässchen offers as its specialities a *Kellerbier* and a *Märzen*; Keesman emphasizes its malty but dry Herren Pils; the secular Klosterbräu has a dark beer; Löwenbräu has a range of products; Mahrs has a relatively well carbonated *Kellerbier* and a delicious, rich dark brew called Wunderburger Liesl. The pale beers of Bamberg all have a dry maltiness.

To the west is the Steigerwald, with woodland walks and scores of small breweries, many with their own taverns. About 24km (15 miles) north of Bamberg, at Pferdsfeld, the Kunigunda Leicht brewery lists its production at 250 hectolitres a year, which probably makes it the smallest in Germany. To the east, in the countryside known as the Frankische Schweiz are more small breweries.

Some towns and villages have communal breweries where members of the public can brew their own beer. Falkenburg, Neuhaus-on-Pegnitz and Sesslach are examples. This facility is generally exercised by barley farmers or tavern keepers. In the days before commercial production, a

communal brewer who had a new batch ready would display
a garland or a six-pointed star outside his house. The latter is
a symbol of the brewer, deriving from alchemy rather than
from any religious significance. In some places this practice
is still followed, although it is also used by small commercial
brewers. Ecclesiastical brewing was significant in the past in
Franconia, but only one monastery brewery remains, the
Klosterbrauerei Kreuzberg at Bischofsheim, north of Würzburg, near the frontier with East Germany.

Where to drink

In Bamberg, the obvious places to stay are the guest-houses
of Brauerei Spezial (Obere König Strasse 10, ☎0951-24304),
which is in the shopping area; or Brauerei Greifenklau
(Laurenziplatz 20, ☎0951-53219) which has a spectacular
valley view. The mandatory stop for a drink is the
Schlenkerla tavern, in Dominikaner Strasse, but other
brewery taps are also worth a visit; the low-ceilinged tavern
of the Mahrs brewery, in Wunderburg, is a delightful
"local". The Steigerwald can be explored from the Klosterbräu Hotel in Ebelsbach (☎09522-235), which specializes in
a dark *Märzen*. To the north, between Bamberg and
Coburg, the Goldener Stern at Ebersdorf (24 bedrooms,
☎ 09562-106163) has a splendid *Zwickelbier*. Northwest of
Coburg, at Gauerstadt, near Rodach, the Wacker brewery
(20 bedrooms, ☎09564-225) has a pale draught beer.
Northeast of Coburg, the Grosch brewery (17 bedrooms,
☎09563-547) in Rodental, on the way to Neustadt, has an
excellent dark beer. In the old brewing town of Lichtenfels,
the Wichert *Gasthof* has a *Kellerbier* but no bedrooms. The
Frankische Schweiz can be explored from the Drei Kronen
brewery inn at Memmelsdorf (☎0951-43001), where an
unfiltered lager and a dark *Märzen* is served. Another Drei
Kronen ("Three Crowns") in nearby Strassgeich produces a
lovely, firm-bodied Kronenbräu Lager with a gravity of 12.7
Plato and a "1308" Pilsener of 12.4 (unusual, in that
everyday lagers usually have lower gravities than their
companion Pilseners). The "1308" is named for the foundation date of this tiny (3,000hl) brewery, which so captured
the imagination of an executive from a large international
company that its name was bought for use on somewhat
lesser beers in Canada and South Africa. This Drei Kronen
has no rooms. Neither does the Schinner brewery restaurant
in Richard Wagner Strasse, Bayreuth, but it does serve an
excellent Braunbier. In Nürnberg, the Altstadt brewery is
an essential visit, with beer on sale by the bottle and available on tap nearby. Regensburg has a number of beer-
restaurants. In Arnulfsplatz, the Kneitinger brewery
produces beer mainly for its own restaurant. The Spital-
garten, in Katharinenplatz, dates from the 14th century and
serves local beer.

Altstadthof

The name indicates "Old Town Courtyard", which is the
corner of Nürnberg where this delightful *Hausbrauerei* is to
be found. The brewery, a bakery and one or two wholefood
shops share a restored courtyard off Berg Strasse. In the Old
Town, in a building dating from the 16th century and with
brewing rights from that time, the *Hausbrauerei* first
charged its traditional copper kettle in 1984, taking care to

use organically grown barley malt and hop blossoms. Fermentation is in open, wooden tuns like those in drawings of medieval breweries and lagering is in wooden hogsheads of the type often kept as museum pieces in large breweries. The year-round product is an unfiltered dark beer with a gravity of 12–12.5 Plato. **Hausbrauerei Altstadthof★★★** beer has a deep, tawny colour, almost opaque; yeasty fruitiness and malty sweetness in the aroma; a yeasty dryness overlaying the rich, smooth, malty palate; dark malt tones in the finish, with some local, Hersbrucker hop coming through. Seasonal *Bock* and *Märzen* versions have also been produced. A tiny antique bottling machine fills the beer into swing-top litres, which are then sold at the brewery in crude wooden six-packs. The beer is also available on draught at two Altstadthof cafes (one, opening at lunchtime, is called the Dampfnudel and specializes in sweet steamed puddings; the other, opening in the evening, is the Schmelztiegl). The brewery has only two full-time employees.

The *Hausbrauerei* was established, initially out of enthusiasm for beery history, by the owners of the Lamms brewery in Neumarkt, south of Nürnberg. Lammsbrau provides not only the yeast but also the water for Altstadt. The *Hausbrauerei* does not have an adequate supply of its own water, nor space for treatment facilities.

EKU

The EKU brewery in Kulmbach boasts the highest gravity of any beer in the world, with its **Kulminator 28★★★ → ★★★★**. As its name suggests, this beer has a guaranteed gravity of 28 degrees – though analysis has revealed levels as high as 30.54. The brewery claims to mature the beer for nine months with a short period of freezing to settle protein. Since this is not done specifically for the purpose of raising alcohol content, Kulminator 28 is not labelled as an *Eisbock*. As the name Kulmin*ator* implies, it is a *Doppelbock* by style, though it is labelled merely as *Urtyp* ("original") and *Hell* ("pale"). In fact it is not especially pale – the great density of malt provides an amber cast – but it is not a dark beer. It has an intensely malty nose and palate, with a strongly alcoholic character. Its alcohol content has been analysed at 10.92 by weight, 13.5 by volume.

The world heavyweight title is contested between Kulminator 28 and the Swiss Hürlimann brewery's Samichlaus (a Christmas beer). Samichlaus has a lower gravity (27.6), a longer period of maturation (a year) and a higher alcohol content (11.1 by weight; 13.71 by volume). While this contest is too hard to resist, such muscle has limited application. These are beers of excellent quality but they would best be dispensed from small barrels suspended from the necks of mountain-rescue dogs. Whether they revive or stun the recipient depends upon the constitution of the drinker. Certainly, in their fermentation, the yeast is stunned by the alcohol it produces. That explains why these beers take so long, and are so difficult to make. Nor do they contain any of the sugars (or, sometimes, enzymes) that are used in the relatively lightweight strong beers (or "malt liquors") of the USA.

EKU also has a dark double bock, simply called **Kulminator★★ → ★★★** (with a gravity of 18.5); a pale, single **Edelbock★★**; a conventional dark export-style beer called

Rubin; a rather full-bodied **Pils★→★★**; and a pleasant **Weizen★**.

The first two initials of EKU stand for Erste ("First") Kulmbach. The "U" derives from the union of two earlier breweries that created the company in 1872.

Hofmark

The traditionalist Hofmark brewery is interesting for a number of reasons: its location, east of Regensburg at Cham on the Bavarian side of the Bohemian Forest, means that its soft water emerges from the same quartz-granite bed as that of Pilsen; it was founded in 1590 and has been in one family for more than 200 years; and it still uses some traditional techniques, not least the method of fining with beechwood chips. It is also unusual in that its premium beer Das feine Hofmark is prepared in two variations: mild and bitter (designations that sound more English than German). Both are firm, smooth, beautifully balanced beers of some complexity. Das feine Hofmark **Würzig Mild★★** has a malt accent; **Würzig Herb★★→★★★** (meaning "dry" or "bitter") has a lovely hop character in both nose and finish. This brewery was a pioneer in the use of swing-top bottles.

Kaiserdom

A full range of beers is marketed under the Kaiserdom label by the Bürgerbräu brewery of Bamberg. Most tend toward the dry maltiness of the region but are unexceptional. However **Kaiserdom Rauchbier★★★** has the distinction of being the only smoked beer exported to the USA.

Kulmbacher Mönchshof

The dark-beer tradition of Kulmbach is best maintained by the "Monks'" brewery. Its **Kloster Schwarz-Bier★★★★** rates as a classic, with a gravity of 12.5, a full, smooth body and a dark-malt palate unrivalled among major labels. The connoisseur of Bavarian dark beers might, of course, prefer the earthier character to be found in some of the many *Hausbrauerei* examples. Mönchshof goes back to the beginnings of monastic brewing in Kulmbach in 1349. It was secularized in 1791, becoming a family brewery, and is now part-owned by Kulmbacher Reichelbräu. Even at the peak of Kulmbach's international repute as a brewing centre, at the turn of the century, Mönchshof was one of the smaller houses. Today, it remains an active exporter, especially to the USA. Its range includes a very full-bodied dark double bock called **Urstoff★★→★★★**; a very flavourful single **Klosterbock Dunkel★★★**; a malty **Märzen★★**; a malty export called **Maingold★★**; and what is for Bavaria an unusually dry **Mönchshof-Pilsener★★**.

Kulmbacher Reichelbräu

If Germany can have *Eiswein*, then it can have icy beer, too. The tradition of *Eisbock* is especially kept alive by Kulmbacher Reichelbräu. *Eisbock* is a strong beer in which alcohol content is enhanced by freezing and then removing the ice. Because alcohol has a lower freezing point than water this concentrates the brew. The resultant **Eisbock Bayrisch G'frorns★★★→★★★★** ("Bavarian Frozen") has a gravity of 24 and an alcohol content of around 8 percent by weight, 10 by volume. It is a most interesting beer, dense and potent.

Reichelbräu, which is named after its founder, has the biggest local sales and offers a full range of styles.

Kulmbacher Schweizerhof

Kulmbacher Schweizerhof was founded in 1834, but since 1980 has been part of the same group as Rauchenfels, Altenmünster and Sailer. It has a range of styles but its principal beer, identified simply as **Kulmbacher Schweizer-hof-Bräu★→★★** ("feinherb aus Kulmbach") is a rather malty Pilsener with a firm, dry palate.

Maisel

Among the four Bavarian brewing companies called Maisel, this one in Bayreuth is by far the biggest. It has also become well known for its speciality brews, notably its highly individualistic **Maisel's Dampfbier★★★**. This is a top-fermenting beer, very fruity, with vanilla-like tones. It has a gravity of 12.2 Plato, is made with a triple decoction mash from four barley malts, hopped with Hallertaus and fermented with its own yeast in open vessels. It emerges slightly redder and paler than a Düsseldorfer Altbier, and about 4 percent alcohol by weight, 5 by volume. It is not pasteurized, even for export to the USA. "Dampfbier" is a registered name, not intended to indicate a recognized style and Maisel earnestly disavows any intention to sound like Anchor Steam (which is different both in production process and palate). In the late 1970s, the brewery decided that, "all beers were beginning to taste the same. We wanted something distinctive. We experimented, and this was the brew we liked." The decision may also have had something to do with the move out of a magnificently castellated and steam-powered brewery of 1887 into a remorselessly modern plant next door. There is an element of nostalgia to a "steam beer" (which is how Dampfbier would, inescapably, translate). For the two Maisel brothers who own the brewery, nostalgia is not a cheap emotion. The entire old brewery has been mothballed, in working order, and is now open for tours, at 10 o'clock each morning, or by appointment.

Meanwhile, Maisel continues in its spotless new brewery to produce an interesting range of products, including three wheat beers. **Weizen Kristall-Klar★★** is, as its name suggests, a crystal-clear beer, very pale, with a champagne-like sparkle and a tannic, apple fruitiness. **Hefe-Weiss★★** is fermented out with a mixture of yeasts, kräusened and given a dosage at bottling. It has a deep bronze colour, an apple-like palate and a big, fluffy body. **Weizenbock★★→★★★**, at 17.5 Plato, has a deep tawny colour, a big body, and a sharpness that recedes into smooth vanilla and licorice tones at the finish.

Rauchenfels Steinbiere

One of the world's oddest speciality beers, **Rauchenfels Steinbiere**, is also among the most drinkable. This is a 1980s revival of a brewing method used before the development of metal kettles. When brewing vessels were made from wood they could not be heated directly, and one method of boiling the brew was to mull it with hot stones. This is said to have been done in Alpine areas where stones could be found that would accept great heat, and sudden cooling, without shattering. The inventive and entrepreneurial German brewer Gerd Borges, on the lookout for new specialities, acquired a quarry with suitable graywacke stones, developed a way of handling the hot stones in a brewery and revived the technique. A clay hearth and a beechwood fire heat the stones, which are held in a steel basket, to a temperature of 1,200°C. The stones are then immersed in a pre-heated brew. The kettle bubbles, hisses, and exhales steam as though it were a volcano. Within a few seconds, the malt sugars in the brew have caramelized on to the stones. In this modern version, the heating function of the stones is less significant than the caramelization of the malt sugars. "Stone Beer" is top-fermenting, but the caramelized malt comes back into play when the cooled stones are placed in the maturation vessels with the brew. At this point, a violent secondary fermentation starts, settling down over a three-week period. **Rauchenfels Steinbiere**★★★ → ★★★★ has a very smoky palate, less dry than smooth, with a long, rounded finish. A companion "stone" Weizenbier is also produced. The beers are made at Neustadt, near Coburg, in an old-established brewery acquired for the purpose.

Schäffbräu

After a bruising collision with the *Reinheitsgebot*, the Schäffbräu brewery now probably produces the purest beer in Germany. Whatever its other claims to fame, it is notable for its "Fire Festival" double bock. **Schäff-Feuerfest**★★★ has a gravity of 25 Plato, and the brewery claims that it is matured for 12–18 months before emerging with an alcohol content of more than 8 percent by weight; 10 by volume. It is a dark, fruity beer, with a low carbonation. Although the brewery recommends Feuerfest as an aperitif, both its name and its prune-brandy palate seem more suited to accompany *crêpes Suzette*. So does its bottle, with wax seal and limited-edition number. The brewery is south of Nürnberg, in the Altmühltal Natural Park at Treuchtlingen.

Schlenkerla Rauchbier

The most famous Bamberg *Rauchbier* is Schlenkerla, produced for the tavern of that name by the Heller brewery. Like Scotch whisky, *Rauchbier* gains its smoky palate at the malting stage. Again as with Scotch, the method stems from the available means of kilning the malt. What the Scots had at hand was peat; the Franconians had beechwood. As more modern methods of kilning evolved, a degree of tradition survived in both Scotland and Franconia, especially in the wooded countryside that surrounds the town of Bamberg.

Ricks of beechwood logs still wait to burn in the tiny maltings (though it has both Saladin and drum systems) of the Heller brewery, which dates from 1678. The traditional brewhouse, in copper trimmed with brass, sparkles. In another room, a whirlpool makes a strange contrast before the open fermenters. Ninety-five percent of the brewery's production is *Rauchbier*, usually at a *Märzen* gravity of just over 13.5 percent. It is made entirely from smoked malt, mashed by double decoction, hopped only once (the magic cone can hardly fight the smoke), bottom-fermented, matured for six or seven weeks without kräusening and not pasteurized. The resultant beer has a smoky aroma and a dryness the moment it hits the tongue, and a full, smoky flavour that lingers in a long finish. Some people have to drink as many as five litre glasses before they begin to enjoy *Rauchbier*. It is, not only among beers but also among all alcoholic drinks, a classic. **Aecht Schlenkerla Rauchbier Märzen★★★★** is the definitive example, and in October, November and December there is a 19 Plato version called **Ur-Bock★★★**. The brewery also has a *Helles*, but even that has a hint of smokiness.

Spezial

The oldest *Rauchbier* producer is believed to be Bamberg's Brauerei Spezial, which dates from 1536. It is an unassuming *Hausbrauerei* in a main shopping street. The Christian Merz family have their own tiny maltings and produce only smoked beers. Their everyday product, if it can be called that, is a *Rauchbier* simply called **Lager**, at 12 Plato. It has a gently insistent smokiness and a treacle-toffee finish. A **Märzen★★★** version of around 13.5 is even smokier in texture, bursting with flavour in the finish. There is also a November **Bock★★★**.

Tucher

One of the two large breweries that dominate the Nürnberg market is Tucher, the other being Patrizier. On their home ground, both have upset beer-lovers by swallowing smaller breweries, but Tucher's exports have brought a welcome taste of Germany to parts of the New World. The brewery has a full range, including a dryish **Pilsener★→★★**; a tasty, malty dark beer called **Alt Franken Export Dunkel★★**; a smooth double bock called **Bajuvator★★**; and a couple of wheat beers, **Weizen★** and **Hefe-Weizen★**. Sad to say, the splendidly bitter **Doppelhopfen** has not been available in recent years.

Würzburger Hofbräu

Würzburg is in wine country and tried, in 1434, to banish its brewers forever. A couple of hundred years later it had acquired a Hofbräuhaus, which still produces pleasant beers, malt-accented but well balanced. Its **Pils★→★★** has a malty nose, a firm body and a hoppy finish. **Burkardus★** (in some export markets **"Bavarian Dark"**) is tawny and translucent with a dry, malty palate. **Oktoberfest★** is on the dark side and quite dry. There is also a **Maibock★**, a **Sympator★** double bock and a **Hefe-Weissbier★★**.

BERLIN

"The champagne of beers" is a soubriquet too generously disposed. It is appropriate only to wheat brews, notably *Berliner Weisse*. Napoleon's troops during their Prussian campaign coined the description "the champagne of the north". Long after Napoleon was vanquished, the same "champagne" was a fitting toast in Imperial Berlin.

"Berlin white beer" has a very pale colour, an insistent sparkle, a fragrant fruitiness in the nose, a sharp, dry palate and a *frisson* of quenching, sour acidity in the finish. It is served in large bowl-shaped glasses, like beer-sized champagne saucers. To soften its acidity, it is often laced with a dash (a *Schuss*) of raspberry syrup, as though it were a *kir royale*. The green essence of the herb woodruff is also sometimes used for this purpose, though this is becoming less common. To complete the presentation, candy-striped straws of white and pink or green may be offered as a decoration. It is a speciality style of beer, produced as a summer refresher by the principal breweries on both sides of the Berlin Wall. Despite its limited, seasonal popularity, its distinctiveness and nobility remains a matter of civic pride.

The term "white" has been used over the centuries throughout northern Europe to describe pale, sometimes cloudy, wheat beers. In the north of Germany it became the practice for such beers to contain a relatively low proportion of wheat and be characterized by a lactic fermentation. No doubt the lactic fermentation was originally accidental, but it is now a feature of the style. There are vestiges of this type of brewing elsewhere in the north, notably in Bremen, but it is mainly associated with Berlin.

Although *Berliner Weisse* beers were once produced in a wide variety of gravities, the quenching quality of this style is best suited by a low alcohol content and this has become the custom. For the same reason, this type of beer is brewed to have only very slight hop bitterness. The classic example, **Berliner Kindl Weisse**★★★★, is produced from a gravity of 7.5 Plato and emerges with an alcohol content of just under 2.5 percent by weight; around 3 by volume. It has only four units of bitterness.

Hops are used in only small quantities and in an unusual way. They are added in the mash tun, in a technique that presumably dates back to their role as a preservative. Either an infusion or decoction mash may be used. Only about a quarter of the mash comprises wheat, which is malted. The rest of the mash is barley malt. A top-fermenting yeast is used, but in a mixture with rod-shaped lactic acid bacteria. The classic method is to bottle without filtration and let the beer undergo a secondary fermentation at 15–16°C (59–62°F). There may then be three or four weeks' cold maturation in the bottle while the yeast settles. After sale, the beer should continue to improve in the bottle for months (but perhaps not years), gaining a greater complexity of aroma in particular. *Berliner Weisse* should be stored in a dark, cool but not refrigerated place. Because there is a sediment, handle the bottle carefully, and because the beer has such sparkle and foam, pour gently, ideally into a large, wide vessel. *Berliner Weisse* should be served lightly chilled or at a natural cellar temperature.

Berliner Kindl Weisse has a little more sharpness than its rival from Schultheiss. These two breweries dominate West Berlin and each produces a wide range of more conventional beers. Schultheiss also owns West Berlin's third brewery, Engelhardt, which does not produce a *Weisse*. These three family names are also used by breweries in the East, together with Bürgerbräu and Bärenquell. The East German Schultheiss and Kindl breweries both produce *Berliner Weisse*.

Where to drink

In summer, *Berliner Weisse* is widely available throughout Germany, especially the north, and readily in outlets served by the parent groups of Kindl and Schultheiss. In Berlin, the cafes of the Kurfürstendamm and the city's beer halls (or "palaces") serve *Weissbier* in summer. It is a popular drink at the writers' and actors' bar and restaurant called Diener, at 47 Grolman Strasse in the Charlottenburg district.

SCANDINAVIA

The northernmost nations of Europe evoke images of icy *fjords* bristling with longboats full of Norsemen inflaming themselves with mead or some early form of beer. Nordic legend certainly lays great stress on brewed beverages, but the modern reputation of Scandinavia in this respect derives from elegant, civilized Copenhagen.

Outside Germany, the Danes did more than anyone to popularize lager brewing, and they did so with great resourcefulness. In 1845, pots of bottom-fermenting yeast were brought from Munich to Copenhagen by the founder of the Carlsberg brewery. In a journey of at least 600 miles (965km), by stagecoach, he is said to have kept the yeast cool under his stovepipe hat and by dousing it with cold water at every stop. In 1883, the Carlsberg laboratory crossed another frontier by isolating for the first time a single-cell yeast culture. Pure bottom-fermenting yeasts were subsequently identified as *carlsbergensis*.

Denmark continues to remember its earlier, top-fermenting wheat beers by producing a barley malt derivative, of low alcohol content, called *hvidtøl*. But it is, of course, best known for pale lagers, brewed in an unusually wide variety of strengths, and typically with a malty mildness of palate.

Not only in tradition but also in consumption of beer per head, Denmark is an important brewing nation. It has, though, only about 30 breweries. Among those, Carlsberg, Tuborg, Wiibroe and Neptun are controlled by United Breweries of Copenhagen, which also has a stake in Jyske breweries (Ceres and others).

Norway has 16 breweries, producing by law all-malt beers, principally clean, crisp Pilseners. Probably the best-known brewery is Ringnes, producing good examples of the style, while the beers of its associate Frydenlunds have more hop character. In the same group are two provincial breweries, Arendals and Lundetangens. Most towns have their own breweries, marketing only locally. One of them – Mack, in Tromsø – is the world's most northerly brewery. In Tromsø, which is north of the Arctic Circle, beer is served with a snack of seagulls' eggs.

A typical Norwegian brewery might produce a Pilsener of 10.5–11 Plato (1042–44), with around 3.6 percent alcohol by weight; 4.5 by volume. Other products may include a summer beer of around 10.5, attenuated to a similar alcohol content and hopped for flowery aroma rather than bitterness; a "Bavarian-style" dark lager of 11–12 (1044–48), less well attenuated, to achieve again a similar alcohol content; a German-style "Export" of 13, 1052, 4.5, 5.6; a Christmas beer of 15, 1060, 4.8, 6; and a dark *Bock* of 17, 1068, 4.9, 6-plus. There might also be a special product marking an anniversary or other celebration, usually at around 11.5, 1046, 3.6, 4.5.

In Norway and Sweden, beers are heavily taxed, and their strength and availability is beset with restrictions. Sweden's laws on beer strength mean that supermarkets sell only low-alcohol or light beers. The former, designated as Class I, have a maximum of 1.8 percent alcohol by weight (2.25 by volume). The latter, Class II, have 2.8 (3.5), from a gravity of at least 10.5 Plato (1042) and often considerably higher. Although such a specification is not unusual elsewhere in the world, Swedes complain that restrictions make it difficult for them to find a beer of a more typically international "medium" strength (which they describe as *Mellanøl*, at 3.6, 4.5). Given this difficulty, serious beer-lovers in Sweden often find themselves in restaurants or state liquor stores where strong beers (Class III, 4.5, 5.6) are available. Thus laws that are intended to favour low-strength beers have the opposite effect, and visitors being entertained in Sweden can gain the impression that the country's beers are unusually full-bodied and strong.

Sweden has 16 breweries, four of which are owned by Pripps and a fifth by its associate Falken (which spells its brand Falcon). Despite the rigid alcohol brackets, most brewers have a wide variety of products. The same product may be brewed in two or three strengths, each clearly labelled as to its class.

The most unusual Swedish beers are two from a company called Till, which has three breweries in the far north. One, with the Viking name **Röde** (Red) **Orm**, is described as a mead. It is primed with honey, and spiced, though it is brewed from barley malt and hopped. It has hints of honey in the aroma and finish. Despite its fierce name, it is a low-alcohol beer (Class I). The other, in Class II, is called **Spetsat**. It is a dark beer seasoned with juniper, angelica and sweet gale (*Myrica gale*, also known as bog myrtle). It has some juniper in the nose and a sweetish, faintly resinous, palate. All three ingredients were widely used in brewing in Europe before the ascendancy of the hop, and may still be found – along with alder twigs – in traditional home-brews in Nordic countries.

Finland has 11 breweries, owned by five companies. The Fins do not tax beer so heavily, since they see it as a temperate alternative to hard liquor. Their alcohol limits on beer are also generally a little higher. Finland's Class I beers may have a maximum alcohol content of 2.25 by weight; 2.8 by volume. Class II (3;

3.75) is generally ignored by brewers. Class III has 3.7; 4.5. Class IV has 4.5; 5.6. The laws also encourage all-malt beers, though some other brewing sugars are allowed. Beers tend to be broadly in the Pilsener style, very clean and firm, with some fruitiness.

Aass

Embarrassingly named (at least to English-speakers) brewery in Drammen, near Oslo. The name means "summit", so perhaps the owning family originally came from the mountains. A small brewery by international standards and only middle-sized in Norway, but an exporter. Range includes the well-matured **Aass Export**★★, firm and smooth, with Saaz hops in the nose; **Aass Bayer Øl**★★, a good example of the Bavarian style; **Aass Jule Øl**★★★, a Christmas beer with a tawny colour and a lovely, nutty finish; and **Aass Bokk**★★→★★★, splendidly creamy.

Albani

Medium-sized indpendent producing a typical range of Danish beers, with some good strong seasonal specialities as well as the popular **Giraf**★★ pale lager (15.4 Plato; 1063; 5.4 percent alcohol by weight; 6.8 by volume) and an all-malt **Porter**★★→★★★ (20; 1083; 6.2; 7.8).

Carlsberg

International name, producing or licensing its beers in at least a dozen countries, some of which have as many as four or five different strengths and styles of Carlsberg. The company also makes at least half a dozen special export beers, and within its own country has yet more. The basic **Lager Beer** (known in some markets as Hof, after the Danish Royal Court)★→★★ has the soft, smooth, malty dryness that is typical of Carlsberg and its home country. The same character can be found in the much stronger **Elephant**★★ (in some markets, Carlsberg '68), which has 16 Plato; 1064; 5.7; 7.1. There is, predictably, a chewier character to the yet stronger **Carlsberg Special Strong Lager**★★★, which represents something of a style in itself. At Easter, Danes have the pleasure of **Carlsberg Påske Bryg 1847**★★★ (17.4; 1069; 6.2; 7.8), which has a lovely, deep-amber colour, a restrained sweetness in the nose and a malty dryness in the finish. A beautifully balanced and delicious beer. A similar brew, of slightly lower gravity, is produced for Christmas. **Gamle Carlsberg Special Dark Lager**★★ is a true Munich-style beer, of conventional gravity. **Gammel Porter** (or **Imperial Stout**)★★★ has a gravity of 18.8; 1075, producing 6.1; 7.5. It is bottom-fermenting, but has a splendidly stouty "burnt toffee" palate. Carlsberg's premises include the world's most beautiful brewhouse, like a cathedral of beer. The founders turned the company into a foundation to support the arts and sciences, and it remains such, despite being a component of United Breweries.

Ceres

While its own **Ceres Pilsner**★→★★ has a classically clean maltiness, this medium-sized Danish company also has hoppier beers from its associate Thor brewery. The group, which also includes the Urban brewery, produces a very wide range of tasty beers in typically Danish styles. A beer colourfully dubbed **Red Eric★★** has a gravity of just under 13; 1058; and an alcohol content of 4.5; 5.6. It is a firm, dry lager, pale in colour despite its name. A pink version was dropped after a Community ruling on food colourings.

Faxe

Unpasteurized beers, sterile-filtered, from an aggressive independent. The principal local product is **Faxe Fad★ →★★** (meaning "draught-style"), at 3.6; 4.5. An export version called **The Great Dane★ →★★** has 4.5; 5.6. In some markets there is a **Fest Bock★ →★★**, at 6; 7.5. Typically Danish beers, perhaps less distinctive than they were a few years ago.

Koff

A genuinely top-fermenting **Porter/Imperial Stout★★★ →★★★★**, dry, very roasty and satisfying, is an especially noteworthy product from this Finnish brewery. Full name Sinebrychoff.

Neptun

A green beer is the speciality product of this house. The beer is called Green Rooster in the American market, Bacchus in Japan, and **Pinsebryg★★** (Whitsun brew) in Denmark. The colour was devised to celebrate the beginning of spring, but it merely distracts attention from a pleasantly soft, dryish palate, big body, and alcohol content of 6; 7.5. Another brewery provides the wort; Neptun ferments and matures.

Polar Beer

Iceland (with only 200,000 people) has just one brewery, and severe laws mean that its local products, a "Pilsner" and (surprisingly) a "*Märzen*-type", have only 6.2; 1025; 1.78; 2.25. However, the brewery does export a well-made **Polar Beer★ →★★** of 13; 1052; 4.2; 5.3.

Pripps

Sweden's biggest brewing company. Its **Nordik Wölf★ →★★** is very well attenuated (9; 1036; 3.8; 4.75). In Sweden, it rates as a Class III beer, and it has more alcohol and flavour, especially hop character, than most competing "light beers" in the US market. In the Swedish market, the brewery is very proud of its **Royal★★**, a Pilsener-style beer with a lot of Hallertau hop in the nose, a soft palate and a spritzy but long finish. Within an extensive range, another interesting product is a sweetish, chocolatey, Munich-style beer with the British-sounding name **Black and Brown★★**. The most distinctive of all the Pripps products is Sweden's only top-fermenting brew, **Carnegie Porter★★★**, which in its reintro-duced Class III version has a big, dry, "burnt" palate.

Spendrup's

Sweden's most aggressive independent. Its all-malt premium **Spendrup's★★** and its super-premium **Old Gold★★** have a lot of hop character, in both aroma and palate.

Tuborg

International name, producing a full range of Danish styles. Tuborg's beers are perhaps a little lighter in body and hoppier than those of its partner Carlsberg.

THE NETHERLANDS

Because it has become the most international of all beer brands, Heineken is not always perceived to be Dutch: to originate from Holland or, as the nation is properly known, The Netherlands. Big names are a feature of brewing in this small country (Heineken, Amstel, Skol – even Oranjeboom and Three Horseshoes are to some extent international brands) and until recently they tended to obscure the presence of interesting middle-sized companies like Grolsch, not to mention the smaller houses like Brand that dot the southern provinces of Brabant and Limburg. There is even a Trappist monastery brewery: Schaapskooi in Brabant. Now, the Dutch are beginning to pay more attention to these small breweries, in addition to which three or four boutiques have been established.

Initially, it tended to be the small houses that were contract-brewing for prospective boutiques. An Arnhem company had a strong ale called Sloth; a firm in Gouda had a copper ale, Kuyt: these ran into hiccoughs. In the northern town of Groningen, a firm called De Munte marketed a contract-brewed dry stout while also producing its own abbey-style Triple, a heavily sedimented ale with lots of hop bitterness, called **Noorderblond**★★ → ★★★.

In the cheese town of Alkmaar, a boutique called the Noorderbierbrouwerij began with a most unusual product: an alcoholic ginger beer, called **8 Oktober**★★★. This is appropriately gingery and beery, if a little too yeasty, and it deserves points for boldness. Early products also included a "white" beer, **Burg-wit,** actually reddish in colour and very tannic; a rather cheesy-tasting **Golden Brown** (6.5 percent alcohol by volume); and a **Winterbier** (7.5), astringent in the nose and sweet in palate.

Near the eastern town of Nijmegen, a boutique called Raaf produces a well-balanced, honeyish ale at 5 percent, known simply as **No 12**★★ → ★★★. The same brewery has a **Nijmeegs Dubbel**★★ (6.5), tawny, fruity and very dry. An ale is also produced for the local Café de Fuik. Also in the east, a prospective boutique in Apeldoorn began with a contract-brewed, claret-coloured, "sweet and sour" beer in Flemish style, called **Palinckx**★★.

In 1985, Amsterdam's first boutique, 't IJ, began with a Triple called **Zatte**★★★, well balanced, with malt and fruit in the nose and lots of hop bitterness in the finish.

Until recently, a typical Dutch brewery would produce a low-alcohol Old Brown (around 9 Plato;

1036; 2–3 percent by weight; 2.5–3.5 by volume); a Pilsener (in The Netherlands, this term indicates the classic gravity of 11–12; 1044–48; with an alcohol content of around 4; 5); a "Dortmunder-style" (some, as might be expected, at around 13.5; 1054; 4.7; 5.9, but others considerably stronger); and a seasonal *Bock* (15.7–16.5; 1063–66; 5–5.5; 6.25–7). Now, new styles are being introduced, often with a Belgian accent. There are 20-odd breweries.

Where to drink

The Dutch pioneered speciality beer bars, and it is doubtful whether any in the world can surpass Café Gollem, in Amsterdam. This has the best elements of Amsterdam's cosy, friendly cafes, while also serving around 200 beers: not the biggest selection in the world, but chosen and presented with knowledge and care. Behind the Royal Palace, turn left into Spuistraat, right into Raamsteeg (☎020-254634. Open 4 o'clock). There are at least 20 specialist beer bars in The Netherlands, and another notable example, in the town of Utrecht, is Jan Primus (27-31 Jan van Scorellstraat ☎030-520347).

Alfa

Small Limburg brewery making exclusively all-malt beers, smooth and well-balanced, with Hallertau and Saaz hopping. Noted for its sweetish **Super-Dort**★★★, the strongest example of the style (16–16.5; 1064–66; 5.5; 7).

Arcen

Revivalist Limburg brewery making a wide range of all-malt, top-fermenting specialities, including the strongest beer in The Netherlands, **Arcener Grand Prestige**★★★ (22; 1088; 8; 10); very dark, with a malty nose, fruity vanilla notes in the palate and a dry finish hinting at licorice; a good, bottle-conditioned, winter ale. Other products include **Arcener Stout**★★★ (16.5; 1066; 5.2; 6.5), which has a smoky dryness; and The Netherlands' first *Altbier*, **Altforster**★★ →★★★, which is dry and rather thin. A range of specialities is also produced under the Hertog Jan name.

Bavaria

Light, malty-tasting beers under the **Bavaria**★ and **Swinkels** names. This brewery, in Lieshout, Brabant, produces a wide range of supermarket and other "own-brand" labels.

Brand

Oldest-established brewery in The Netherlands. This Limburg company has attracted attention in the United States by marketing its pleasant **Pils**★★ in a porcelain-style bottle, as Royal Brand. This beer has a malty nose, light body, and dry finish. The super-premium, all-malt **Brand Up**★★ →★★★, dry and hoppy, is a much more interesting beer (12.5; 1050; 4.25; 5.5). A pale (actually, amber) *Bock* called *Imperator* ★★ →★★★ is also all-malt, as its palate suggests (16.5; 1066; 5; 6.5). A new strong, all-malt brew (19.5; 1078; 7; 9) called **Sylvester**★★★, is available regularly, despite its New Year name. It is highly unusual in that, while its primary fermentation is with a "bottom" yeast, its secondary – in both tank and bottle – is "top". Bottle-conditioning takes about 15 weeks. The beer has a dense head, a bronze colour, a malty nose, a suggestion of alcohol in the palate, and a dry hoppiness in the finish. A nice, warming, winter beer.

Breda

This Brabant town gives its name to a company making the once-famous **Three Horse(shoes)**★ beers (generally fresh-tasting, with some hoppiness), and now linked with Rotterdam's **Oranjeboom**★ (whose products tend to be firmer in body), as part of Allied Breweries (with the bland **Skol**★ labels). A confusion of similar-tasting beers, with export markets also having the low-cost **Royal Dutch Post Horn**.

Budels

Small Brabant brewery with several interesting new products: **Budels Alt**★★→★★★ is in the German style but from the relatively high gravity of 13.5 (1054; 4.4; 5.5). **Parel**★★→★★★ is a top-fermenting pale beer of 14 (1056; 4.8; 6). **Capucijn**★★→★★★ (16; 1064; 5.2; 6.5) is first bottom- and then top-fermented. It is a most unusual beer, with hints of smoked applewood. All of these beers are notably smooth, and are not pasteurized.

Dommels

Brabant brewery owned by Artois, of Belgium. **Dominator Dommelsch Speciaal**★★, a strong (4.8; 6), very pale lager, dry and lightly fruity, is a new product. A similar *speciaal* is produced by the sister brewery in Hengelo.

Grolsch

The pot-stoppered bottle was set to be phased out in the 1950s, but consumers objected. It helped **Grolsch**★★ become a cult beer, first in The Netherlands, more recently in export markets. Judged (as it now must be) among the bigger-selling Dutch Pilseners, Grolsch has a hint of new-mown hay in the nose; a soft, fluffy body; and a dryish palate. It is unpasteurized.

Gulpen

Small Limburg brewery already known for one speciality, and now gaining attention for a second. The original speciality, **X-pert**★★→★★★, is a super-premium Pilsener with a notably full colour, a gravity of 12 (1048; 4; 5), and a lot of Tettnang hop in both aroma and palate. It is kräusened, and well-matured. The newer product, **Mestreechs Aajt**★★★, is a revival of a regional speciality, with a nod in a southerly direction. It is a sour-and-sweet summer beer, claret in colour, and with some wild fermentation. It is brewed from a refreshingly low gravity of 8.5 (1034; 3.2; 4), and matured for a year. It is ironic that Gulpen should intentionally produce a sour beer. In the days before refrigeration, if beer in a brewery went sour, it would be sold off as malt vinegar. Gulpen's vinegar was so popular that the company continues to produce it (by less empirical methods), and also makes mustard.

Heineken

International trade (in beer even before tea, spices and diamonds) has always been a way of life in The Netherlands, a tiny but densely populated nation pushing into the sea. Heineken was the first brewery in the world to export to the United States at the repeal of Prohibition, and the company now controls the production of more beer in the international market than any rival. Its principal product, **Heineken Lager Beer**★ →★★, is in the Pilsener style, and in its production the company stresses the use of summer barley and a total process time of not less than six weeks. The beer has a characteristically refreshing hint of fruitiness, only a light hop character, and a spritzy finish. In the Dutch market, the company produces a full range of local styles. It also has specialities like the tasty, though bottom-fermenting, **Van Vollenhoven Stout**★★ →★★★ (16.2; 1065; 4.8; 6). Seasonal *Bock* beers have been marketed locally under the Heineken, Hooijberg and Sleutel names, in what seems to be ascending order of dryness. A full range of beers is marketed internationally under the Amstel brand. These are generally lighter, and sharper, in palate (see also Canada). A third international brand is Murphy (see Ireland). The company also has substantial stakes in the local brewing industries of France, Italy and several smaller countries.

De Kroon

Very small Brabant brewery. A new speciality called **Egelantier**★★ is a bronze, bottom-fermenting beer of conventional gravity but full body. The Dortmunder-style **Briljant**★★ (12; 1048; 5.2; 6.3) seems to have developed more of its own character in recent years. It has a malty nose, firm but surprisingly light body, and dry palate.

De Leeuw

Small Limburg brewery. It is to be hoped that the soft, all-malt **Jubileeuw**★★ (originally produced for the brewery's centenary) has a permanent place in the range. This is a pale, bottom-fermenting beer of conventional gravity. **Super Leeuw**★★ (13.5; 1054; 4.7; 5.9) is a well-liked Dortmunder. These beers are unpasteurized.

Lindeboom

Small Limburg brewery noted for its dry **Pilsener**★★ and a pleasant **Bock**★★.

De Ridder

Small Limburg brewery noted for its creamy, fruity, Dortmunder-style **Maltezer**★★. The products of this brewery do not seem to have changed in character since it was acquired by Heineken.

Schaapskooi, Trappist Monastery

Proud monastery, near Tilburg, recently much more assertive in its brewing activities. The basic **Schaapskooi Trappisten Bier**★★★ has a copper colour, a sherryish nose, and a gently malty palate, with fruity undertones (4 percent alcohol by weight; 5 by volume). There is a more pronounced fruitiness to the yeasty, dry **La Trappe**★★★ →★★★★ (17 Plato; 1068; around 5.5; 7) which is also a little paler. Slightly paler again – though still full in colour – is a Trappist beer of similar gravity and strength, but maltier in character, brewed under the name **Koningshoeven**★★★ and marketed by Allied Breweries in The Netherlands.

BELGIUM

The secret is out. Beer-drinkers have begun to realize that Belgium has the most diverse, individualistic brews in the world. Its cidery, winey, spontaneously fermenting *lambic* family pre-date the pitching of yeast by brewers and its cherry *kriek*, strawberry *framboise* and spiced "white" brews pre-date the acceptance of the hop as the universal seasoning in beer. Other countries have monastery breweries but it is only in Belgium that the brothers have evolved their own collective style. Whether produced in the country's five monastery breweries or in a secular plant, "abbey"-style beers are always strong, top-fermenting and bottle-matured. They often have a heavy sediment and a fruity palate, sometimes evincing hints of chocolate. Within these characteristics, however, there are substantial differences between the brews, and a couple of sub-categories, but that is the way of Belgian beer. Some Belgian specialities are hard to categorize, although most are top-fermenting and many are bottle-matured. No country has a more diverse range even within the bottle-matured group – the Belgians are keen on this means of conditioning and sometimes refer to it as their *méthode champenoise*.

In a Belgian cafe, the list of beers will identify at

least one member of the *lambic* family (occasionally a sweet *faro*, often a sparkling *gueuze*); perhaps a honeyish "white" beer (*witbier* or *bière blanche*) from the village or a brown (*bruin*) from the town of Oudenaarde; a local *spécial*; and a strong, bottle-conditioned monastery (*abdij* or *abbaye*) brew. There may also be a Belgian *ale*, as well as local interpretations of English, Scottish and sometimes German styles. This is in an ordinary cafe; there will be a far greater categorization in a cafe that makes a feature of speciality beers, listing them by the hundred.

After decades of decline when they were regarded as "old-fashioned", speciality beers began to enjoy a revival in the late 1970s. They are a joy to the visiting beer-lover, although it is necessary to know what to order. A request simply for "a beer" is likely to be met by a mass-market Pilsener.

With the revival of interest in speciality beers within Belgium, more of them have also entered export markets. They present a bewildering choice. As always, the selection of beers reflects both history and geography. The influence of the brewing customs of the surrounding nations has been accepted with shrewd selectivity by the Belgians, yet they have also contrived to be conservative and inward-looking to the point that their principal regions maintain their own traditions. The country is divided not only into its Dutch-speaking north (Flanders) and French-speaking south (Wallonia) but also has a German-speaking corner in the east and a bilingual knot around the city of Brussels. Some styles of beer are perceived as belonging not to a region but to a province, river valley, town or village.

The Belgians like to talk about beer as their reply to Burgundy. They suggest that beer is to them what wine is to France. Cheese might be an even better comparison. The beers of Belgium, like the cheeses of France, are often idiosyncratic, cranky, artisanal. Some drinkers could never learn to enjoy one of the cloudy, sour specialities of the Senne Valley any more than they could acquire a taste for a smelly cheese. In both cases, the loss would be theirs. This is drink at its most sensuous.

In its native gastronomy, Belgium is a land of beer, seafood and – after dinner – the world's finest chocolate. It is a land of German portions and French culinary skills. Beer may be served, with some ceremony, at a family meal, and might well have been used in the cooking. Other countries have the odd dish prepared with beer, but Belgium has hundreds. The Belgians even eat hop shoots, as a delicacy, in the brief season of their availability, served like asparagus, with poached or scrambled eggs.

Beer is also a central theme in Belgium's history and culture. St Arnold of Oudenaarde is remembered for having successfully beseeched God, in the 11th century, to provide more beer after an abbey brewery collapsed. He is the patron saint of Belgian brewers, some of whom display his statue by their kettles. (French-speakers can, if they prefer, remember another beery miracle, that of St Arnold at Metz.) The 13th-century Duke Jan the First of Brabant, Louvain and Antwerp has passed into legend as the King of Beer: "Jan Primus" has been corrupted into "Gambrinus", by which name he is remembered not only in Belgium but also in Germany, Czechoslovakia and far beyond. Jan Primus is said to have been an honorary member of the Brewers' Guild, although their present gilded premises on Brussels' Grand' Place were not built until 1701. Today, the "Brewers' House" is the only building on the Grand' Place still to be used as the headquarters of a trade guild. A small museum in its cellars is open to the public.

Today's Confederation has about a hundred members, and that represents roughly the number of breweries in Belgium. The figure has been declining for some years, although recently a number of new micro-breweries have opened. Many Belgian breweries are family-owned, which can lead to problems when there is no clear succession. But however much the number of breweries fluctuates, the tally of beers increases, with new specialities constantly being launched. At any one time, there are probably more than 500 Belgium beers on the market.

FLANDERS

Flemish painters like Bruegel and the aptly named Brouwer depicted the people of their home state as enthusiastic beer-drinkers. It has been like that for a thousand years. As Emperor of Europe, Charlemagne took an interest in brewing, and perhaps he brought the news from Aix to Ghent. The nationalistic Flemings might, however, secretly resent their famous artists' depiction of beery excess. They take pride in being hard-working, and the Early and Late Flemish schools of painting were made possible by the prosperity of Flanders at different times as an exporter of beer as well as textiles, and as a commercial centre. Flanders emerged as a principal component of the new Belgium in 1830, and has in recent years reasserted itself through the trading prosperity of the river Scheldt – with beer exports once again on the upswing.

As a region, Flanders stretches from the Dutch side of the Scheldt to a slice of northern France. Politically, it comprises the Belgian provinces of West and East Flanders, Antwerp and Limburg.

West Flanders, with its 15th-century canalside capital Bruges, has traditionally been known for its sour, burgundy-coloured style of beer – the classic example is Rodenbach.

The province is well served by small breweries and has two of the strongest beers in Belgium, from the revivalist Dolle Brouwers and the monastery brewery of Westvleteren.

East Flanders, with the proud city of Ghent as its capital, is noted for slightly less sour brown ales, produced in or near the town of Oudenaarde, which has a cluster of small breweries to the east.

The province and city of Antwerp is noted for the beautifully made De Konick beer (a copper ale). The province also has the monastery of Westmalle, which created the Triple style of abbey beer, and in the south, the strong, golden ale called Duvel, the potent, dark Gouden Carolus and the well-liked Maes Pils.

Limburg has a less gilded capital, the pretty little town of Hasselt, which is known for the production of *genever* gin. It is a thinly breweried province but has the distinctive Sezoens beer from the Martens brewery, Cristal Alken, an especially well-respected Pilsener beer.

Where to drink

The biggest selection of beers in any one cafe in the world is probably that at Het Grote Ongenoegen (9 Jeruzalemstraat) in the Old Town of Antwerp. This specialist cafe has more than 1,000 beers, although it seems to have lost some of its energy since the departure of the original owner. The publicity attracted by the collection at Het Grote Ongenoegen helped to make specialist beer bars fashionable in Belgium. The best in Antwerp, although service varies from the obliging to the dour, is the small cafe Kulminator (32–34 Vleminckxveld) with 350–400 beers. Patersvaetje (1 Blauwmoezelstraat) has about 80 beers.

There are good selections in many other places, although Belgian cafes in general do not always offer much to eat. Where they do, Flanders is at its best with seafood. Vagant (25 Reyndersstraat) has some interesting beers and gins, and offers herring in season (in the same street, De Groote Witte Arend marries beer with fine art and recitals of chamber music). De Arme Duivel (in the street of the same name) has *kriek* on draught, and mussels in season; 't Waagstuk (20 Stadswag) has 60 beers and offers fish dishes; Fouquets (17 De Keyserlei) has beers, oysters in season and desserts.

After Antwerp, the largest city in Flanders is Ghent, which has a popular and well-run specialist beer cafe called De Hopduvel ("The Hop Devil", at 10 Rokerelsstraat). The Hopduvel also features the growing number of Belgian cheeses. Bruges, too, has an excellent beer cafe, a pubby place that also specializes in pancakes. It is called 't Brugs Beertje (5 Kemelstraat) and has an adjoining shop selling unusual brews by the bottle. Farther afield, the Limburg town of Hasselt has adjoining beer and gin bars in the town centre in an establishment called the Hasselt Cafe (38 Maastrichterstraat). The cafe also has its own juniper beer, called Dikkenek ("Thick Neck", a self-mocking nickname for the people of Limburg). Nearby, the Hemelrijk cafe (in the street of the same name) specializes in beer and whisky. Not a town for the abstemious.

Cristal Alken

The hoppiest of the principal Belgian Pilseners is **Cristal Alken**★★ → ★★★. This well-made Pilsener with a notably pale colour, fresh, hoppy nose; very clean, crisp palate and a smooth dryness in the finish. It is hopped principally with blossoms, including Saaz for aroma, fermented at relatively cold temperatures, lagered for a respectable period and not pasteurized. Cristal is a much-loved beer and its character has been maintained despite a change in the ownership of the brewery. It has also been retained as the exclusive property of the brewery in the village of Alken in Limburg. There were fears, which have been proved groundless, that production might ultimately be shared with a sister brewery in East Flanders, whose **Zulte**★★ is a good example of the sour, burgundy-coloured style of the region. Both breweries are owned by Kronenbourg, of France.

De Dolle Brouwers

"The Mad Brewers", they call themselves. It is a typically Flemish, sardonic shrug on behalf of a group of enthusiasts who rescued from closure a village brewery near Diksmuide, not far from Ostend. As a weekend project, they renovated the brewery, which dates from the mid 19th century and is a classic of its type. (Tours welcome; ☎051-502781.) They specialize in strong, top-fermenting beers, all bottle-matured. The house speciality is **Oerbier**★★★, very dark and smooth, with a sweetness that is offset by licorice tones (original gravity 1100; alcohol content 6 percent by weight; 7.5 by volume). There are also several seasonal products: the brassy-coloured, honey-primed **Boskeun**★★★, an Easter beer of about 8 percent by volume; the pale, dry-hopped **Arabier**★★★, for summer, with a similar alcohol content; and **Stille Nacht**★★★, a claret-coloured Christmas brew, with hints of apple in its aroma and palate, and an alcohol content of around 9 percent. With an original gravity of around 1120 (12 degrees Belgian), this matches West-vleteren's Abt, although that has a higher alcohol content, having been known to weigh in at 10.6 percent by volume.

De Koninck

A classic. This perilously drinkable, copper-coloured, top-fermenting beer fits in stylistically somewhere between an English ale (a fruity "best bitter") and a smooth Düsseldorf *Altbier*. For all its complexity of character, it pursues an unassuming occupation as the local beer of Antwerp, from the city's only brewery. The company stayed with top-fermentation when other big-city breweries were switching to Pilseners. Its sole product is **De Koninck**★★★, an all-malt beer of 12 Plato, brewed by direct flame in a cast-iron kettle. It is cold-conditioned and emerges with an alcohol content of a little over 4 percent by weight and 5 by volume. De Koninck has an excellent malt character, a yeasty fruitiness and a great deal of Saaz hoppiness, especially in its big finish. Its full palate is best experienced in the draught form, which is unpasteurized. Opposite the brewery, at the Pilgrim Cafe (8 Boomgardstraat), drinkers sometimes add a sprinkle of yeast to the beer. In the heart of Antwerp, the beer is available at the city's oldest cafe, Quinten Matsijs (17 Moriaanstraat) and at Den Engel (3 Grote Markt).

Duvel

This means "Devil" and is the name of the world's most beguiling beer. With its pale, golden sparkle, **Duvel**★★★★

looks superficially like a Pilsener. Its palate is soft and
seductive. Beneath its frothy head, behind its dense lacework, this all-malt, top-fermenting beer has the power (6.7
percent alcohol by weight; 8.2 by volume) to lead anyone
into temptation. The pale colour is achieved with the help of
the brewery's own maltings; Styrian and Saaz hops are used;
a very distinctive yeast imparts a subtle fruitiness (reminiscent of Poire Williams); the cleanness and smoothness is
enhanced by both cold and warm maturation; and, in the
classic, sedimented, version, the *mousse* develops from
bottle-conditioning. Duvel is customarily chilled as though
it were an *alcool blanc*. It is produced by the Moortgat
brewery in the village of Breendonk near Mechelen/Malines.
Other Moortgat products include tasty, abbey-style beers
under the **Maredsous★★** label, for the monastery of that
name. Duvel is sometimes compared with the various
monastic Triple beers, but this is self-evident heresay. Duvel
is lighter in body, less sweet, more delicate. It is the original,
and therefore classic, example of what has become a distinct
style. Broadly in this style are **Deugniet★★**, **Hap-
kin★★ → ★★★**, **Ketje★**, **Lucifer★**, **Sloeber★★** and **Teutenbier★**.

Gouden Carolus

This is the classic strong, dark ale of Belgium. Its name
derives from a gold coin from the realm of the Holy Roman
Emperor Charles V, who grew up in the Flemish City of
Mechelen (better known to the outside world by its French
name, Malines) where this beer is brewed. **Gouden Carolus**
has a dense, dark colour, a gentle, soothing character, a hint
of fruitiness in the finish and, from a gravity of 19 Plato, an
alcohol content of 6 percent by weight; 7.5 by volume. A
lovely after-dinner beer; or, better still, a nightcap.

Kwak Pauwel

The odd name derives from an antique Flemish speciality.
This revival, a strong (9 percent by volume), garnet-
coloured, top-fermenting brew, is notable for its licorice
aroma and palate. Licorice is actually added; the character
does not derive from the malt, as it does in some dark brews.
Kwak Pauwel★★★ is a hearty, warming brew. When it first
appeared in Belgium, it won attention by being served in a
"yard of ale" glass, of the type allegedly handed up to
coachmen in times past when they stopped for a restorative
drink.

Liefmans

Liefmans is the classic brown-ale brewery in Oudenaarde
where such products are a speciality. The brewery's basic
brown ale, known simply as **Liefmans★★ → ★★★** is made from
at least four styles of malt and a similar number of hop
varieties. It spends an extraordinarily long time in the brew
kettle – a whole night – and is cooled in open vessels. It is
pitched with a pure-culture, top-fermenting yeast that has a
slightly lactic character, imparting the gentle sourness
typical in such beers. It has six weeks' warm-conditioning in
tanks and is then blended with a smaller proportion of a
similar beer that has had eight to ten months' conditioning.
It has an original gravity of around 12 Plato (1048) and an
alcohol content of 3.7 percent by weight; 4.6 by volume.
  The longer-conditioned "vintage" brew is bottled

"straight" as **Liefmans Goudenband★★★★** (Golden Band) and is surely the world's finest brown ale. After tank-conditioning, it has 3–12 months' bottle-maturation (without dosage) in the brewery's *caves*. It is called a *provisie* beer, indicating that it can be laid down. If it is kept in a cool (but not refrigerated) dark place, it will continue to improve, perhaps reaching its peak after two years. For a brown ale, it is unusually spritzy and very dry, with a finish reminiscent of Montilla. It has an original gravity of about 13 Plato (1052), and an alcohol content of 4.4; 5.5. The brown ales are also used as the basis for the unusual **Liefmans Kriek★★★**, which has a notably smooth body, a sour-and-sweet palate and a port-wine finish. It has an original gravity of 18.25 Plato (1073), 5.76 by weight; 7.2 by volume. Liefmans craft-brewing approach is emphasized by the use of tissue-wrapped bottles. These appear in a variety of sizes including, for very good customers, hand-filled Nebuchadnezzars containing enough beer to fill 20 normal bottles.

The town of Oudenaarde also has brown ales from its Cnudde and Clarysse breweries, the latter under the Felix label, and in a less sour style from Roman. Similar beers are made nearby by the wonderfully artisanal brewery of Crombe in Zottegem and Van Den Bossche in St Lievens-Esse, and there are many more distant imitators.

Maes

A flowery, "Riesling" bouquet imparts distinctiveness to **Maes Pils★★ →★★★**. In other respects the brewery is unusually faithful to the Pilsener tradition, extensively using malt produced in Bohemia specifically for Maes and Saaz blossom hops. Maes is also painstaking in its use of open cooling vessels and a very slow, cold fermentation in the "double", Darauflassen method. Lagering is for two to three months and the result is a light, soft beer, definitely dry but not assertively so. Maes is one of the principal Belgian Pilseners and is very well made for a relatively mass-marketed beer. The brewery is in the village of Waarloos, north of Mechelen. The company also produces two top-fermenting beers for the abbey of Grimbergen, a Flemish village near Brussels. **Grimbergen Double★★** is a dark, fruity beer, with a chocolatey palate; it has a gravity of 15.8 Plato and an alcohol content of 5.2 percent by weight; 6.5 by volume. **Grimbergen Tripel★ →★★** is paler, fruity, but with a more winey character; it has a gravity of 19.6 Plato and an alcohol content of 7.2 by weight; 9 by volume.

Rodenbach

The unimaginative are apt to consider Rodenbach's beers undrinkable, yet they are the classics of the "sour" style of West Flanders. They gain their sourness, and their burgundy colour, in a number of ways. The sourness derives in part from the top-fermenting yeast a blend of three strains that has been in the house for 150 years, and from cultures resident in wooden maturation tuns. The colour, too, originates partly from the use of reddish Vienna-style malts but also probably from the caramels and tannins extracted from the oak of the tuns. These vessels, made from Slavonian oak, from Poland, are uncoated. They make a remarkable sight, each tun standing vertically from floor to ceiling. The smallest contains 15,000 litres of maturing beer;

the largest 60,000 litres. There are 300 in all, filling several halls, as though this were a winery or a brandy distillery. When the maturing beer has attained its typical palate, it is stabilized by flash pasteurization so does not mature in the bottle and is not intended for laying down.

The basic **Rodenbach**★★★ →★★★★ is a blend of "young" beer (matured five to six weeks) and "vintage" brews (matured 18 months to two years). The longer-matured beer is also bottled "straight" as **Rodenbach Grand Cru**★★★★. The basic Rodenbach has an original gravity of 11.5–11.75 Plato, emerging with 3.7 percent alcohol by weight; 4.6 volume. The Grand Cru has an original gravity of 15, but an alcohol content of only around 4.1; 5.2. The gravity is heightened by the use of non-fermented sugars and the alcohol content is diminished because some of the fermentation is lactic. There is both a sharpness and a restorative quality about these beers: perfect after a game of tennis. The Grand Cru has a slightly bigger palate and a smoother texture. Even then, some Belgians add a touch of grenadine, as though they were making a red *kir*. The Rodenbach brewery is in Roeslare, the centre of an agricultural area.

Several breweries in West Flanders produce similar beers to Rodenbach's but none with such a distinctive character. Examples include Paulus from Van Eecke; Oude Piro from Bevernagie; Bacchus from Van Honsenbrouck; Petrus from Bavik; and Vichtenaar from Verhaege. In East Flanders, beers very much in this style are produced under the name Bios by Van Steenberge.

St Louis

The widely marketed St Louis beers of the *lambic* family, including a novel strawberry brew, come from the Van Honsenbrouck company in Ingelmunster. In buccaneering fashion, this brewery tackles a wide variety of "speciality" styles and carries this off surprisingly well on occasion. St Louis **Gueuze Lambic**★ may be a trifle on the sweet side but the **Kriek Lambic**★ →★★ is well balanced, if a little bland. The **Framboise**★★ is full and fruity. The strawberry **Bezebier**★★★ has to win points for effort. It has a rich strawberry aroma and is sweet when young, drying to a considerable tartness as it ages. In addition to its **Bacchus**★ →★★ (see previous entry), the brewery has an interesting top-fermenting speciality called **Brigand**★★. This is an amber, strong brew, with a secondary fermentation in its corked bottle. It has a gravity of 20 Plato, emerging with 7.2 percent alcohol by weight; 9 by volume. While it superficially resembles a *saison* in its immense liveliness and fruitiness, it has a more rounded texture and its palate is less citric, more reminiscent of soft fruit.

St Sixtus

See Westvleteren, Trappist Monastery of St Sixtus

Sezoens

While seasonal *saison* beers for summer are a recognized style in the French-speaking part of Belgium, they are less evident in Flemish tradition. **Sezoens**★★★ has the same connotation, but is the registered trademark of a distinctive and delightful product from the Martens brewery, in the Limburg village of Bocholt. It has a delightful label, too, showing a well-clad personification of winter handing the beer to a sunny "Mr Summer". Sezoens is a pale, golden top-fermenting brew of 13.5 Plato, with 4 percent alcohol by weight; 5 by volume. It has a fresh, hoppy aroma (Saaz is used), a firm, clean, notably dry palate, and plenty of hop character throughout, especially in the finish, where the hearty dryness is that of the Northern Brewer variety. At the moment, this product is not bottle-conditioned though it might be in the future. In all of these respects, Sezoens is quite different from the amber, stronger, yeastily fruit *saison* brews of French-speaking Belgium. Martens also produces a rather German-tasting **Kwik Pils**★★. Devotees who track these beers down to their far-flung home village should arrange in advance to visit Martens' museum (Brouwerij Martens Museum, Dorpstraat 32, Bocholt, Belgium B3598; ☎011-461705), which is open by appointment only. In Brussels, Sezoens is the speciality of the cafe De Ultieme Hallucinatie (316 Koningsstraat/Rue Royale), in an Art Nouveau house near the Botanical Gardens.

Stropken

The aniseed finish in Stropken makes it especially interesting among the several idiosyncratic speciality beers launched in Belgium, and especially in Flanders, during the 1980s. With its flowery bouquet, fruity start and firm, creamy body, it is the beer world's answer to *pastis*. The first Stropken was assertively spicy, but this subsequently yielded to a more refined Grand Cru version. **Stropken Grand Cru**★★ → ★★★ is a well-made, top-fermenting beer, with an original gravity of 17.5 Plato and an alcohol content of around 5.5 percent by weight; 6.75 by volume. The name Stropken is an ironic Flemish reference to the halters that the rebellious Lords of Ghent were obliged to wear by Emperor Charles in the 16th century. Stropken, originally produced as the house brew at the Hopduvel specialist beer cafe in Ghent, is now produced under contract by the Slaghmuylder brewery also in East Flanders. Slaghmuylder produces well-made abbey-style brews and an unusual, copper-coloured all-malt, bottom-fermenting speciality beer of conventional gravity called **Cornel**★★ → ★★★, beautifully balanced, with a hoppy dryness in the finish.

Westmalle, Trappist Monastery

The classic example of the pale, Triple style of Belgian Trappist brew is produced by the monastery of Westmalle, a village northeast of Antwerp. The monastery, established in 1821, has brewed since its early days, though it was slow in making its beer available commercially, and remains one of the most withdrawn of the Trappist monasteries. Visits are not encouraged, though the brewery can sometimes be seen by appointment. The smart, traditional copper brewhouse is in a strikingly 1930s building. It produces three beers. The "Single", confusingly known as **Extra**, is available only to the brothers; a shame, since this pale, top-fermenting brew is a product of some delicacy. The **Double**★★ is dark brown, malty, but quite dry. It has an original gravity of around 16 Plato and an alcohol content of about 5.5 by weight; just under 7 by volume. The **Triple**★★★★ offers an unusual combination of features, being a strong, top-fermenting beer of pale, almost Pilsener, colour. Its mash is entirely of

Pilsener malts from Czechoslovakia and France but, in the classic procedure, candy sugar is added in the kettle. There are three hopping stages, using Fuggles, a number of German varieties and Saaz. The brew is fermented with a hybrid house yeast, then has a secondary fermentation of one to three months in tanks, and is given a priming of sugar and a further dosage of yeast before being bottled. It is warm-conditioned in the bottle before being released from a gravity of around 20 Plato, it emerges with an alcohol content of around 6.4 percent by weight; 8 by volume. With its faintly citric fruitiness, its rounded body and its alcoholic "kick", the Triple expresses a very full character within six months of leaving the monastery, though bottles from 1927 are still in good condition. Westmalle is jealous of the individuality of its product, but several secular breweries produce beers in a similar style, using the designation Triple (in Flemish, Tripel). Good examples include Vieille Villers Triple from Van Assche; Witkap from Slaghmuylder and the slightly fuller-coloured Affligem from De Smedt.

Westvleteren, Trappist Monastery of St Sixtus

The strongest beer in Belgium comes from by far the smallest of the country's five monastery breweries. This is the monastery of St Sixtus, at the hamlet of Westvleteren, in a rustic corner of Flanders, near the French border and between the coast and the town best known by its French name Ypres (Ieper in Flemish). Although it overlooks a hop garden, the monastery produces beers in which malty sweetness is the predominant characteristic, with spicy and fruity tones also notable. As well as being tiny, the brewhouse is antique. Its own output is limited – artisanal Trappist beers, bottled without labels and identified by the crown cork – though further supplies are produced by arrangement in a nearby commercial brewery. From the monastery's own output there is no Single, and the basic beer, with a green crown-cork, is called **Double★★**. Then comes the **Special★★** (red crown-cork), drier, with hints of vanilla and licorice, a gravity of around 15 Plato and an alcohol content of about 4.8 percent by weight; 6 by volume. The **Extra★★** (blue) has more fruity, acidic tones and some alcohol character (20 Plato; 6.4; 8). Finally, the strongest beer in the monastery (and the country) is the **Abbot★★★★** (yellow), very full-bodied, creamy, soft and sweet. This is sometimes known as a 12-degree beer, its gravity in the Belgian scale. That works out at about 30 Plato (1120) and the beer has around 8.48 percent alcohol by weight; 10.6 by volume.

These beers can be bought by the case at the monastery and sampled next door in the Cafe De Vrede, but they are less easy to find elsewhere. Their crown-corks identify the beer as Westmalle, while the commercially produced version has a label and is designated St Sixtus. The commercially produced counterpart to Abbot, with a yet yeastier character (very lively, and with an acidic finish) is exported to the USA simply as **St Sixtus★★★**. This is remarkable in that the producing brewery, St Bernard, is itself very small. St Bernard is in Watou, near Poperinge. Its local rival Van Eecke produces a similar range of tasty yeasty, abbey-style brews, and a hoppy speciality called **Poperings Hommelbier★★→★★★**.

BRUSSELS AND BRABANT

Within the extraordinarily colourful tapestry of Belgian brewing, the most vivid shades are to be found in the country's central province, Brabant, and especially around the capital city, Brussels. If the Germanic north of Europe and the Romantic south intertwine in Belgium, it is in the province of Brabant and the city of Brussels that the knot is tied. As the nearest thing Europe has to a federal capital, Brussels has some lofty French kitchens, but it also takes pride in the heartier *carbonades* of what it terms *"cuisine de biere"*, in which several restaurants specialize. On its Gallic avenues, it has some splendid Art Nouveau cafes, but the Grand' Place and the older neighbourhoods are Flemish in flavour and so is the beer.

To the east, the Flemish village of Hoegaarden is the home of the Belgian style of "white" beer. Louvain (in Flemish, Leuven) is the home of Stella Artois and the biggest brewing city in Belgium. The greatest splash of colour by far is, however, Brussels. Although it has one conventional brewery, Brussels is the local market for the *lambic* family, the most unusual beers in the world, with palate characteristics that range from a hint of pine kernels to a forkful of Brie cheese. *Lambic* is produced in the city itself and, in great variety, by a cluster of specialist brewers and blenders in the Senne Valley.

The Senne is a small river that runs diagonally, often underground, from northeast to southwest through Brussels. There used to be *lambic* breweries on both sides of the city and even today *lambic* is served as a local speciality on the eastern edge of the city at Jezus-Eik. South of Brussels it is served at Hoeillaart-Overijse, where Belgium's (dessert) grapes are grown. However, it is on the western edge of Brussels that production is concentrated today spreading out into the nearby scatter of farming villages collectively known as Payottenland. Traditional *lambic*-makers brew only in the winter, and the number in production at any one time varies. Some have closed in recent years, but it is not unknown in such cases for a brewery to reopen.

There are a couple of *lambic* breweries within the western boundary of Brussels itself and a further eight or nine active ones in Payottenland. There are also about half a dozen companies that contract or buy brews which they then ferment, mature or blend in their own cellars. A further two or three breweries beyond the traditional area also produce beers of this type (notably St Louis and Jacobins, both from West Flanders). With 20-odd houses producing *lambic* beers to varying degrees of authenticity, and seven or eight derivative styles, some available in more than one age, there are usually about 100 products of this type on the market, though many are obtainable only on a very limited scale and in specialist cafes.

The *lambic* family are not everybody's glass of beer, but no one with a keen interest in alcoholic drink would find them anything less than fascinating. In their "wildness" and unpredictability, these are exciting brews. At their best, they are the meeting point between beer and wine. At their worst, they offer a taste of history, as though one of those stoneware jars of beer had been lifted from the canvas of a

Bruegel or Brouwer.

The basic *lambic* is a spontaneously fermenting wheat beer, made from a turbid mash of 30–40 percent wheat and the rest barley. The barley is only lightly malted; the wheat not at all. The boil can last three to six hours and the brew is hopped very heavily but with blossoms that have been aged to reduce their bitterness. The hops are used for their traditional purpose as a preservative; their bitterness is not wanted in a fruity wheat beer. In the classic method, the brew is taken upstairs to the gable of the roof, where vents are left open so that the wild yeasts of the Senne Valley may enter. The brew lies uncovered in an open vessel, and consummation takes place. The brew is allowed to be aroused in this way for only one night, ideally an autumn evening, and only the wild yeasts of the Senne Valley are said to provide the proper impregnation.

After its night upstairs the brew is barrelled in hogsheads, where primary and secondary fermentations take place, further stimulated by microflora resident in the wood. For this reason, *lambic* brewers are reluctant to disturb the dust that collects among the hogsheads, which are racked in galleries with no temperature control.

Brewers outside the traditional *lambic* area who wish to make a beer of this type have been known to acquire a barrel of a Senne Valley vintage to use as a starter. In the classic method the brewer never pitches any yeast. No doubt it was originally just a question of supply, but some barrels used in the maturation of *lambic* originally contained claret, port or sherry – the last reminiscent of whisky-making in Scotland. Like the whisky-maker, the *lambic*-brewer wants his barrels to respond to the natural changes in temperature.

The primary fermentation takes only five or six days, the secondary six months. If a brew of less than six months is made available for sale, it is customarily identified as young (*jong*) or "fox" (*vos*) *lambic*. The classic maturation period, however, is "one or two summers" and occasionally three.

Terminology is imprecise, not least because of the two languages in use (and Flemish manifests itself in several dialects). *Lambic* may appear as *lambiek* and both the beer and yeast are said to derive their name from the village of Lembeek, in Payottenland. In its basic form *lambic* is hard to find, but it is served on draught in some cafes in the producing area. The young version can be intensely dry, sour, cloudy and still, like an English "scrumpy" or rustic cider. The older version will have mellowed, settled, and perhaps be *pétillant*.

A blended version of young *lambic* sweetened with dark candy sugar is known as *faro*. If this is then diluted with water, it becomes *mars*. Sometimes cafes provide sugar and a muddler. If the sugared version is bottled, it is effectively chaptalized and develops a complex of sweetness in the start and fruity sharpness in the finish. If young and old versions of the basic beer are blended in the cask to start yet a further fermentation, the result, sparkling and medium-dry, is known as *gueuze-lambic*. This term is also sometimes used to describe a version that is blended and conditioned in the bottle, though such a product is properly known simply as *gueze* and is the most widely available member of the family. The bottle-conditioning may take three to nine months, though the beer will continue to improve for one or two years after leaving the brewery and will certainly last for five. Because the atmosphere in the brewery is dusty and perhaps damp, some small brewers feel it pointless to label their bottles but do put a dab of whitewash on the bottle to show which way up it has been stored.

The version in which cherries have been macerated in the cask is known as *kriek*. If raspberries are used, it is called *framboise*. Strawberries (*aardbeien*) and even grapes (*druiven*) have also been used. The cherry version is a very traditional summer drink in the Brussels area, and the original method is to make it with whole fruit, which ferment down to the pits. Another technique is to macerate whole fruit in juice and add the mixture to the brew.

The original beer is brewed from a conventional gravity of 12–13 Plato (1048–52), though the density and alcohol content varies according to dilution, blending and maceration. A basic *lambic* has only about 3.6 percent alcohol by weight; 4.4 by volume. A *gueuze* might have 4.4; 5.5. A *kriek* can go up to 4.8; 6.

Even with all of these variations at their disposal some cafes choose to offer their own blend, perhaps to offset the sourness of a young *lambic* with the fruitiness of a mature one. Such a blend may be offered as the *panache* of the house. These beers are sometimes accompanied by a hunk of brown bread with cheese, onions and radishes. A spready *fromage blanc*, made from skimmed milk, is favoured. Or a salty *Brusselsekaas* might be appropriate. The beers are served at a cool cellar temperature of around 10°C (50°F). In the USA they have proved themselves to be elegant aperitifs, over ice, as though they were vermouth.

As if such colour were not enough, there are a number of ale breweries in Brabant, especially northwest of Brussels.

Where to drink

In Brussels: Beer-lovers who also enjoy Art Nouveau will appreciate the cafe De Ultime Hallucinatie (31b Rue Royale). Something a little later, reminiscent of the bar in a railway station of the period, is offered by the wonderful 1920s, Mort Subite (serving the *lambic* beers of the same name) at Rue de Montagne-aux-Herbes Potagères, not far from Grand' Place. Another *lambic* cafe, even closer to Grand' Place, is Bécasse, in an alley off Rue Tabora. Easily drinkable and sweetish *lambic* beers are brewed for the house by De Neve and served with snacks in a cosy "Dutch kitchen" atmosphere. On Grand' Place, La Chaloupe d'Or has a wide selection of beers. Another cafe in the "Dutch kitchen" style, also in the centre of the city, is 't Spinnekopke at Place du Jardin aux Fleurs, with a good range of well-kept beers. Not far away, Place Sainte Catherine has several atmospheric cafes selling *lambic* beers.

Around the edge of the city centre there are several outstanding specialist beer cafes: La Houblonnière, a student spot with hearty hot food, in Place de Londres; Le Miroir, with a knowledgeable owner, some unusual speciality beers and a "coffee shop" atmosphere, at Place Reine Astrid in Jette; Moeder Lambic, which also has a restaurant, at Chausée de Waterloo; Au Père Faro, in Chaussée d'Alsemberg, Uccle; and Bierodrome, with jazz, at Place Fernand Cock in Ixelles.

In Louvain/Leuven, the town-centre cafe Domus in Tiensestraat has a wide selection of beers and brews its own Munich-style pale lager.

In Payottenland, every village has at least one cafe serving *lambic* beer. In the aptly named village of Beersel, there are two cafes that blend their own *lambic*. One, Drie Fonteinen, has hand-pumps. The other, Oude Pruim, also specializes in *boudin* (black pudding, or blood sausage). Beersel has a 13th-century castle that can be visited in summer or on winter weekends.

Artois

A major European brewing company that is the biggest in Belgium. The name derives from a family, not the region of northern France. **Stella Artois★** is a Pilsener-style beer with a hint of new-mown hay in the nose. Artois, based in Leuven, also produces a "Danish"-style premium lager called **Loburg★** and the top-fermenting **Ketje★**. Products of its subsidiaries include **Wiel's★**, a local Pilsener in Brussels; **Vieux Temps★** and **Ginder★**, both Belgian-style ales, and the **Leffe★★** and **Tongerlo★★** ranges of abbey-style ales.

Belle-Vue

In so far as the phrase "mass-market" can be applied to *lambic* beers, it describes the relatively bland and sweet **Belle-Vue★** products from the sizeable Vandenstock brewery in Brussels. The same company owns the excellent De Neve *lambic* brewery in Payottenland at Schepdaal. In its unfiltered form, **De Neve Lambic★★→★★★** has an almondy, aperitif dryness.

Boon

A well-respected blender of *lambic* beers, Frank Boon (pronounced "Bone") has contributed much to the revival of interest in *lambic* styles since he started to blend his own products some years ago at the former De Vit brewery in, appropriately, Lembeek. Boon's *lambic* beers are aromatic, very lively, fruity and dry. He makes a speciality of offering a variety of ages and even of *caves*. His speciality blends are labelled **Mariage Parfait★★★**. Other blenders include De Koninck (no connection with the Antwerp brewer of the same name), Hanssens and Wets.

Cantillon

Tiny, working "museum brewery" producing *lambic* beers in Brussels. Well worth a visit at 56 Rue Gheude, Anderlecht (☎5214928). Its beers are smooth, with a sustained head, dry and with a sharply fruity finish. A full range of *lambic* beers is produced, and the **Framboise Cantillon★★★★** is a classic.

De Troch

Very small *lambic* brewery in Wambeek in Payottenland. Despite its small scale it exports to France where its beer is well-regarded. **De Troch★★★** beers are generally on the dark side, quite full in body, and rather carbonic. There is also a blender called De Troch in Schepdaal.

Eylenbosch

The extreme dryness and woodiness formerly found in the Eylenbosch *lambic* beers seems to have retreated since the brewery was rented to new management. The beers are still dry but balanced with hints of sweetness against a smoother background. Distinctiveness has been traded perhaps for a broader acceptability. An Eylenbosch speciality has been the **Festival Supergueuze**★★★, which has more than three years' maturation before being bottled, according to the brewery which is at Schepdaal, in Payottenland.

Girardin

A good, traditional *lambic* brewery in Payottenland at St Ulrik's Kapelle. Girardin produces big-bodied, fruity and rather bitter beers. Its **Lambic Girardin**★★★ is a well-regarded example of the basic style.

Haacht

Beyond its everyday beers (usually on the malty side) and a pleasant Belgian ale called **Aerts 1900**★★ this brewery, in Boortmeerbeek, has made some effort to promote a **Gildenbier**★★★. This is an unusual, Belgian style of top-fermenting dark brown beer that is notable for its rich sweetness. It may have limited application – as a restorative, perhaps – but is a part of tradition. This example has a hint of iron in the nose and licorice tones in the finish. The style was originally local to Diest, not far away on the northeast border of Brabant. Revivalist examples are also made by the brewery De Kluis and by Gouden Boom of Bruges.

Hoegaarden "White"

Hoegaarden is a village in the far east of Brabant that is famous for cloudy "white" wheat beers. There were once 30 breweries in the area producing beers in this style. The last closed in the mid 1950s and a decade later a revivalist brewer re-started production on a small scale. This unlikely venture has proved to be both a critical and commercial success. The brewery is called De Kluis and the beer **Hoegaardse Witte**★★★★. It has a very old-fashioned specification: in percentages, 45 wheat, 5 oats and 50 barley. The wheat and oats are raw, and only the barley is malted. This strange brew is also old-fashioned in that it is spiced, with coriander and curaçao, both of which were once commonly used before the universal adoption of the hop as a seasoning. A top-fermenting yeast is used and there is a further dosage in the bottle, with a priming of sugar. The nature of the grist and the use of a slowly flocculating yeast in the bottle help ensure the characteristic "white" cloudiness. The beer has a conventional gravity of 12 Plato, and emerges with an alcohol content of 3.84 percent by weight; 4.8 by volume. As it ages, it gains a refractive quality known as "double shine", and its fruity sourness gives way to a honeyish sweetness. A similar beer, aromatic and pale but stronger (18.4 Plato. 6; 7.5) and made exclusively from barley malt, is called **Grand Cru Hoegaarden**★★★.

Also in a similar style is a slightly darker beer, **Echte** ("real") **Peeterman**★★★. The darker hue comes from torrefied barley malt and it is a beer of conventional gravity. The name derives from the church of St Peter in nearby Louvain, a city that once had its own "white beer" tradition. Another Peeterman, also from eastern Brabant, is made by Verlinden of Lubbeek, and there is a sweet, cidery version in broadly the Louvain tradition from De Kroon of

Neerijse. This is called **Dubbel-Wit** and is, indeed, very cloudy. White beers in the Hoegaarden style are also made in Flanders by Riva (whose Wittekop is exported to the US) and Gouden Boom (which calls its entrant, with civic pride, Brugs Tarwebier).

Meanwhile, the Hoegaarden brewery's taste for experimentation is unquenchable. Another of its products is called **Forbidden Fruit. Verboden Vrucht**★★→★★★ (Le Fruit Defendu) is a claret-coloured, all-malt, strong ale of 19.5 Plato (6.4; 8), which combines a spicing of coriander with a hefty helping of Challenger and Styrian aroma hops. The spicy, sweet fruitiness is very evident in the aroma, and the earthy hoppiness in the palate. A very sexy strong ale, as its label implies.

Lindemans

This classic Brabant farmhouse brewery in *lambic* country at Vlezenbeek, Payottenland, seems an unlikely location from which to attack world markets. Nonetheless, its craftsman-made **Faro**★★★→★★★★, **Gueuze**★★★→★★★, **Kriek**★★→★★★ and **Framboise**★★★ are variously well-known in The Netherlands, France and the USA. In their whitewashed brewery the Lindemans family have seen *lambic* beer, once written-off as a "farmers' drink", capture the imagination of wine-lovers. In so doing, their products have lost a little of their sharpness and become a trifle sweeter, but they remain authentic and interesting examples of their style.

Mort Subite

The name may mean "Sudden Death", but it derives simply from a dice game played at the famous Mort Subite cafe in Brussels. Despite the Bruxellois joke "from beer to bier", the Mort Subite brews are not especially lethal. On the contrary, they have a conventionally modest alcohol content. They are brewed by the De Keersmaeckers in Payottenland. The family have been brewers since the 18th century and still have some cellars dating from then, though their 1950s brewhouse is modern by *lambic* standards. Their beers, including a **Faro**★★, a **Gueuze**★★ and a **Kriek**★★, have in the past varied from being sharp to being on the bland side. Recently there have been some rather sweet, "beery" bottlings.

Palm

Typically Belgian ales are produced by this medium-sized family brewery in the hamlet of Steenhuffel, to the north-west of Brussels. In Belgium, a top-fermenting beer of no regional style is often identified simply as a "special" to distinguish it from a Pilsener. Hence **Spéciale Palm**★★, now exported to the USA under the more precise name **Palm Ale**. It has an original gravity of around 11.25 Plato and its yeast is a combination of three strains. Palm Ale has a bright, amber colour; a light-to-medium body; a fruity, bitter-orange aroma and a tart finish.

Timmermans

Widely available *lambic* beers made by traditional methods at Itterbeek in Payottenland. Timmermans' **Lambic**★★→★★★, **Gueuze**★★→★★★ and **Kriek**★★→★★★ are all fruity and acidic but easily drinkable.

Vanderlinden

Excellent *lambic* beers, produced at Halle in Payottenland. Vanderlinden's **Vieux Foudre Gueuze**★★ → ★★★ has a full colour, a dense, soft, rocky head and a palate that is smooth and dry, with a "sour apple" tartness. **View Foudre Kriek**★★ → ★★★ is lively, with lots of aroma, starting with hints of sweetness and finishing with a dry bitterness. The brewery also has a fruity **Framboise**★★ → ★★★. Its house speciality **Duivel**★★★ is an odd combination of a *lambic* with a conventional top-fermenting beer.

FRENCH-SPEAKING BELGIUM

Perhaps it is the softness of the language: summer beers called *saisons*, winter-warmers like Cuvée de l'Ermitage and Chimay Grand Reserve, aperitifs like Abbaye d'Orval. Or maybe the rolling, wooded countryside, occasionally hiding a brewery in its folds. The French-speaking south seems a restful, contemplative place in which to drink. Just as there are fewer people in the south, so the breweries and beer styles are thinner on the ground, but they are rich in character.

Contemplative beer drinking (an aperitif here, a digestif there) suits the pace. No gastronome would go to Belgium without wishing to taste the hams, pâtés and game of the Ardennes – the sprawling forest that occupies much of the south, forming and straddling the borders with France, Luxembourg and Germany. This is country for touring rather than tourism. The Ardennes are the dominant feature of French-speaking Belgium, especially east of the river Meuse, and to the outsider they identify the region more readily than its official name, Wallonia.

When, as sometimes happens, a beer menu in Belgium lists "Wallonian specialities" (in whichever language), it is referring to *saisons* and monastery beers from four provinces. Among these, the province of Hainaut (with interesting industrial archaeology around the cities of Mons and Charleroi) has the most breweries, including the celebrated one at the abbey of Chimay. The province of Namur, named after its pleasant and historically interesting capital city, has the Rochefort monastery brewery. The province of Liège, also named after its principal city, has the Jupiler brewery, producing the biggest-selling Pilsener in Belgium. This province also has the German-speaking pocket in which the Eupener Brauerei produces an excellent Pilsener and a stronger, amber Kapuciener Klosterbrau. The Belgian province of Luxembourg (which borders on the sovereign state of the same name) has the Orval monastery brewery.

Where to drink

Almost every town in Belgium has at least one specialist beer cafe, and there are many in the French-speaking provinces. Good examples include: in Mons, Le Bureau, on Grand Rue, and La Podo, in Marché aux Herbes; between Brussels and Charleroi, at Nivelles, Le Pado; near Namur, at Jambes, Escapade, and – a little further away – Le Relais de la Meuse, at Lustin; between Namur and Liège, at Huy, Tavern Big Ben; in Liège, Le Cirque d'Hiver and Le Pot au Lait; south of Liège, in the direction of the Ardennes, Le Faudrée, at Angleur.

Bush Beer

This distinctive and extra-strong brew takes its name from that of the family Dubuisson (*buisson* means "bush") by whom it is made, in the village of Pipaix near Tournai in the province of Hainaut. Retaining the botanical theme, the family re-named the beer Scaldis, after a local flower, for the American market, to avoid conflict with the US brewers Busch. Under either name, **Bush Beer/Scaldis**★★★ might be more accurately described as an ale. It has a copper colour, a gravity of 9.5 Belgian degrees (24 Plato; 1095) and an alcohol content of 7.34 percent by weight; 9.4 by volume. Produced with a top-fermenting yeast matured for three months, dry-hopped and filtered but not pasteurized, it emerges with a chewy, malty, perhaps nutty, palate and with a hoppy dryness in the finish.

Chimay Trappist Monastery

The best-known and biggest monastery brewery in Belgium. Its long-serving brewmaster, Father Théodore, is a greatly respected figure in the industry, and Chimay's products have been a model for many others. They are, in the monastic tradition, top-fermenting strong ales, conditioned in the bottle. Within this tradition, the Chimay beers have a house character that is fruity, both in the intense aroma and the palate. Beyond that, each has its own features. Each is distinguished by its own colour of crown cork (*capsule*). The basic beer, **Chimay Red**★★★, has a gravity of 6.2 Belgian degrees, 15.5 Plato, 1063, with 5.5 percent alcohol by weight; 7 by volume. It has a full, copper colour, a notably soft palate and a hint of blackcurrant. The quite different **Chimay White**★★★ has a gravity of 7 Belgian; 17.35 Plato (1071) and an alcohol content of 6.3; 8. It has a firm, dry body, slender for its gravity, with plenty of hop character in the finish and a quenching hint of acidity. This noble beer is very highly regarded by the brewery, but it does not have the most typically Chimay character. A return to type is represented by the **Chimay Blue**★★★★, which has a gravity of 8; 19.62 (1081) and an alcohol content of 7.1; 9. This has, again, that characteristically Chimay depth of aromatic fruitiness – a Zinfandel, or even a port, among beers. Chimay Blue is vintage-dated on the crown cork. If it is kept in a dark, cool place (ideally 19°C (65°F), but definitely not refrigerated), it will become markedly smoother after a year and sometimes continues to improve for two or three, drying slightly as it progresses. After five years, it could lose a little character, but some samples have flourished for a quarter of a century. A version of Chimay Blue in a corked 75 cl bottle is called **Grande Reserve**. The larger bottle size and different method of sealing seem to mature the beer in a softer manner. With different surface areas and air space, a slightly larger yeast presence and the very slight porosity of cork this is not fanciful.

The full name of the abbey is Notre Dame de Scourmont, after the hill on which it stands near the hamlet of Forges, close to the small town of Chimay in the province of Hainaut. The monastery was founded in 1850, during the post-Napoleonic restoration of abbey life. The monks began to brew not long afterward, in 1861–62. They were the first monks in Belgium to sell their brew commercially, introduced the designation "Trappist Beer" and in the period after World War II perfected the style. The monastery was damaged in the war and has been extensively restored, but in traditional style. It has a classic copper brewhouse and very modern fermentation halls.

The monastery also makes a cheese, called Chimay, of the Port Salut type. A restaurant not far from the monastery sells both beer and cheese. In the area, a favourite local dish is the spiced trout *escavèche* derived from the tastes and cooking techniques of occupying forces during the period of the Spanish Netherlands. There are also several local recipes featuring Chimay beers.

Cuvée de l'Ermitage

Hermitages were the first homes of monks in the western world and there were many in the forests of Hainaut in the early Middle Ages, but no one is certain which of two sites gave their name to this brew. It is certainly worthy of being enjoyed in a reflective moment, though not necessarily to the ascetic taste. **Cuvee de l'Ermitage**★★★ is a very dark and strong all-malt brew of 18.7 Plato, with an alcohol content of 6 percent by weight; 7.5 by volume. It is produced from three malts and heavily hopped with an interesting combination of Kent Goldings and Hallertaus (both for bitterness) and Northern Brewer and Saaz (both for aroma). It has a distinctively creamy bouquet, a smooth start, with hints of sweetness, then a surprising dryness in the finish – almost the sappiness of an Armagnac. **Cuvée** is the local speciality of the old Union brewery at Jumet, on the edge of Charleroi. The brewery produces a range of top-fermenting beers for its parents, Maes and Watney.

Jupiler

The biggest-selling Pilsener beer in Belgium takes its name from Jupille, near Liège, where it is produced by a brewery that for many years rejoiced in the odd name Piedboeuf. In recent years, the company itself has become known as Jupiler. Although it has lost some of its hoppiness, **Jupiler**★ remains dry and soft and is a pleasant enough mass-market beer. The company has recently acquired Lamot and Krüger.

Orval Trappist Monastery

There is a purity of conception about both the brewery and the monastery of Orval. The brewery provides its own distinctive interpretation of the monastic style and offers just one beer: **Orval**★★★★. This brew gains its unusual orangey colour from the use of three malts produced to its own specification, plus white candy sugar in the kettle; its aromatic, aperitif bitterness derives from the use of Hallertau and (more especially) Kent Goldings, not only in the kettle but also in dry-hopping; its characterful acidity comes from its own single-cell yeast in its primary and secondary fermentations and a blend of four or five bottom cultures in a slow bottle-conditioning. As to which of these procedures is most important in imparting the *gout d'Orval*, there may be some debate. The triple fermentation process is certainly important, but the dry-hopping is perhaps the critical factor. The beer has an original gravity of 13.5 – 14 Plato (1055 +) and emerges with an alcohol content of more than 4.5 percent by weight, around 6 by volume. Its secondary fermentation lasts for five to seven weeks, at a relatively warm temperature of around 15°C (60°F). Its bottle-conditioning, regarded by the brewery as a third fermentation, lasts for two months, again at warm temperatures. The beer should be kept in a dark place, ideally at a natural cellar temperature. If it was bought in a shop, give the beer a few days to recover its equilibrium and pour gently. It should improve for about a year and, although its character may then diminish, it could keep for five years.

This is a short period in the life of an abbey that was founded in 1070 by Benedictines from Calabria, rebuilt in the 12th century by early Cistercians from Champagne and sacked in several conflicts along the way, in the 17th century leaving most of the ruins that stand today. From the 18th century, there are records of brewing having taken place in the restored abbey, which was then sacked in the French Revolution. The present monastery, with its dramatic, dream-like purity of line, subsumes Romanesque-Burgundian influences in a design of the late 1920s and 1930s. The monastery makes its beer, crusty brown bread and two cheeses, of the Port Salut and (in a somewhat distance interpretation) Cheddar types, and sells them to tourists in its gift shop.

Meanwhile, in its corner of the province of Luxembourg, not far from the small town of Florenville, the "valley of gold" dreams. Legend says that Countess Mathilda of Tuscany lost a gold ring in the lake in the valley. When a fish recovered the ring for her, Mathilda was so grateful that she gave the land to God for the foundation of the monastery. The fish with the golden ring is now the emblem of Orval and its beer.

No other beer can be said to match the character of Orval, but there are secular products in a broadly similar style. An example from this part of Belgium is the beer of the new micro-brewery at Montignies sur Roc. From Flanders, there is Augustijn, produced by the Van Steenbergen brewery.

Rochefort Trappist Monastery

A low profile is perhaps appropriate to a Trappist monastery and it cannot be said that Rochefort, in the province of Namur, has any clear image. The first impression created by its beers is that they are classic examples of the Trappist style and certainly very well made. If they have a house characteristic, it is a subtle chocolate tone. **Rochefort★★★** has beers at 6, 8 and 10 Belgian degrees.

Saison Régal

This is the most widely available *saison* beer, from the Du Bocq brewery of Purnode in the province of Namur and Marbaix in Hainault. **Saison Régal★★** is neither the strongest nor the most efflorescent example of the style, but it is a useful introduction. It has a gravity of around 13 Plato (1052) and around 4.5 percent alcohol by weight; 5.6 by volume. It is produced with a mash of more than 90 percent malt, pale and crystal, has a Kent Goldings accent in the hopping (with also Hallertau and Saaz) and spends a month stabilizing in closed tanks. The beer has a full, amber colour, a surprisingly light but firm body, and a teasing balance between aromatic hoppiness and fruitiness. The brewery also produces a characterful strong ale, **Gauloise★★ → ★★★**. (This has nothing to do with the well-known brand of cigarette.) The beer celebrates those most brave of Gauls, the early Belgians. Gauloise is available 6 and 8 degrees Belgian gravity, producing slightly higher figures for alcohol by volume. Du Bocq produces a great many other products, in some instances marketing the same beer under more than one name. It is a colourful old brewery, but this practice of "label-brewing" does not win friends in Belgium.

Saison Silly

"Saison" is emphasized in English-speaking markets to prevent this name from sounding too silly. In fact, Silly is the name of the village in Hainaut where the beer is made. In Belgium, **Saison Silly★★ → ★★★** has a gravity 13.75 Plato, a firm body, a hint of intentional, quenching sourness in the palate and a sweeter, soft finish. The *saison* sold in the US is **Speciale Enghien★★★**, which has a higher gravity, at around 20 Plato, with a softer, rounder palate, quenchingly acidic but notably clean in its long finish. A companion of 15 Plato is called **Doublette Enghien★★ → ★★★**. Beers in this *saison* style usually have a big, rocky head; good lacework; a full, amber colour; a firm but sometimes quite thin body and a delicate balance between sour acidity and sweet fruitiness; with a soft, clean finish. They are usually bottle-conditioned and often dry-hopped. Other examples include *saisons* Dupont, Pipaix, Roland and Voisin. These artisanal *saisons* come in corked wine bottles and are something of a speciality in the western part of Hainaut.

There are beers that are not described as *saisons* but are similar in style. These include the Allard and Groetembril range from Hainaut and La Chouffe from a new micro-brewery in the province of Liège.

THE GRAND DUCHY OF LUXEMBOURG

Although it shares its name with a province of Belgium, and has economic ties with that country, the Grand Duchy of Luxembourg is a sovereign state. In the matter of beer, the Grand Duchy leans in the opposite direction, towards Germany. It even claims that its Purity Law is similar to that of Germany, though it does, in fact, permit adjuncts. The typical product range of a Luxembourgeoise brewery includes a relatively mild Pilsener; a slightly more potent brew, perhaps in the Export style; and a bottom-fermenting strong beer, sometimes seasonal.

Luxembourg has five brewing companies, each with just one plant. The biggest, just, is Diekirch, which has a fairly big-bodied, clean-tasting, all-malt **Pils★★**, with a good hop aroma. There have also been occasional sightings of a stronger (4.9 by weight; 6.1 by volume) pale, bottom-fermenting beer called **Premium★★** from Diekirch.

The second largest brewery (in which Artois, of Belgium, has a small stake) is Mousel et Clausen, with the Royal-Altmünster brand. Then comes Brasserie Nationale, of Bascharage, with the Bofferding and Funck-Bricher labels. The small Simon brewery, of Wiltz, produces some excellent beers. So does the tiniest of them all, Battin, of Esch, with its Gambrinus label.

FRANCE

As well as making the world's most complex wines, France has a beer tradition stretching from the beginnings of brewing. It is most evident in the north: the Flemish corner of France specializes in top-fermented beers; Alsace and Lorraine in bottom-fermented brews. A link has even been forged with Britain, with the opening of a Breton ale brewery, Brasserie de Deux Rivières, in Morlaix.

Between Valenciennes and the Belgian border, at Crespin, there was once a monastery that is remembered in a tart, fruity, bottle-conditioned, abbey-style beer, **Réserve St Landelin★★★**, from the local Rimaux brewery. Just south of Valenciennes, Duyck produces **Jenlain★★→★★★★**, a classic *Bière de Garde*, with a deep, amber colour, fruity nose and hints of licorice in its long finish. In the tradition of this style, it is a top-fermenting brew, all-malt, 16 Plato (1064; 5.2; 6.5), not pasteurized, although it is filtered (ideally, it should not be – the original idea of a *Bière de Garde* was that it could be laid down).

The area between Valenciennes, Lille and Boulogne is the heartland of this style. Good examples include the bottle-conditioned **La Choulette★★★**, counter-pointing a citric fruitiness with a hoppy dryness; the beautifully balanced **Réserve du Brasseur★★→★★★**; the lively, soft, **La Cave des Pères★★→★★★**; the malty **Petite Suisse★★→★★★**; the perfumy, strong **Septante 5★★→★★★**; and the profoundly fruity **Ch'ti★★→★★★**, which appears in dark and pale versions. Outside France, the easiest to find are the relatively hoppy **St Léonard★★→★★★** and the malty **Lutèce★★**, from Paris.

The Lille area also has the world's strongest pale (truly golden) lager, **La Bière du Démon★★★** (21.7; 9.6; 12). For its weight, this beer is surprisingly dry, but with honeyish tones. It is brewed by Enfants de Gayant, who also own the Boxer brewery in Switzerland. George Killian's **"Irish Red"★★→★★★** is brewed by Pelforth of Lille (16.8; 1067; 5.3; 6.6) in a malty, full-bodied interpretation that also characterizes the brewery's darker **Brune★★**. Both are top-fermenting. Pelforth and Union de Brasseries (whose brands include **"33"** and **Mützig**) are part-owned by Heineken.

A yet more unusual speciality, **Adelscott★★★** (16.2; 1065; 5.2; 6.5) is produced with whisky malt, which in this case imparts a very light smokiness. It is brewed by Fischer/Pêcheur, a major independent based in Alsace. This region is also the base of Kronenbourg, the biggest brewer in France. Its beers are generally fruity and slightly sticky. The premium product is the relatively dry **1664★→★★**.

England, Wales and Scotland are the only nations in which the principal brewing tradition is to produce ales. Ireland is the only nation in which the principal tradition is to produce stouts.

These island nations were at the peak of imperial arrogance when the rest of the world started to abandon such top-fermenting brews in favour of bottom-fermenting lagers, in the mid and late 19th century. Imperial power may be a mixed blessing, but there is something to be said for national pride.

Even to the British, their ales and stouts present a taste which has first to be acquired. The writer Graham Greene, whose own family have a renowned brewery, recalls in his book *A Sort of Life* that he "hated" his first pint but that when he tried a second, he "enjoyed the taste with a pleasure that has never failed me since". The delights afforded by the classic draught ales of the British Isles might be compared to the pleasures offered by the red wines of Bordeaux. Both have subtlety of colour; a fresh fruitiness; dashes of sweetness and counter-strokes of dryness; and sometimes a hint of oak. The dry stouts of Ireland have the qualities ascribed by Hugh Johnson in his *World Atlas of Wine* to true Amontillado sherries: "Dry and almost stingingly powerful of flavour, with a dark, fat, rich tang".

In Britain, the seeker after "real" ales will look out for the designation "cask-conditioned" at the point of sale, and for hand-pulled pumps, the most common (though not only) form of dispense. A British ale served as cask-conditioned draught is like a Bordeaux wine bottled at the château.

In 1986, Britain's "Big Six" brewing companies (Bass, Allied, Whitbread, Watney, Courage, Scottish and Newcastle) had 39 breweries; the old-established independents had 81; new boutiques, all established within the previous decade, had 91; and there were 76 brewpubs, most of them equally new. Among these, 278 out of 287 produced cask-conditioned ales.

Where to drink

Of Britain's 70,000 pubs, half serve the cask-conditioned product. Among those, the 5,000 chosen each year for the *Good Beer Guide* are the ale-lovers' favourites. This invaluable guide is published by the Campaign for Real Ale (34 Alma Road, St Albans, Herts AL1 3BW), and available from WH Smith and other bookstore chains. Not every visitor to Britain has time to visit all 5,000 although it is praiseworthy to try. Most visitors land in London, where there are some good "real ale" pubs, but where out-of-town brews can be expensive and badly kept (to be fair, most don't travel well).

A much more satisfying experience will be obtained if the drinker does the travelling, whether for a long weekend or for a browse of two or three weeks around the British Isles. Below, the ale territories are viewed anti-clockwise from London. Since Britain has not only a great many pubs but also a huge range of ales, only those of special interest or reputation (and not all of those) can be detailed, and scores are accordingly high. The ★ and ★→★★ ales generally did not make the list.

LONDON AND THE SOUTH

The capital has two classic breweries, Young's and Fuller's. In Central London, Young's is well served at the Lamb (94 Lamb's Conduit St, Bloomsbury); Fuller's at the Star Tavern (6 Belgrave Mews West, Belgravia). The breweries are both on the west side of town, in Wandsworth and Chiswick respectively, whence their pubs generally fan outward toward pretty London "villages" like Richmond. Lamb's Conduit St also has the Sun, famous for its wide range of out-of-town ales. Not far away (at 208 High Holborn) is another such specialist pub, the Princess Louise. Another, near Waterloo Station, is the Hole in the Wall (5

Mepham St), with ales from one of the longer-established London boutiques, Godson-Chudley. The Beer Shop (8 Pitfield St, near Old St Underground station) has a wide selection of bottled products, and has its own boutique (tours: ☎739 3701). London has many brewpubs. None stands out for its beers, but the Firkin chain is famous for having popularized the idea. A good example is the Frog and Firkin (41 Tavistock Crescent, Westbourne Park Underground, near Portobello Road market).

Where to drink: long weekends

West to Oxford along the Thames Valley, where every brewery offers good, country ales. Go via Marlow (Wethered's ales, a Whitbread subsidiary, try the Royal Oak); Henley (Brakspear's: Three Tuns); Abingdon (Morland's: the Ox Inn or the riverside Old Anchor); and Oxford (Morrell's: lots of good pubs; try the King's Arms, 40 Holywell St). Return via the B474 to visit the Royal Standard of England (Marston's Owd Roger) at Forty Green, near Beaconsfield.

South to Brighton. Via Horsham (King and Barnes: the Stout House) or Lewes (lovely, buttery-malty ales from Harvey's/Beard's: the Brewer's Arms); and Brighton (the Raven boutique brewery has its ales at the Coachmaker's Arms, 76 Trafalgar St; Alexandra Becket's at the Queen's Head, 69 Queen's Road).

East to Canterbury, via Maidstone (Goacher's: the Pilot, 3 Upper Stone St) and Faversham (Shepherd Neame at the Sun; Fremlin's, a Whitbread subsidiary, at the Phoenix). Canterbury Brewery's ales can be found in its home town at the Millers Arms in Mill Lane.

Brakspear

Among a remarkably good crop of breweries in the Thames Valley, Brakspear, at Henley, is outstanding. Its "ordinary" **Bitter★★★★** (1035), hoppy from its nose to its lingering finish, is the classic example of this English style.

Fuller

Persistent award-winner. Beautifully balanced ales, with hoppiness being countered by fruitiness as gravities ascend. Delightful "ordinary", **Chiswick Bitter★★** (1035+); complex "special", **London Pride★★ →★★★** (1041+); renowned **Extra Special Bitter★★★★** (1055+). The bottled **Golden Pride★★★ →★★★★** (1084–92) has the colour, smoothness and warming finish of a cognac. The brewery is on the way into London from Heathrow

Gale

The corked and bottle-conditioned **Prize Old Ale★★★ → ★★★★** (1092–98) has such a dry fruitiness, and alcoholic warmth, as to be reminiscent of a Calvados. This dry fruitiness characterizes the range. The brewery is about 60 miles (96 km) from London, on the edge of Portsmouth.

King and Barnes

Country brewery specializing in "real" ale. Malt, hop and fruitiness beautifully balanced in ales like **Festive★★** (1050). The brewery, at Horsham, Sussex, is an interesting blend of tradition and modern technology.

Shepherd Neame

The Queen Court vineyard, growing a prize-winning Müller-Thurgau, is owned by this brewery. Since the location of both, the country town of Faversham, is in the 'Grande Champagne' of the English hop, it seems a shame that Shep's no longer grow their own East Kent Goldings. After a period of flirtation with other hops, the brewery is, however, now re-emphasizing this wonderfully aromatic local variety. The hop bitterness comes through most strongly in the "ordinary" **Masterbrew Bitter**★★★ → ★★★★ (1036). **Shepherd Neame Stock Ale**★★★ (1037) is dark and dry, with a lot of character for its gravity. **Invicta**★★ (1044) is a "best" bitter with a nice balance of hop and malt.

Watney

Bête rouge of the "real ale" movement, though past sins should by now be forgiven. Perhaps because of the house yeast, its London cask ales are not as characterful as devotees would wish. Albeit a minor category, **Mann's Brown Ale**★★★ (1034–5) is a classic example of the southern style. **Stingo**★★★ (1076) is a dark barley wine in a distinctively dry interpretation, with a touch of burnt stoutiness. Watney's affiliate Truman produces more assertive ales.

Whitbread

A well-ordered portfolio of 30 or 40 products (each with its own specification) includes about 15 middling-to-good "real" ales from local subsidiaries (the company has eight breweries). National bottled products include the definitive sweet or "milk" stout (both brewed and primed with lactose), **Mackeson**★★★★ (1038–42 in Britain; higher in the Americas). Surprisingly, this brew is not filtered, just fined. The brewing world's answer to Bailey's Irish Cream perhaps? Whitbread also has **Gold Label**★★★ → ★★★★ (1098; 8 percent alcohol by weight; 10 by volume), a classic pale barley wine, which spends three hours in the brew-kettle, has its own yeast and in the bottled (but not canned) form is unpasteurized. Strong and warming, but mellow. The brewing world's answer to whisky?

Young

Fiercely independent London brewery serving real ale in all of its pubs. Its "ordinary" **Bitter**★★★ → ★★★★ (1036), soft and complex, is still a classic, despite being less assertively dry than it once was. Its **Special**★★★ → ★★★★ (1046) is beautifully balanced, with a malty finish. Its bottled **Ramrod**★★ (1046) has a smooth bitterness and an interesting balance of maltiness and strength. **Young's Export Special London Ale**★★★ (1062–3) has, when it is fresh, a massive bouquet of floral East Kent Goldings. **Old Nick**★★★ → ★★★★ (1084) is a classic dark barley wine, warming, with some liqueurish fruitiness (a hint of banana?) in the finish.

EASTERN ENGLAND

From London, a round-trip east for two or three days will reveal some intensely traditional ales and interestingly rural (if often flat) countryside. The first stop would be one of the villages near Chelmsford, where Ridley's brewery sells its very hoppy, dry beers, often from wooden casks.

Further down the road, Ipswich has pleasantly hoppy ales from Tolly Cobbold. Beyond Ipswich, the road heads for the main destination, the pretty little harbour town of South-wold, the home of Adnams brewery.

Further north in Norwich, the boutique brewery Wood-forde has its very hoppy ales at the Plasterers' Arms, in Cowgate, and the Rosary Tavern, in Rosary Road. From Norwich, the road runs through The Fens to Wisbech, where Elgood's fruity **Bitter**★ →★★ is brewed. Further west lies Oakham, home of the famous Ruddle's brewery, which has no pubs of its own. Ruddle's ale can be found in Peter-borough, at the Still, in Cumbergate. South of Peter-borough, Paine's makes very fruity, strawberry-ish ales at St Neots, on the way to Cambridge.

From Cambridge, the route presents a tough problem: to the east lies Bury St Edmunds, with the classic Greene King brewery; to the west is Bedford, home of Charles Wells. Whichever the way home, pass through Hertford, home of McMullen's, noted for its lightly dry **A.K. Mild**★★ →★★★.

Adnams

Noted wine merchants as well as brewers. It seemed like a Scotch whisky allusion, too, when British beer-writer Roger Protz observed that he found a salty, tangy, "seaweedy" character in Adnams' tawny ales. Perhaps this is merely suggested by the maritime location but there does, indeed, seem to be a salty dryness along with the firm body and herby hop character. The **Mild**★★ (1034), **Bitter**★★ (1036) and **Extra**★★★ (1044) are all distinctive and very complex.

Greene King

Graham Greene, as a celebration of his 80th birthday, mashed a special "edition" of the family brewery's **St Edmund Ale**★★★ (1056–62). This pale strong ale has a surprising crispness in its malty palate. The brewery is better known for its very fruity draught ales, especially **Abbot**★★★. Greene King also owns Rayment.

Ruddles

Regards itself as an ale specialist. The characteristically fresh fruitiness of English ales is more evident in Ruddle's draught products than their bottled counterparts, though the latter are still enjoyable. The **Bitter**★★ →★★★, with lots of Fuggles character but a gravity of only 1032, shows just how much palate can be found in a very light English ale. There is a greater Goldings character in the persistently award-winning **County**★★★ (1050).

Wells

Home of the full-bodied **Bombardier Ale**★★ (1042), a "special" bitter with a creamy texture and a dry maltiness, well-liked in Britain and a sought-after export.

YORKSHIRE AND THE NORTHEAST

Instead of being happy to be England's biggest county, Yorkshire has always felt itself to be a nation in its own right, steadfastly preserving its customs. Even today, its brewing tradition of using double-deck fermentation vessels leaves it with a family of yeasts that are as headstrong as a York-shireman. Perhaps that is why the character of its ales has been better sustained than that of the brews from the counties further north, clustered around the city of Newcastle.

An ale tour might follow the Pennine hills and dales, whose villages are always within easy reach of the big industrial cities. In South Yorkshire, the city of Sheffield has a brewpub, the Frog and Parrot (Division St ☎0742-21280), which has in recent years brewed a winter (October and November) dark ale, aiming for a world-record gravity of 1125 and a commensurate alcohol content. Although the record has not yet been ratified, **Roger and Out**★★★ → ★★★★ is immensely potent yet soft and smooth. Sheffield has two breweries owned by Bass, one producing the tasty **Stone's Best Bitter**★ → ★★. It also has a Whitbread brewery, producing **Trophy Bitter**★. Yet a third sizable brewery, owned by Vaux, produces the under-rated Ward's ales. In the nose, they seem malty, but there is a dense interplay of hop and yeast in a full flavour and texture that is typically Yorkshire. Vaux also has malt-accented ales from the Darley brewery, not far away in Doncaster.

In West Yorkshire, Wakefield has a boutique called Clark's, with an adjoining pub, the Henry Boon, in West-gate, selling its flowery **Bitter**★★ (1038). Halifax has a Watney subsidiary, Webster, making dry ales with a pleasantly oily texture. Keighley, near Bradford, has a classic brewery, Timothy Taylor's. Leeds has another classic, Tetley's. In East Yorkshire, a boutique called Old Mill has a herby, hoppy **Traditional Bitter**★★ (1037).

In North Yorkshire, the village of Tadcaster became for reasons of its water an important brewing centre. It has the classic Sam Smith's; former family rival (now part of the Courage group) John Smith's, producing a pleasantly drinkable **Bitter**★ → ★★ with some Yorkshire character; and a Bass brewery with several local ales. North Yorkshire has, not far from Ripon, in the village of Masham, the classic Theakston brewery, owned by Matthew Brown.

Further north, there are lovely, nutty ales from Cameron's in Hartlepool. Nearby, a Whitbread brewery produces sweetish ales at Castle Eden.

Vaux has its principal brewery at Sunderland. Its **Samson** ★ → ★★ is a hoppy, fruity "best" Bitter. Its range also includes **Double Maxim**★★★ → ★★★★, a brown ale in the higher-gravity style (around 1045) regional to the North-east; not so much brown as amber red, with a full, crystal-malt character, its sweetness steadied with an underlying hint of dry roastiness. Its neighbour and more famous rival **Newcastle Brown Ale**★★★ (1045) is less malty. Newcastle Breweries' other products include a hoppy cask ale called **Exhibition**★ → ★★. In something of a revival of the city's tradition, Newcastle now has a boutique, called Big Lamp, and producing an intensely hoppy-tasting **Bitter**★★.

Samuel Smith

Classic exponent of the Yorkshire brewing system, ferment-ing in "stone" (actually, slate), double-deck vessels, which make for a circulation of the yeast. The character developed by the yeast in this system produces brews with a very full texture. "Sam's" products also have their own roundness. They are often thought to be malty, but they also have a great deal of interwoven hop character. While British drinkers seek them out as cask-conditioned draught (always from the wood), export markets have to make do with bottled products. Britain's "Strong" (1048) **Pale Ale**★★★ has become chic in the US. So, at the same gravity, have Britain's **Strong Brown**★★★, known in the US as Nut Brown (it is, indeed, nutty-tasting) and the delightfully named **Nourishing Strong Stout**★★★ (again, 1048), confusingly offered to Americans as Porter (it is arguably dry enough, but surely too full-bodied for that designation?). If the British have a serious complaint it is that they cannot buy the silky **Oatmeal Stout**★★★ → ★★★★ (1048) or a new **Imperial Stout**★★★ → ★★★★ (1072), immensely rich, with a flavour of slightly burnt currants on a cake.

Tetley

Classically creamy Yorkshire ale, **Tetley Bitter**★★★ (1035.5), comes from this independently minded outpost of Allied Breweries.

Theakston

Never mind the spelling, **Old Peculier**★★★ (1058–60) is a strong dark ale with a sweet richness that is positively embracing in the cask-conditioned draught. In bottled form, it is as satisfying as a chaste kiss. If it is chilled, so is the kiss.

Timothy Taylor

A splendidly Yorkshire-sounding brewery, in the land of the Brontës (or, if you prefer it, Rugby League). A quirky but wide, and excellent, range includes a hoppy "best", **Landlord**★★ → ★★★ (1042) and the beautifully balanced, dark **Ram Tam**★★ (1043).

SCOTLAND

A cold country that specializes in rich, warming ales. Scotland, and especially Edinburgh, were once known throughout the world of brewing for their strong ales. The quality and diversity of these products was pummelled by brewery takeovers in the 1960s, and the dust has yet to settle, despite the arrival of one or two boutiques.

Among the British giants, Bass has two Scottish breweries, mainly concerned with the better-than-average Tennent's lagers. They also have one or two cask ales, and a pleasant strong brew called **Fowler's Wee Heavy**★★ (1067–73). Allied brews Skol in the brewing town of Alloa, and has a cask ale called **Archibald Arrol's 70/-**★★ (1037), with a typically Scottish maltiness in the entrance but a surprising hop acidity in the finish. Watney owns Dryborough, whose dark, malty **Eighty**★★ (1042) has a good Scots accent. The nation's own giant, Scottish and Newcastle, produces a variety of products under the McEwan and Younger labels. Vaux has the excellent Lorimer and Clark brewery. Belhaven and Maclay are the only old-established independents, both cherished.

Good ranges of Scottish ales can be found in Edinburgh at the Guildford Arms (West Register St, in the city centre) and the Starbank Inn (on the waterside at Newhaven); and in Glasgow at the Bon Accord (153 North St) and the Victoria Bar (159 Bridgegate).

Alice

Boutique in the Highland capital of Inverness. Principal product is the intensely fruity and dry **Alice Ale**★ (1040).

Argyle

Boutique in Edinburgh, brewing a full-bodied, dark, Scottish-accented ale, **Argyle 80/-**★★.

Belhaven

With monastic beginnings and a site in a harbour village at Dunbar (between Edinburgh and the border), Belhaven has romance enough. It probably still has the finest ales in Scotland, too, although its performance has experienced the upheavals of takeovers and modernizations. Its **70/- Heavy**★★ →★★★ (1035–6) is a beautifully balanced beer; its maltier **80/- Export**★★★ →★★★★ (1041–2) is perhaps the classic Scottish draught ale.

A bottled version of the Export is gaining popularity in the US as Belhaven Scottish Ale.

Borve House

Brewpub/boutique on the remote Outer Hebridean island of Lewis. Britain's most northerly brewery produces the delightful **Borve Ale Extra Strong**★★ →★★★ (1085), with a smoky aroma, a full palate and a long, intense finish.

Devanha

Aberdeen boutique producing a sweetly fruity **80/- Pale**★ (1042).

Greenmantle

An interesting balance of malt and hop in **Greenmantle Ale**★★ (1038). Boutique at Broughton, near Biggar, Lanarkshire, in the south of Scotland.

Lorimer and Clark

Old-established small brewery in Edinburgh, especially noted for its strong Scottish ale (1080; 5.7; 7.1), available on draught in its home country as **Caledonian**★★★ →★★★★, and also marketed in the US as MacAndrew's.

Maclay

The lesser-known of Scotland's old independents, probably because its ales can be hard to find outside its home town of Alloa. Rarity value aside, there is a school of drinkers that favours Maclay's as the best ales in Scotland. They are, though, a tad too hoppy to be regarded as classically Scottish. Perhaps the national taste is most evident in the **60/- Light**★★★ (1030).

McEwan/Younger

In Scotland, the ale known as **80/-** or **IPA**★★ (1042) is enjoyed for its fullness of flavour. In England, the richer and darker **Younger's No 3**★★ (1043) has a small cult following. In Belgium and the US, another dark brew, **McEwan's Scotch Ale**★★★ (1088), packs a more obvious punch.

Strathalbyn

Boutique at Dalmuir, near Glasgow. Its **Strathalbyn II**★★ →★★★ (1043) is a rich, malty-fruity Scottish ale.

Traquair

A manor house (perhaps even a castle?) in which Bonnie Prince Charlie once took refuge. Like any other large residence, it had its own brewery, enterprisingly put back into operation by the present Laird in 1965. The castle can be visited (☎0896-830323). Its principal product, **Traquair House Ale**★★★★ (1073–1080), is the classic example of a dark Scottish ale, rich and full without being excessively sweet: not unlike a good port.

THE NORTHWEST

South of the Scottish border, the Lake District and Lancashire are dotted with breweries all the way to Manchester, which has a cluster of its own. The trouble with breweries in the Northwest is that they keep buying each other.

It is to be hoped that independence can be preserved by the region's classic country brewery, Jennings, of Cockermouth, Cumbria – a "real ale" specialist, producing a wonderfully hoppy **Bitter**★★→★★★ (1035), with a hint of fruity sourness in the nose and a tingle at the back of the tongue.

Elsewhere in the county, Carlisle has a Theakston brewery, but that company belongs to the Blackburn firm of Matthew Brown (which has itself been the subject of takeover attentions from Scottish and Newcastle). The old Cumbrian Brewers, of Workington, also belongs to Matthew Brown, whose own ales are pleasant but unexceptional. In Ulverston, Hartley's is known for its beautifully balanced "best" Bitter, **XB**★★→★★★ (1040), but the brewery is now owned by Robinson's, of Stockport. Lancaster lost a brewery in 1985 after a takeover by another Blackburn company, Thwaites (itself well-known for a malty but dryish **Best Mild**★★, at 1034). Lancaster's survivor, Mitchell's, produces pleasantly smooth ales. The Manchester company Boddingtons owns the nearby Oldham Brewery and Higson's, of Liverpool.

Despite all of this activity, there remains a remarkable selection of ales. Greater Manchester has (apart from the interestingly malty ales of Wilson, a subsidiary of Watney) some very dry brews. These include those of Chester's, a subsidiary of Whitbread, as well as several independents. The once-revered pale **Bitter**★★ of Boddingtons has lost a little of its character, but each of the smaller breweries has its own partisans. **Robinson's Best Bitter**★★→★★★ (1042) has lots of hop character in aroma as well as palate, and a big body. This brewery also has a strong (1079) dark ale called **Old Tom**★★★, surprisingly dry for its gravity, with a lot of alcohol character in the finish. The small Lees brewery has a similar product but of less personality, called **Moonraker**★★ →★★★ (1072). Holt's ales are extremely hoppy, and its **Bitter**★★★ (1039) is a local classic. The smallest of the old-established Manchester breweries is Hydes, easily overlooked, it certainly should not be. Its ales are deceptively drinkable, but with a great deal of character in the finish.

Between Manchester and Liverpool, the town of Warrington has the independent Burtonwood brewery, producing creamy-textured ales; a Tetley branch brewery; and the acquisitive Greenall Whitley (making unexceptional ales itself, and having taken over Wem, Davenport's and Shipstone, among others).

BURTON
AND THE MIDLANDS

The most famous brewing centre in Britain is Burton, a small and rather scruffy town between the West Midlands city of Birmingham and the East Midlands cities of Derby and Nottingham. Burton originally became a brewing centre because of the qualities of its water, and its renown grew when its brewers were the most active in the popularization of pale ales.

Burton Ale★★ →★★★ (1047.5) is a full-bodied premium Bitter, with the fruitiness that typifies the town's brews. It is produced by Allied's brewery in Burton. Another member of the Big Six, Bass, has a brewery – its original and most famous – in Burton. Within the premises is a museum of brewing (☎0283-45301). **Draught Bass**★★★ (1044) is regarded among today's draught pale ales as being the original. Its distinctive fruitiness is slightly sour and its body gentle for the gravity, yet these negative-sounding features make for a unique character, irresistible to its admirers. The sedimented **Worthington White Shield**★★★ →★★★★ (1052) is its bottled counterpart. The brewery has sought to retain the character of these two products, though the yeast is no longer bred and trained in the old circulatory system of linked wooden barrels, known as Burton Unions.

The Marston brewery does to some extent use Burton Unions, and its **Pedigree**★★★★ (1043) is surely today the classic English draught pale ale (or "best" Bitter). It has the Burton fruitiness but also a balancing maltiness, the two blending into a nutty finish. Marston also has a soft, complex dark ale at the same gravity, **Merrie Monk**★★ →★★★, and a rich strong ale, **Owd Roger**★★ →★★★ (1080).

The old Everards brewery in Burton is being restored as the Heritage Museum, and in that guise will continue to produce ale. The somewhat newer Burton Bridge boutique produces ales very much in the town's tradition. **Bridge Bitter**★★ →★★★ (1042) has a big, plummy aroma and a fruitiness that carries right through to its soft finish.

Away from Burton, palates and styles change. In the West Midlands, both dark and pale milds are traditional, and there is often little to distinguish the latter from the region's characteristically sweet "bitters". The area also has no fewer than three out of the four original brewpubs in Britain (that is to say, the old ones that had continued to operate before the new wave).

Not far from the Welsh border, in the Shropshire village of Bishop's Castle, is the Three Tuns (☎0588-638797), a pub with its own traditional tower brewery. Also in Shropshire, near the town of Telford, at Madeley, is Mrs Lewis's All Nations (☎0952-585747). Yet more urban is Ma Pardoe's Old Swan (☎0384-53075), at Netherton, near Dudley. This brewpub, nothing short of an institution, was recently threatened with demise, and saved with the help of CAMRA, The Campaign for Real Ale.

An eight-pub brewery may be small, but it has to be regarded as a free-standing independent. In nearby Brierley Hill, behind its Vine pub (locally known as the Bull and Bladder), is Batham's, a classic small Midlands brewery. Its **Bitter**★★ →★★★ (1043) has a subtly balanced Midlands maltiness in palate and body with a light hoppiness in the finish. Its local rival in Dudley is Holden's, not a great deal bigger, with a characteristically malty range.

The regional giant, Wolverhampton and Dudley Breweries, enjoys considerable success with its ales, and is noted for the medium-dark Hanson's and Banks' **Milds**★★. Davenport's dark **Mild**★★ and soft **Bitter**★★ have the light, sweetish maltiness that is so characteristic of the West Midlands, and it is to be hoped that this character will be retained after a recent takeover by Greenhall Whitley. Bass has a West Midlands brewery making only Mild. On these grounds, its fruity **Highgate Mild**★★★ should surely be regarded as a classic (it has a gravity of 1036; most of its local rivals are just under, or around, this figure). Oddly, one of its favoured local rivals, Ansell's **Mild**★★ →★★★ (with a coffeeish aroma and palate), is now brewed outside the area. Several of Ansell's former workers started the excellent Aston Manor boutique, in Birmingham.

In the East Midlands, the city of Leicester has a working beer museum at Hoskins (133 Beaumanor Rd, ☎0533-661122), which was England's smallest brewery before the boutiques began. Hoskins produces excellent, firm-bodied ales, with a nutty start and a hoppy finish. The brewery's founding family left to form a new company, also in Leicester, producing a couple of hoppy Bitters under the name Hoskins and Oldfield.

The East Midlands' other big city, Nottingham, has no fewer than three well-established breweries: one, with the curious name of Home, produces notably well-rounded ales; Hardy and Hanson's sweetish ales are unexceptional; Shipstone's are still enjoyable and hoppy, though less so since the brewery was acquired by Greenall Whitley. Nottinghamshire also has the Mansfield brewery, a recent convert to "real ale", although in export markets its lager beers are easier to find.

The outstanding brewery of the East Midlands is away from the cities, on the coast: Bateman's, of Wainfleet, near Skegness, in Lincolnshire. Its "best" Bitter, **XXXB**★★ →★★★ (1048), is full of hops in aroma and finish, with a mighty draught of malt to keep them apart. Sad to say, the brewery's future has been clouded by family difficulties and takeover prospects.

WALES

The Welsh seem to have been known for their mead before they brewed ale. They even used honey to spice their ale in Saxon times (another antecedent for the sweet character of ales on the Celtic fringe?). They no longer do that, nor do they have their own distinctive style of brewing. They once had a style of ale called *cwrwf*, but no one else in the world could pronounce it, so nobody ever established what it was. It is equally hard today to dragoon a pronunciation out of Felinfoel, a Welsh brewery that nonetheless exports to the US.

Admirers of the writing of Dylan Thomas might find themselves in the area of Swansea, near which is Llanelli, famous for Rugby Union and the manufacture of tinplate. Britain's first canned beer was made here, by Felinfoel. Today the brewery is known for good-quality ales, including a very fruity **Bitter**★ →★★ (1038) and a nuttier "best",

Double Dragon★★ (1040). Felinfoel is part-owned by Buckley, which is in the same town. Buckley has a lightly fruity
Best Bitter★ →★★ (1036), with both malt and hop coming
through in the palate. There is a fruitiness, too, in Crown's
ales, notably its **Special Best Bitter**★ →★★ (1036). Brain's
ales, however, are distinctively malty. Brain's "best" Bitter,
called **S.A.**★★ →★★★, is a delicious ale from a classic brewery
in the centre of Cardiff, capital of Wales.

Bass has Welsh Brewers, producing pleasant ales under
the Hancock's brand. Whitbread and Allied have breweries
whose products are of no special interest. At the opposite end
of the scale, one or two boutiques have opened. In the border
town of Monmouth, the Queen's Head Hotel, in St James's
Street, has its own boutique, whose products include a
strong ale called Brain Damage. In Central Wales, the
Samuel Powell boutique is in Newtown, Powys.

THE WEST COUNTRY

The most westerly brewery in Britain is also one of the
oddest. It is the Bird in Hand brewpub, in Paradise Park, at
Hayle, Cornwall. The name derives from the fact that
Paradise Park is a garden in which rare birds are bred. It
supports itself by attracting visitors – and by selling them
three hearty ales in its pub.

An earlier brewpub, in fact one of the original four, is also
a popular stopping place for visitors to Cornwall; the Blue
Anchor, in Helston, produces a range of strong ales under the
name **Spingo**★★ →★★★. Cornwall also has the old-established
independent St Austell brewery, with a very full-flavoured
and well-balanced ale called **Tinners' Bitter**★★ (1038), after
the local mining industry.

The centralized big brewers have found distribution
difficult along the craggy coasts and hilly countryside of the
thinly populated West, so brewpubs and boutiques bristle
through Devon and Somerset, around Bath and Bristol, and
into Gloucestershire. There are too many to visit on a single
tour, and they are as prolific and fragile as mushrooms.

In Totnes, the Blackawton Brewery, founded in 1977, is
now Devon's oldest. Among the older-established examples
in Somerset, and producing excellent ales, are Golden Hill
and Cotleigh (both in Wiveliscombe), and the Miners' Arms
(Britain's first new brewpub, except that it was actually a
restaurant; now in Westbury-sub-Mendip). In the county of
Avon, Butcombe and Smiles were both pioneers. Pubs
specializing in boutique brews include the Masons' Arms, in
Taunton; the Star (23 Vineyards); King William (Thomas
St) and Bladud Arms (Lower Swainswick), all in Bath.

An ale-tour on this route might continue to arc north
through Gloucestershire (more boutiques: like Three Counties, Cirencester, and Uley) to the Cotswold Hills. There, the
prettiest brewery in Britain is to be found: Donnington, at
Stow-in-the-Wold, producing malt-accented ales of great
subtlety. Still in Cotswold country, but no longer in the
West, Hook Norton, at Banbury, has a magnificently
traditional tower brewery and some delicious, dry ales.

An alternative route (or the southern half of a round-trip)
would sample the ales of the four old-established, independent, country breweries in Dorset: Palmer's of Bridport
(very pretty, with lightly hoppy ales); Devenish of

Weymouth (light, dry ales); Hall and Woodhouse, of Blandford Forum (lightly fruity) and Eldridge Pope of Dorchester (with several well-known specialities). There would then be a sampling of the ales from the classic boutique of Ringwood (in the New Forest) and the old-independents Gibbs Mew (Salisbury), Wadworth (Devizes) and Arkell (Swindon). Among several boutiques in Wiltshire, the drinker would most certainly not miss Archer's (also Swindon).

Courage

This member of the national Big Six has its principal production of cask-conditioned ales in the West, in Bristol. Its **Directors' Bitter**★★→★★★ (1046) is a British classic: a cask-conditioned "super-premium", with a firm, medium-to-full body, a malty palate with fruity undertones, but most notable for its dry-hopped quality. Courage's Bristol brewery laid down a new stock of **Imperial Russian Stout**★★★★ (1104) in 1986. The company's brewery near Reading produces **Bulldog**★★★, a warm-conditioned, bottled pale ale that is a minor classic.

Eldridge Pope

Britain's most potent bottled brew, **Thomas Hardy's Ale** ★★★★, is produced by this old-established company in Dorchester. Much of Hardy's work was based in and around the town, and he wrote lyrically of the local beer. For a Hardy festival in the 1960s, the brewery produced a celebration ale, and has continued to do so ever since. Thomas Hardy's Ale is produced in numbered, limited editions. It is a bottle-conditioned dark ale of 1125.8; 9.98; 12.48. When young, it is very sweet, but it dries with age: a hint of oloroso sherry? Perhaps this is suggested by the fact that Eldridge Pope has its own soleras in Jerez, producing its own range of sherries. It also uses the sherry casks for the maturation of Scotch whisky.

The company is also known in Britain for a super-premium Bitter called **Royal Oak**★★ (1048), with a notably soft, fresh, fruity character. Although this product is dry-hopped, with Goldings, their character is more evident in **Pope's 1880**★★ (1041), a premium, bottled ale.

Ringwood

The godfather of boutique breweries in many parts of the world is Peter Austin, founder of Ringwood. After leaving an established brewery, he set up his own, in the New Forest, and as a consultant has since helped many others to do the same thing. His ales all have a firm body, a dry maltiness, and plenty of hop character. Ringwood **Fortyniner**★★ (1049) and **Old Thumper**★★ (1060) are both widely admired.

Wadworth

Classic country brewery that has quietly won the respect of ale-lovers everywhere. Its **Henry Wadworth IPA**★★ (1034) has a hoppy acidity; its **6X**★★ (1040), often served from the wood, is bigger than its gravity would suggest, with a more obvious fruitiness. In the darker **Farmer's Glory**★★→★★★ (1046), the two elements reach a hefty balance: the hoppiness in the start is almost herbal, and there is a rich fruitiness in the finish.

IRELAND

The land of dry stout, the style of beer famously typified by Guinness. While the best-known dry stouts of Ireland are produced by Guinness, of Dublin, there are also fine examples from two other brewers, Murphy and Beamish, both in Cork, the second city of the Republic.

It is commonly held that the Guinness in Ireland is better than that sold elsewhere. This is true of the draught product in so far as the fast turnover encourages the brewery not to pasteurize. **Draught Guinness★★★→★★★★** in Ireland therefore has a freshness, and perhaps a softer character, than its counterpart in other countries. In both Ireland and Britain, the bottled product is supplied in pubs (but not necessarily in other outlets) in unpasteurized form, under the designation **Guinness Extra Stout★★★**. It may be far less creamy, but the yeasty liveliness imparted by bottle-conditioning, and the lack of any pasteurization, frees the full, hoppy intensity that characterizes Guinness.

Despite their fullness of both flavour and body, dry stouts tend to have fairly standard gravities in Ireland: around 1037-40, with an alcohol content in the region of 3.5 by weight, 4.3 by volume. The same is true in Britain, but the various American and Continental markets get their stouts at anything from 1048 to 1060-plus. Tropical countries have the version of Guinness known, rather quaintly, as **Foreign Extra Stout★★★→★★★★**, at 1073. This highly distinctive, extra-strong stout is first slightly soured in its conditioning, then pasteurized for stability. It thus has a hint of sharpness to balance its immense weight.

Murphy and Beamish are both excellent dry stouts, each with their own distinctive characters. **Murphy's Stout★★★** is firm-bodied, with a roasty character. **Beamish★★★** is very creamy, only medium-dry, with some chocolate notes. The Murphy brewery has recently received considerable investment from its owners, Heineken. Beamish is also owned by a large brewing company, Carling O'Keefe of Canada. (It is coincidental that the original O'Keefe came from Cork.)

Ales are a minor category in Ireland, although the number of brands has increased in recent years. Guinness, together with Allied Breweries of Britain, has a company called Irish Ale Breweries. They have breweries in Dundalk and Kilkenny. Irish ales are generally full in colour (often reddish), full-bodied, sweet, sometimes with hints of butteriness. While this last characteristic would be unacceptable in a lager, it is a distinguishing feature of some ales. Irish Ale Breweries' products are, in ascending order of sweetness: **Macardle's★→★★** and **Phoenix★→★★**; **Perry's★→★★**; **Smithwick's★★**; and the newer **Twyford's★★**. There is also a **Smithwick's Barley Wine★★★**.

The most Irish-tasting ale is arguably **Dempsey's★★★**, from a boutique brewery in Dublin. This is available cask-conditioned in its local market, although "real ale" is not widely understood in Ireland. In the North, cask-conditioned ales have been produced by boutique breweries or brewpubs like the Down Royal, near Lisburn, County Antrim; the Hilden Brewery, also near Lisburn; Herald, at Coleraine; and Maiden Oak, in Derry.

Among lagers **Harp★→★★** is native Irish, but without any specifically Hibernian character.

SOUTHERN EUROPE

The fastest-growing consumption of beer in Europe is in Italy, where the bright young things of prosperous northern cities like Milan regard wine as a drink for their parents. Brewers in other European countries have poured their most sophisticated beers into the Italian market, and now local companies are responding with their own specialities.

Such influences reached their peak in 1985, when a lover of English ales started to produce one in a brewpub in Sorrento (The English Inn ☎0818-783684). This is the tiniest brewery in Italy, but several others remain in private ownership, ranging from the very small Menabrea through the middle-sized and well-respected Forst to Peroni, the country's largest (its **Nastro Azzuro**★→★★ and the very similar **Raffo**★→★★ are well-balanced Pilseners).

A classic family-owned brewery (with its "moustachioed man" trademark) is Moretti of Udine, north of Venice. In winter, the adjoining restaurant serves a yeastily unfiltered version (ordered as *integrale*, meaning "whole") of the basic **Moretti**★★ beer, which in its normal form is a clean and lightly spritzy Pilsener. Moretti is also very proud of its export-style **Sans Souci**★★ (15 Plato; 1060; 4.5; 5.6), which has a flowery hop aroma and a smooth, malty finish. The brewery also has a higher-gravity (16; 1064; 5; 6.25), all-malt version of a Munchener dark, called **Bruna**★★ →★★★. Its most specialized beer, however, is the deep red **La Rossa**★★★ (18; 1072; 6; 7.5), that is also all-malt, as evidenced by its rich aroma and palate.

A beer in the style of a "red ale", **McFarland**★★→★★★ (13.5; 1054; 4.4; 5.5) is made by Dreher (now owned by Heineken). The most exotic speciality, a deeper copper-red in colour, is **Splügen Fumée**★★★, made with medium-smoked Franconian malts, by Poretti (in which United Breweries of Copenhagen has a share).

Elsewhere in Southern Europe, Spain has some pleasantly dry Pilseners and a good few double *Bock* beers (at around 17; 1068; 6; 7.5). On Malta, the top-fermenting specialities of the **Farsons**★★★ brewery are all worthy of attention: a genuine **Milk Stout** (1045); a darkish mild ale, **Blue Label** (1039); a very pale, dry ale called **Hop Leaf** (1040); and a darker, fuller-bodied ale, **Brewer's Choice** (1050). Greece has, for reasons no one can remember, a German-style law insisting upon all-malt beers. Yugoslavia, on the other hand, is a hop-growing country, so that ingredient tends to be emphasized by its brewers. Some, like Karlovačko, also have a bottom-fermenting **Porter**★★★ (1064).

CANADA

Against an easily conjured backdrop of mountains, forests, wildlife and lakes, the brews of Canada have in recent years won attention far beyond their own country. Romance must take some of the credit. By far the greatest part of Canada's brewing takes place where the people live: in cities, and not far from the border. The major Canadian breweries do equally well in their home market by producing under licence heavily advertised brands from across the same border.

For the beer-drinker in search of true variety and individuality, a much more interesting inspiration in recent years has been manifested by the emergence of "boutique" (or, in Canada, sometimes "cottage") breweries. The French word may be coy, but surely less so than the English-language designation, even if these new breweries are concentrated in Anglophone Canada. In the mid-1980s, new boutiques and brewpubs were opening more frequently in Canada than anywhere in the world.

Since the everyday beers of Canada are slightly higher in both original gravity and alcohol content than their cross-border counterparts, they do in these respects manifest a slightly fuller flavour. However, the difference in alcohol content is exaggerated by the Canadians' sensible use of the volume system. The principal Canadian brews have an alcohol content of 5 percent by volume, amounting to 4 in the "by weight" system used across the border. Their US counterparts have between 3.9 and 3.2 by weight.

The fullness of flavour also derives from the huskiness of six-row barley, which is widely used. Set against this is the lightening and sweetening effect of large proportions of corn, often in the form of syrup – and modest hopping rates. Although they are by no means alone in this, Canadian brewers have a considerable propensity for advertising beers as being "smooth" when "bland" might be more honest.

A more interesting feature of Canadian brewing is the extent to which ales survive, in Ontario and – especially – Quebec. The major breweries' ales are golden in colour, usually made with "top" yeasts and fermented at notably warm temperatures, producing a subtle but distinctive fruitiness. As ales go, they are lightly hopped, even in comparison with some of their US counterparts. The "Canadian taste" – a fullness that is not altogether of flavour but also of texture – is even more apparent in the ales. There are also one or two half-hearted porters and stouts from the major brewers. Much more assertive speciality products are being made by some of the boutiques.

The most unusual range – including a *Weissbier*, an *Alt* and a brew in the style of California's Anchor Steam Beer – was proposed in 1985 by an embryonic company in Vaudreuil, near Montreal. At the same time, it was announced that a new brewery was to be built in Prince Edward Island, the only Canadian province without one.

Thus influences go full circle. The boutique brewery renaissance began in Britain, crossed to the USA, and progressed from California through the Pacific Northwest into British Columbia before beginning to move across Canada to some notably English-sounding places (Windsor, Ontario, being another prospective site). As the various Canadian provinces relaxed their laws to make this possible, there was also a loosening of restrictions on the availability of imported beers. Beer-drinking in Canada was becoming a great deal more interesting.

Where to drink

A brewpub revolution promises to liberate Canadians from the grip of tied taverns and state-monopoly liquor stores. It began in 1982, at the Troller Pub, in Horseshoe Bay, a yacht marina and ferry terminal linking the city of Vancouver with the island of the same name. That year, the Troller began serving its own ales, albeit brewed (in accordance with the law of the time) at a separate premises – less than 100 metres away. Since then, there have been periodic changes both in the range of products and their character, but the basis has been all-malt ales and porters; hopped with blossoms; primed, fined and cask-conditioned, but served under pressure, at around 10°C (50°F). The house **Bay Ale**★★★ is an impressive, copper-coloured bitter, with lots of North American hop in its bouquet, palate and finish. **Royal Ale**★★★, an excellent "best" bitter, is still hoppy but with a bigger, more malty, body. **Bay Gold**★★ is paler and drier.

The Troller offered the first cask-conditioned ale in North America, and was within 100 metres of being the first brewpub. A couple of years later, one of its principals, John Mitchell, crossed to Vancouver Island, where he was allowed by a change of law to found an undisguised brewpub. The pub is called Spinnakers, and is in the island's principal town, Victoria (308 Catherine Street). Despite being a town of only about 70,000 people, Victoria is the provincial capital of British Columbia. The pub serves an outstanding range of top-fermenting, naturally conditioned brews, some by gravity from the cask, others by hand-pump for cellar tanks. **Spinnaker Ale**★★★, at an original gravity of 1042, has a straw colour, a hoppy nose, a dry, very smooth palate and a slightly acidic finish. Mitchell's **Extra Special Bitter**★★★ → ★★★★, at 1049/50, has a copper colour, with a lovely balance of malt, hop and yeasty fruitiness. There is a very full hop flavour in the finish. **Mount Tolmie Dark**★★★, at 1047, has a tawny colour and a rich, chocolatey dryness. **Empress Stout**★★★ → ★★★★, at 1052, is extremely dry, and smooth.

Spinnakers was soon sharing its thinly populated island with more brewpubs: the Prairie Inn at Saanich; the Terminal Hotel at Nanaimo; and the Leeward at Comox. All passed up the opportunity to add to the variety, and settled for lagers of the type brewed to perfection by the majors. The Prairie Inn's "Black Malt Steam Beer" turned out merely to be a thin-bodied dark lager.

Both on the island and the British Columbia mainland, a number of free-standing boutique breweries were established. In 1985, Alberta introduced a bill to approve brewpubs, and there were hopes that the same would soon happen in Saskatchewan. In Manitoba, the Nobleman Brewing Company started to produce Canadian-style light and dark ales of no special character for a disco-pub called Friday's, in the Travelodge Hotel in Winnipeg; even by Canadian standards, this conjunction must strain the patience of the beer-lover. Enthusiasts in Ontario were still lobbying for brewpubs long after the first free-standing boutiques there had been established. Quebec was slow off the mark, too, though its laws on drink are in general the most liberal in Canada. The nation's extremities seem to be best lubricated: another early brewpub was Ginger's Tavern on Hollis Street, Halifax, Nova Scotia. Ginger's serves a **Best**★★★ ale inspired by the Ringwood products in England. Also British-inspired, though wholly independent, is the vigorous CAMRA Canada, in the vanguard of the revolution.

Amstel

This Dutch *alter ego* of Heineken has acquired the brewery formerly owned by Henninger, of Germany, as a North American outpost. Amstel and Henninger brands are produced by the brewery, in Hamilton, Ontario – along with the more Canadian-sounding **Grizzly**★, which is sweetish and slightly fruity.

Brick

Sizable boutique, in Waterloo, Ontario. Produces a pleasant, all-malt beer called **Brick's Premium Lager**★★. Malt accented, but with a hop balance.

Bryant's

Boutique at Maple Ridge, British Columbia. Products have varied, but have included a pale, hoppy, and rather acidic **Bitter**★★, available only locally.

Campbell River

Boutique, Vancouver Island, British Columbia. Too early to rate.

Carling

"Black Label" is still an international brand, but its Canadian parent has long settled for being one of the "Big Three" in its home country. **Carling Black Label**★ has a smaller sale in Canada than the company's misnamed **Old Vienna**★, which is slightly less dry. By Canadian standards, the Carling products are in general dry and rather thin. The full name of the company is Carling O'Keefe, the latter identifying its principal ale. **O'Keefe Ale**★ is carbonic and fruity, but there is a little more hop character in **Buckeye Ontario Special Ale**★→★★. Like its competitors, Carling

O'Keefe has a wide range, and branch breweries have some local labels. The company is part of the international Rothman group, which is based in South Africa.

Conner's

A boutique ale-brewery on the edge of Toronto. Too early to rate.

Granville Island

The "island" is a trendy and touristy shopping area in a restored neighbourhood of the city of Vancouver. The brewery is a sizable boutique, producing well-made beers according to the *Reinheitsgebot*. **Island Lager**★★→★★★ has a soft, malty body and a dry, hoppy finish. **Island Bock**★★★ has a tawny colour, a dense head, a malty aroma, and a balancing dryness in the finish.

Island Pacific

A more truly insular boutique – on Vancouver Island. Its **Gold Stream Local Lager**★→★★ is an all-malt brew, but early samples have been unbalanced toward fruitiness, and slightly harsh.

Labatt

Biggest of Canada's brewers in recent years; controlled by a splinter of the Bronfman (Seagram's whisky) family. Its beers lean toward a perfumy sweetness, most evident in its big-selling, Pilsener-style **Labatt's "Blue"**★. A new premium, **Labatt's Classic**★→★★, is disappointing, despite being an all-malt, kräusened beer. The principal ale, **Labatt 50**★, is agreeably aromatic but unexceptional. Its **IPA**★★★ is by far its most distinctive brew. This ale has a conventional golden colour, a little hop in the aroma, and a firm body, with a honeyish malty sweetness in the finish. **Labatt's Velvet Cream Porter**★→★★ is closer to being a sweet stout.

Molson

Oldest-established of the Big Three, and still controlled by the Molson family. Of the three giants, it offers perhaps the most characterful products overall. In recent years, the Hallertau hop character in some products seems to have diminished, accenting their softness and fruitiness. The company's basic lager, **Molson Canadian**★, has some hop in the nose, and a yeastily fruity palate. Its basic ale, **Molson Golden**★, is light and rather bland. Its **Export**, also marketed as **Molson Ale**★→★★, has slightly more hop character and considerably more of the fruitiness of warm fermentation. **Molson Stock Ale**★★ has a more definite hop character, and malty body. An ale counterpart to a malt liquor, originally styled Brassée d'Or, but compounded to the ugly **Brador**★★★, has an alcohol content of 5 percent by weight, 6.25 by volume, and represents an interesting variation. Molson also offers Canada's best example of a **Porter**★★★, from its brewery in Barrie, Ontario.

Moosehead

Sizable regional brewing company, with plants in Nova Scotia and New Brunswick, though its frontier image is more apparent in the American market. Moosehead's beers have a delicacy of hop character, with a hint of Saaz, a firm body, and a grassy yeastiness. Its local brew, **Alpine★→★★**, has a little more character than **Moosehead Canadian Lager★**, which is marketed in the USA. **Moosehead Export★** is a sweetish ale. **Moosehead Pale Ale★→★★** is drier. **Ten Penny Stock Ale★★** is slightly darker and more characterful, and fractionally stronger.

Mountain Ales

The mountains are on the border, whence it is a short distance to this boutique brewery in Surrey, an outer suburb of Vancouver. Several ales have been produced. Some have been outstanding, but consistency has been a problem, especially when they have had to travel any distance. At its best, **Mountain Premium★★→★★★**, a copper-coloured ale, has a fruity nose; a very soft, malty palate; and a lightly hoppy finish. **Mountain Malt★★→★★★** is a darker, tawny ale with a smooth palate, hoppier than its English inspiration, Newcastle Brown. Both are all-malt.

Northern Breweries

Former Carling breweries sold to the employees through the unions. A positive notion, but uninteresting beers.

Old Fort

Regional independent, formerly owned by the entrepreneur "Uncle Ben" Ginter, in Prince George, British Columbia. Produces several Pilsener-type beers, including the robust **Pacific Gold★** and the more mellow **Yukon Gold★**.

Rocky Mountain

Another former Ginter brewery, in Red Deer, Alberta. Its premium product, **Gold Peak★**, is a Pilsener-style lager with a fresh, light aroma.

Upper Canada

Sizable boutique, in Toronto. Its unusual **Upper Canada Ale★★★** has a full, tawny colour; a pronouncedly fruity aroma (pears in cream, perhaps?); a rounded body; a rich, roasty, malt character; and a late bitterness from Hallertau aroma hops. Its **Upper Canada Lager★★★** has a very tasty malt character, again balanced by a hoppy finish. It is a very assertive and well-balanced beer. Both are *Reinheitsgebot* brews, naturally carbonated and unpasteurized. The brewery has shareholding links with Granville Island.

Victoria Brewing

Boutique in Victoria on Vancouver Island. First product is a sweetish, thin-tasting amber lager. Too early to rate.

Wellington County

Cask-conditioned ales, hopped with Fuggles and East Kent Goldings, and boutique-brewed in the town of Guelph, Ontario. One of the founders of the town was a member of the Arkell family, who own a brewery in Swindon, Wiltshire, England. In his honour, the Guelph brewery calls its "best" bitter **Arkell★★★**. This has an original gravity of 1038; a dry, malty start; a nutty palate, with refreshingly fruity undertones; and a hoppy finish. The brewery's "super-premium", **Wellington County★★★**, has a gravity of 1052, an aromatic fruitiness; and a hearty smack of hops from start to finish.

THE UNITED STATES

It is widely believed that there are fewer brewing companies in the United States than there were four or five years ago; in fact, the number has been increasing since the early 1980s. Closures have been outstripped by openings, albeit of tiny, "boutique" breweries.

It is assumed that there is a lesser choice of beers brewed in the United States; perhaps surprisingly, today's selection (although not universally accessible) is broader than it has been since Prohibition. It is recognized that, in volume, there has been a growth in the production of lighter, blander beers; it is not so readily grasped that, in numbers of products, there has been a far greater growth in speciality beers: not only "super-premium" Pilseners but also lagers in the Vienna and Munich styles; ales and stouts; even the odd *Altbier* and several wheat beers.

The lightness of body and palate in mainstream American beers leads some consumers to believe that they are especially low in alcohol. This is not so. Some states stipulate that anything labelled "beer" (as opposed to "malt liquor" or "ale") must not exceed 3.2 percent, but that figure represents alcohol by weight. In volume terms, this amounts to 4 percent, a level not unknown in other parts of the world. A "light" or low-price beer might be around this level in whatever state it is bought. A premium or super-premium beer has, though, in most states an alcohol content of between 3.6 and 3.9 by weight (4.5–4.8), from a gravity of 10.75–11.25 Plato (1043–1045). Most American ales have an alcohol content of around 4.25–4.75 by weight (5.3–5.9), 12.25–12.5 Plato (around 1050). Malt liquors may have a similar alcohol content, or may go up to around 6.5 (8).

The mainstream American beers are a derivation from the Pilsener style. What makes them characteristically American is their lightness of both body and palate. When, not satisfied with this, American brewing companies developed the category "light beer", it was like Volkswagen announcing that it would extend its range by starting to build small cars.

Although one or two "super-premium" brands of American-style Pilsener beer are made from all-malt mashes, the lightness of body is usually achieved by the use of other grains, often in proportions as high as 40 percent. One or two premiums use rice, but corn (maize) is more common, in the form of flakes or grits or (especially in cheap brands) as a syrup. The lightness of palate is achieved by low hopping rates, with units of bitterness often as low as 13 and rarely higher than 17.

It is the skill of the big American brewers to produce beers in this way while also seeking a clean, lightly crisp, taste. In so doing, they walk a faint line between delicacy and blandness.

THE EAST

The renaissance of traditional beer styles in the United States has a special relevance for the East. Having been the first part of the country to be settled, the East has the oldest brewing tradition, rooted in Colonial times, and still with an inclination toward ale. This has now been given a new life by boutiques like the Manhattan Brewing Company, New Amsterdam and Newman's, upstate in Albany. While these breweries have the assertiveness of youth, a more restrained approach to ale is offered by large breweries like Genesee (of Rochester, New York) and, with its McSorley's label among others, Schmidt (of Philadelphia). Pennsylvania, better known for its German tradition, is still one of the states best blessed with independent breweries. It has half a dozen, most of them very small.

Where to drink

"The biggest selection of beers in the United States" is a claim that has in recent years been offered by several bars and restaurants in the United States, but the consistent leader has been the Brickskeller (1522 22nd Street NW) in fashionable Georgetown in the heart of Washington, DC. Underneath a hotel, this brick-lined cellar stores many hundreds of beers (the number increases all the time), even to the extent of admitting that the age of some "endangered species" may render them of less interest to drinkers than to can collectors. In much the same spirit, genuine buffalo stew has been known to feature on the menu.

Despite its being an institution, New York City's most famous pub P.J.Clarke's (915 3rd Ave and 55th St) has no great claims in respect of beer; surprisingly, its branch in Macy's department store seems more interested. The biggest selection of beers in a bar is at the Peculier [*sic*] Pub (182 W 4th St, between 6th and 7th Avenues), in Greenwich Village; on weekdays, owner Tommy Chou does not open until 4 o'clock in the afternoon. For beer-lovers, another mandatory call – in the East Village – is McSorley's Ale House (15 E 7th St, between 2nd Avenue and Cooper Square). Although it was founded in 1854, McSorley's attracts a young crowd to drink its house pale and dark brews (produced by Schmidt's). For more interesting beer, the bar-restaurants of the Manhattan and New Amsterdam breweries should not be missed. The biggest selection of beers in a store is in the Village at the Waverley Deli (327 6th Ave, between 3rd and 4th Streets). Many other stores have good selections, and beers are well represented at the famous gourmet food shop of Dean & DeLuca (121 Prince Street) in SoHo.

Boston's most celebrated old tavern is Jacob Wirth's, (1868, 31 Stuart and Eliot); its "famous dark beer" has been supplied by more than one brewery over the years, and recent samplings have been rather thin, soft and fruity. On Harvard Square, Cambridge, the old-established Wursthaus bar and restaurant has a large beer-list, though not as extensive as is claimed.

Boston Beer Company

The Bostonian revolutionary politician Samuel Adams may have known more about tea parties, but his name has been appropriated by a fine, new beer, created by this small brewing company based in his home town. **Samuel Adams' Boston Lager**★★★ first appeared in 1985, and was judged best-of-show at that year's Great American Beer Festival, in Denver. On the day, it had more Pilsener character than any other beer in America. It is an all-malt beer, brewed from the relatively high gravity of 12.5 but to a conventional alcohol content of around 3.5 percent by weight, with kräusening and dry-hopping. It has a dense head, a huge hop aroma – its outstanding characteristic – and a big body. The Boston Beer Company was established by a young entrepreneur, and the product is made to his specifications in an old-established East Coast brewery.

Champale

Malt liquor specialist in Trenton, New Jersey. Its **Champale** comes in versions flavoured with citrus fruits and grenadine, but owes more to novelty than tradition.

Chesbay

Boutique, whose full name is Chesapeake Bay Brewing. **Chesbay Gold**★ →★★ is Pilsener with a dry fruitiness. **Chesbay Amber**★ is a medium-dark beer with a rather light body. The brewery is at Virginia Beach, Virginia.

Eastern Brewing

Specialist in low-price and supermarket brands. Brewery in Hammonton, New Jersey.

Geary

Boutique ale-brewery announced for Westbrook, Maine.

Genesee

The biggest specialist brewer of American-style ales, and a major regional independent, in Rochester, New York. Its ales are the principal examples of their styles, but it would be hard to rate such diffident brews as classics. **Twelve-Horse Ale★★→★★★** is golden in colour, with a fleeting fruitiness of aroma and palate, and a very lightly creamy texture. A proportion of this top-fermented brew is blended with a lager to produce **Genesee Cream Ale★★→★★★**. Both have an underlying sweetness. Genesee now produces the Fred Koch brands, including the malty **Jubilee Porter★★**.

Iron City

The brand is better known than its parent, the Pittsburgh Brewing Company. **Iron City★** has lost some of its character in recent years. **Iron City Dark★→★★★** is, however, one of the more full-flavoured examples of a Munich-style American beer. The brewery has also produced many novelty brands aimed at can collectors.

Jones

Small brewery founded in 1907 by a Welsh family in Smithton, Pennsylvania, and still owned by them. Produces the clean-tasting **Stoney's Beer★→★★**, proclaimed to contain no additives, and the light **Old Shay Cream Ale★**.

Latrobe

Small, beautifully equipped brewery in Latrobe, Pennsylvania, making only **Rolling Rock★★**, a very clean-tasting beer that has a cult following in the East. Rolling Rock has some rice adjunct, is brewed with spring water, and blossom-hopped with American varieties.

Lion

Small, old-established, brewery in Wilkes-Barre, Pennsylvania, noted for the (bottom-fermented) **Stegmaier Porter★→★★**, with its pronounced licorice character.

Manhattan Brewing Company

Despite a great beer tradition, and much-bruited civic pride, New York City lived for almost a decade without a brewery until this boutique was established in the mid 1980s. The Manhattan Brewing Company is in SoHo, on Thompson St, at Broome, between 6th Avenue and W Broadway. A brew-kettle decorates the outside of the building, and others embellish the bar and seafood restaurant. The company also has drayhorses fit to cause heart attacks among New York cabbies. The splendid products are all top-fermenting, and are tank-conditioned and fined for serving at the brewery under pressure. The principal brews are a pale, **Golden Light Ale★★→★★★** (1044), lively and dry, with a hoppy finish; an aromatic, fruity, but beautifully balanced **Royal Amber★★★** (1048); and a smooth, dry **Special Porter★★★** (1056).

F.X.Matt

The present Francis Xavier Matt is the third generation of his family to run this small brewery in Utica, New York. Its products, which tend toward a creamy softness, include: a full and fruity Pilsener-type beer called **Matt's Premium ★→★★**; **Maximus Super★★**, a malt liquor of 5.25–5.5 percent alcohol by weight; the top-fermenting **Utica Club Cream Ale★★**; and a new super-premium Pilsener, **Saranac 1888★★**, which is an all-malt, exclusively two-row, brew, hopped with Cascades and Hallertaus, and kräusened.

New Amsterdam

The first revivalist beer of New York, though initially production time was rented upstate at the Utica brewery. New Amsterdam's own brewery and tap room opened its doors in 1985, in the city's Chelsea neighbourhood, at 235 11th Avenue and 26th Street. **New Amsterdam Amber Beer★★→★★★** has an appropriately full colour (perhaps it should have been called New Vienna?) and a pleasant Hallertau and Cascade hop character, but with warm fermentation providing a degree of ale-like fruitiness. Having started with this gently different beer, the parent Old New York Brewing Company has since added a dry-hopped version, which is described as **New Amsterdam Ale ★★→★★★**. The brewery can be seen from the Tap Room, which serves a cosmopolitan range of snack meals.

Newman's

The first boutique brewery anywhere in the East, but Newman's has never had the credit it deserves. Its misfortune is to be in Albany, which may be the state capital but is an unimaginable distance – about 140 miles (225 km) – from downtown Manhattan. Those miles are along the stately Hudson valley, and Albany – an elegant city that was once the centre of ale-brewing in America – is worth a visit to sample the Newman's products in their draught form. In this form, they are fined in the cask, then stabilized by cold conditioning. They have in general a soft, tasty character. The local specialities are **Albany Amber Ale★★→★★★** (1042), malty and spicy; a **Pale Ale★★★** (1045) with a copper colour and a lot of floral hop character; and a seasonal **Winter Ale★★★** (1050), dark and chocolatey but dry.

The brewery also has a product in a paler copper colour, at 1036, which is top-fermenting but described nonetheless simply as being Newman's "beer". This fruity but well-balanced brew is available in a good many states, in the bottle, as **Albany Amber Beer★★**.

Schmidt

Major regional brewer, with a lovely, old plant in Philadelphia, interesting yeasts and one or two colourful specialities. These brews are cherished by beer-lovers, but Schmidt's attitude toward its position as their provider is not always clear.

The regular **Schmidt's★→★★** and the similar **Rheingold ★→★★**, its New York brand, are slightly fruity and fairly full-bodied. The company also produces the golden-coloured **McSorley's Cream Ale★★**, bottom-fermented but with a degree of hop in the nose and palate. There is a similar character to **Prior Double Dark★★**, which seems to have lost something of its fullness. Recent sightings of **Tiger Head**★★, a top-fermenting, golden-coloured ale, have been rare.

Straub

Very small, old-established brewery in St Mary's, Pennsylvania. **Straub Beer**★→★★ is a fairly light-bodied lager, with a longish, dry finish.

Yuengling

The oldest brewery in the United States. Yuengling, founded in 1829 and still family owned, is best known for its **"Celebrated Pottsville Porter"**★★, which has a soft, medium to full body, a mild hopping, but a dash of roasty dryness in the finish. The brewery, in Pottsville, Pennsylvania, also has **Lord Chesterfield Ale**★→★★, English-sounding but American in style, with a flowery hop aroma and a golden colour. Both are actually bottom-fermented. There are several other products, all pleasant but none exceptional.

THE MIDWEST

Most Americans would identify their nation's greatest brewing region as the Midwest, but that is no longer true except in Germanic tradition. From its business base in Detroit, Stroh's is a growing brewery company, but it no longer produces beer in its home city. Chicago has, at least for the moment, no brewery; in St Louis, Anheuser-Busch prospers but Falstaff has long gone; worst of all is the plight of Milwaukee, supposedly the brewing capital of the United States. Of its three famous names, Miller is now in the hands not only of tobacconists but also of grocers (a situation not unique to American breweries). Pabst is a shadow of its traditions; and Schlitz no longer brews in the city it claims to have made famous. Despite the cluster of breweries in Wisconsin, no Midwestern state makes as much beer as California.

One giant set to restore some tradition is Heileman (of La Crosse, Wisconsin), which is building a boutique brewery (though it will no doubt avoid such a California-sounding description) in Milwaukee. The Milwaukee area is, indeed, gaining several boutiques. Meanwhile, several old-established small breweries have begun to give more emphasis to speciality beers. Some have done so under new ownership and new names, notably Hibernia (formerly Walters of Eau Claire, Wisconsin) and Rhömberg (formerly Pickett's Dubuque Star in Iowa).

Where to drink

The workaday cities of the Midwest are not the best places in the United States in which to find a fancy selection of beers, though Chicago is notable for the survival of German tastes. It is the only city where these vestiges of the past form a bridgehead to the new awareness of beer. The most famous beer tavern in Chicago, in The Loop, is The Berghoff (17 W Adams St), founded in 1898. The Berghoff has its own beer (brewed by Huber, and similar to Augsburger), an 80ft stand-up bar, and a lunch counter that becomes an oyster bar in the evening, and a restaurant. Also in Chicago, the Weinkeller, in Roosevelt Road, Berwyn, is a liquor store and tavern with a wide selection of beers. The German bar Resi's, on Irving Park Road, west of Lincoln, is appropriately chauvinistic. Milwaukee has two famous beer taverns: Karl Ratzsch's (320 E Mason) and Mader's (1037 N 3rd Ave).

Anheuser-Busch

The world's biggest brewing company, headquartered in St Louis, Missouri (the gateway city to Middle America), and producing between 60–70 million barrels a year, its capacity shared between ten of its own plants across the nation. Anheuser and Busch were related by marriage, and the company – formed in 1865 – is still controlled by the family. Oddly, the family name is appropriated to a low-price brand of beer, **Busch**★, this having originally been the local brew for St Louis. The Royal Court brewery of Bohemia inspired the name **Budweiser**★→★★ for the world's first consciously mass-marketed (ie national "premium") beer. A Bohemian brewing town also inspired America's first "super-premium" beer, **Michelob**★★, from the same company. The delicacy of these two beers was developed over the years from four principal influences: the use of a proportion of rice (traditionally 30 percent in Budweiser and 25 in the fuller-bodied Michelob) to provide lightness and "snappiness"; a complex hop blend of more than eight varieties (notably Oregon Fuggles), in at least three additions, to impart complexity of aroma and palate; a house yeast that confers a very subtle, apple-like fruitiness; and fining over beechwood chips, to ensure a clean character. Recently, the company has re-emphasized, under the Michelob brand, its **Classic Dark**★, but this has less character than it promises.

Ballantine

Once East Coast classics, these top-fermenting ales are now produced in Fort Wayne. The basic **Ballantine Ale**★★ is in the American golden style. The dry-hopped, wood-aged **Ballantine IPA** (India*n* Pale Ale?)★★★ has a copper-colour. Although it has lost some of its character over the years, it remains an interesting brew. It has a gravity of 1076 and 5.6 percent alcohol by weight (7 by volume). **Narragansett Porter**★★ is dry but rather thin.

Capital

New boutique at Middleton, Wisconsin. Producing lager beers with a German accent. Too early to rate.

Cold Spring

Very old small brewery in Cold Spring, Minnesota. "Super-premium" **Cold Spring Export**★★ is a little fuller-bodied than most beers of its type, with some Cascade aroma.

Geyer

The smallest of the old-established breweries in the United States and the one with the most antiquated plant. Geyer, in Frankenmuth, Michigan, is unusual in that its principal product is a copper-coloured "dark" beer. Despite its colour, **Frankenmuth Bavarian Dark**★★ has a light, dry palate.

Heileman

Often thought of as a regional brewery, perhaps because its flagship products have anonymous names. In part by acquisition of companies whose own leading brands have been sensibly retained, Heileman is now fourth among the six brewing groups that dominate the United States. Its base brewery is in La Crosse, Wisconsin, and it plans to open a boutique under the old Blatz name downstate in Milwaukee. Heileman makes a point of kräusening. This is, however, less evident in its rather limp **Old Style**★ than its spritzy **Special Export**★★. Subsidiaries include Blitz-Weinhard and Rainier.

Hibernia

A new company, established by an American Irishman (hence the name) at the old Walter brewery, in Eau Claire, Wisconsin. Hibernia's emphasis is on speciality beers of excellent quality. Its year-round speciality is a pale lager called **Eau Claire All Malt**★★→★★★, smooth and tasty but surprisingly dry. It does, however, also make a point of its seasonal brews. These include a bronze-coloured, hop-accented, top-fermenting **Winterbräu**★★; a fresh, soft, soothing **Dunkelweizen**★★★→★★★★ (a dark wheat beer, for summer), with hints of chocolate and vanilla before a refreshing acidity in the finish; and a copper-coloured, malt-accented but well-balanced **Oktoberfest**★★★. Some of the Walter's range are still produced.

Huber

Old-established brewery in Monroe, Wisconsin. Recently acquired by new owners. Known for its **Augsburger**★★, which is a Pilsener-style beer with a touch more hop bitterness than most of its competitors. It is a well-made example of an American beer. The same can be said for **Augsburger Dark**★★ and **Huber/Augsburger/Rhinelander Bock**★★→★★★ (4.6 by weight; 5.75 by volume).

Hudepohl

One of two old-established small breweries in Cincinnati. Its speciality is a malty super-premium lager called **Christian Moerlein**★★★, after an early brewer in the city. This is a *Reinheitsgebot* brew, with plenty of body and a full, smooth finish. The brewery made a malty, copper-coloured brew of considerable character to celebrate its Jubilee; perhaps this should be substituted for the rather thin **Hudepohl Oktoberfest**★→★★. The original brewery was known as Buckeye (see page 27) because it was on Buckeye Street (now East Clifton Avenue).

Kalamazoo

Home-brew boutique in Michigan. Too early to rate.

Leinenkugel

Old-established small brewery in Chippewa Falls, Wisconsin. Has won a cult following for its light, flowery premium beer, known simply as **Leinenkugel**★→★★ (by devotees, as "Leiny"). Also a pleasantly malty, tawny **Bock**★★ (5; 6.25).

Miller

Owned by Philip Morris, and with marketing skills to match. Known for **Miller Lite**★. Its new "Genuine Draft" version of **Miller Highlife**★ is lightly malty and dry. **Plank Road**★ also new (and taking its curious name from a brewery address), has a similar character but with a faintly more perfumy palate. Though lack of pasteurization is a bonus, the product itself is not of great interest.

Mill Stream

Boutique in the "Colonies" of the Amana sect, in Minnesota. Lager beers. Too early to rate.

Pabst

Long ago, **Pabst Blue Ribbon**★ was a classic premium beer. Perhaps its slightly savoury character, and hint of chewiness, has led some of today's Americans to see it as a smokestack beer. The image has not been dispelled by a new owner.

Point

Old-established small brewery in Stevens Point, Wisconsin. Unlike many of its contemporaries, this brewery has nurtured strong local support; its **Point Special**★★ also emerged as top beer in a tasting organized by the feisty Chicago columnist Mike Royko. It is a full-bodied, and well-balanced, beer. A well-made **Bock**★★ is also produced.

Rhömberg

Original name, now restored, of the former Pickett's brewery, in Dubuque, Iowa. Under new but still fairly local (Milwaukee) management, this brewery is now producing a beautifully balanced beer, with a pale copper colour, that is broadly in the Vienna style. It has the typical maltiness of aroma, and of palate (emerging more clearly with every sip) but it is never sweet, and has a definitely hoppy finish. Although this product is called simply **Rhömberg All Malt**★★ → ★★★, it is best identified by its blue label. While most breweries give a special designation to their dark beers, Rhömberg does so with its **Classic Pale**★★ (brown label), which has an aromatic nose, a full texture, and some sweetness in the finish.

Schell

Old-established small brewery that has enlivened its range with the lightly aromatic, dry, firm-bodied, all-malt, kräusened and well-matured **August Schell Pilsner**★★; a fruity, almost liqueur-ish **Weiss**★★★; and a nicely dark and rich but rather sweet **Ulmer Braun**★★. The brewery, in New Ulm, Minnesota, has a small deer park.

Schoenling

Smaller of the two old-established small breweries in Cincinnati. Schoenling specializes in the sweetish, mellow **Little King's Cream Ale**★★ → ★★★. A taste of Americana.

Sprecher

The first new brewery in Milwaukee since 1947. A boutique making pale and dark lagers. Too early to rate.

Stroh

A fast-spreading brand-name since this Detroit-based company went national by acquiring Schlitz and Schaefer. Stroh makes a point of using direct flame to fire its kettles. This traditionalist technique of "fire-brewing" pre-dates the more common use of steam-heating. The flames create hot spots in the kettle, and the swirling brew has the briefest of flirtations with caramelization, thus acquiring a tinge of sweetness to be found in **Stroh's**★ → ★★, which is otherwise unexceptional. The same character is more evident in the fuller-bodied super-premium **Signature**★★. The old Schlitz super-premium **Erlanger**★★ is a firm-bodied all-malt brew, but of no great distinction. The label describes it as a *Märzenbier* but it bears no relation to the German style.

Vienna

The Austrian capital has inspired many beers over the years, but the latest is an outstanding example. A talented young brewer in Milwaukee founded Vienna Brewing Inc, and also uses the city's name to identify his product. **Vienna All Malt Lager Beer**★★★ is an assertive but beautifully balanced brew. It is true to the Viennese style in its colour and maltiness, but also has a great deal of hoppy dryness. It is produced for its creator by a small brewery in Wisconsin.

THE WEST

The principal areas for the cultivation of both the wine-grape and the hop in the United States were originally the northeast and are now the northwest. The grape commands the valleys of northern California, and has spread into Oregon and Washington State. The hop has moved more decisively, gradually deserting northern California for the two states beyond. Oregon and Washington (especially the latter, in its Yakima Valley) are hop-growing areas of international standing.

Although the success of boutique wineries created a precedent for the new brewers, they do not like the soubriquet. They dislike it precisely because it may make them sound fashionable and therefore ephemeral. It does, though, explain them to the consumer: a boutique makes, on a small scale, a hand-crafted product of individuality and personality; it does not seek to compete with the mass-produced goods (however well-made and competitively priced) of the department store. The new generation prefer the term "micro-brewer". Perhaps that has a ring of Silicon Valley, but it could as well evoke the computer consoles of the giant breweries, nationally owned, in which the prosperous, populous, West is now also the leader.

Where to drink

The West is the land of outdoor drinking: at the mountain, the cookout, the beach, the boat. Nonetheless, it also has many restaurants and bars that boast very large selections of beers. Distinguished voices have praised, for example, the range at the Old Chicago pizza restaurants in Denver and nearby Rocky Mountain towns. (This is also the country of the Great American Beer Festival, by far the biggest sampling of US brews, on Memorial Day weekend, at the beginning of June.) Throughout the West, a deft hand is employed by Restaurants Unlimited, in its eclectic and stylish establishments: a good example, favoured by West Side folk in Los Angeles, is Cutters in Santa Monica.

San Francisco has a famously eccentric beer bar called Tommy's Joynt at Geary and Van Ness; a more restrained selection of beers at the pub in the St Francis Hotel; and a few vintage taverns and restaurants (like Schroeders on Front Street); probably the best retail selection of beers in the United States is at the gourmet food store in The

Cannery; and the KQED international beer festival is in early July. In nearby San Mateo, there is also a good selection at the Prince of Wales pub (16 E 25th Avenue).

The first brewpubs in the United States were established in northern California in 1983–84. One, appropriately, is in an old hop-growing area (now known for its wines). This is the Mendocino Brewing Company, in the town of Hopland, about 100 miles (160km) north of San Francisco on Highway 101, which heads on to the Redwood National Park and the Oregon state line. Tourists stop to buy champagne magnums filled with the fruity **Red Tail Ale★★**, or to sample the chocolatey **Black Hawk Stout★★**. East of San Francisco, toward the white wine country of the Livermore Valley, Buffalo Bill's (1082 B Street, Hayward) offers a fluffy yeasty lager that defies rating. The Redwood brewpub produces top-fermenting beers in Petaluma, close to the wine country of Sonoma Valley.

Portland, Oregon, already lauded for Henry Weinhard's Private Reserve, has become a very interesting brewing town with the addition of three boutiques (the closure of General Brewing, across the river, was no great loss to beer-lovers). Old-established sampling spots include Produce Row (204 SE Oak) and the Horse Brass Pub (4534 SE Belmont). Four pubs specializing in draught are run by beer-freak Mike McMenamin, whose Hillsdale (1505 SW Sunset Boulevard) produces its own flippant specialities.

Seattle, too, has become an American beer capital. Local boutique brews are heavily featured at J.C. Fox (2307 Eastlake Avenue E., near Lake Union), Murphy's (2110 N 45th Street, near the university) and Cooper's, with a startling array of local draughts (8065 Lake City Way). There are smaller, but well-chosen, beer selections at the Westin Hotel; the Mark Toby, a hangout for cafe society (90 Madison Street); Place Pigalle, with a bistro ambience (81 Pike Street); and another Cutters, with an imaginative and varied menu of light meals (Pike Place Market). Near the Kingdome sports stadium F.X. McRory is a tavern-style restaurant with a wide range of beers and Bourbons.

Seattle has many more attractions for the beer-lover, but nor should such an enthusiast leave the state without taking the drive – about 120 miles (193km), over mountains and desert – to the hop-growing town of Yakima, to visit Grant's brewery and pub.

Anchor Steam

The renown of this small San Francisco brewery has gradually spread across the nation, though its particular claim to fame is not always understood. The point is that its principal product, **Anchor Steam Beer★★★★**, is made by a process unique to the United States (and, for more than 60 years, to this brewery). Anchor Steam Beer is thus not only a brand but also the sole example of a style. It is also a wholly original way of brewing, and not a dilution of a European style (as are such minor categories as cream ales, malt liquors and light beers). Anchor Steam Beer is produced by bottom-fermentation but at high temperatures and in unusually wide, shallow vessels, in a method once typical of the Bay Area. This technique marries some of the roundness of a lager with the fruitiness of an ale. Irrespective of the technique, Anchor Steam Beer also has a firm body and plenty of hop character, both in the aroma and the finish.

The brewery also makes a number of top-fermenting styles: a rich, creamy **Anchor Porter★★**; a very aromatic and bitter, dry-hopped **Liberty Ale★★★**; a light, delicate interpretation of a **Wheat Beer★★ →★★★**; and an occasional **Old Foghorn Barley Wine★★★ →★★★★** (7 percent alcohol by weight; 8.75 by volume) that is surprisingly lively for its weight, with an intense interplay of malt, hop and yeasty fruitiness. From Thanksgiving each year, a Christmas Ale is available. Each "vintage" has a deliberately different character, and these brews are not to be missed. The Anchor brews are all produced to a very high quality, naturally carbonated, and only flash-pasteurized. Being an old-established brewery (though "rescued" in more recent times), and having grown beyond being tiny to being merely small (about 40,000 barrels a year), Anchor is not a boutique, though its example has inspired many.

Blitz-Weinhard

Best known for its super-premium **Henry Weinhard's Private Reserve★★ →★★★**. When this product was launched, in what were for American beer-drinkers the bland 1970s, the brewery took the revolutionary step of admitting that it employed hops. Even more daringly, the hops were permitted to announce themselves with a bouquet. Such extrovert behaviour is less noticeable in today's climate of boutiquery but, among super-premium Pilseners, Henry's is still one of the more aromatic, and in the light style that is characteristic of western examples. The same lightness of character underlies the dry **Henry Weinhard Dark★ →★★** and the gently fruity **Blue Boar Ale★ →★★**, described as "Ireland-style", a claim as valid as its grammar. Blitz-Weinhard, with its brewery in Portland, Oregon, is owned by Heileman.

Boulder

Barely a boutique, if that term could ever have been applied to a brewery that began in a goat-shed. Now, it is not so much a micro as a macro, with a purpose-built brewery that is architecturally reminiscent of a modern church. **Boulder Extra Pale Ale★★ →★★★** has a fruity aroma, a soft palate and an assertively hoppy finish. **Boulder Porter★★ →★★★** has a hint of licorice in the aroma, a firm body, a dry, roasty palate, and a rather quick finish. An intense **Boulder Stout★★★** is occasionally produced. The brewery is in Boulder, Colorado.

Bridgeport

Boutique in Portland, Oregon, producing the characterful **Bridgeport Ale★★ →★★★**, notably sweet, but with smoky undertones, a soft, full body and an attractive ruby colour. The brewery also has the well-balanced **Bridgeport Stout★★ →★★★**. Although the name Bridgeport is more familiar to local beer-lovers, the company is called Columbia River Brewing. It was founded by the Ponzi family, owners of a well-known Oregon winery. A pub is planned.

Coors

The biggest single brewery plant in the world, despite its remote Rocky Mountain location in Golden, Colorado. From the outside, it looks like an atomic power station; inside, it is one of the world's most beautiful, and remarkable, breweries. Its pristine, tiled brewing halls are lined with rows of traditional copper vessels – a tub of blossom hops by every kettle – capable of producing 25 million barrels a year. The traditionalism of the Coors family extends to a dislike of pasteurization, instead of which the beer is filtered to an unusual degree. From the seeding of its own barley to the production of its own packaging, Coors takes astonishing care over its product. The best of brewers guard their beers as though they were their children; perhaps Coors is extra-protective because its beer is so innocent. The basic **Coors★★** must surely be the lightest and cleanest premium beer in the world, with just a hint of maltiness to remind the drinker that this is not pure Rocky Mountain spring water. In recent years, Coors has experimented with a considerable number of further brands. The unlikely sounding **George Killian's★★** started out as a licensed re-creation of an Irish Red Ale, but its character has diminished. The brewery's latest product, for a separate company formed by Coors, Molson and Kaltenberg, is a beer called **Masters★**, aromatic, smooth, lightly fruity, and designed for a mass audience.

Excelsior

Boutique lager brewery in Santa Rosa, California. Too early to rate.

Grant's

Hop Country boutique producing some of the most distinctive brews in America. With a long background in both the hop-growing and brewing industries, Bert Grant makes assertive products to his own taste, and sells them in his own pub in Yakima and elsewhere throughout the northwest, where they enjoy a dedicated following. Grant spent the first two years of his life in Dundee, on the strength of which he called his first product **Scottish Ale★★★**. Despite its full body and malty firmness, this is less Scottish than American, with its Cascade hop accent in both its huge aroma and its emphatic bitterness (1050–55; around 4.5 by weight, 5.6 by volume). This was followed by an appropriately more attenuated **IPA★★★**, at just under 1050, with an immense hop character, especially in its long finish. Among a number of more idiosyncratic brews, Grant's has won special attention for its "Russian" **Imperial Stout★★★ → ★★★★** (at around 7, 8.5), in which the typical "Christmas pudding" palate is underpinned by a dash of honey and dried, again, by hefty hopping. Since their launch, some of these products seem to have diminished slightly in their richness, and it is to be hoped that standards can be maintained.

Hale's Ales

Well-made, unfiltered, English-style ales from a boutique brewery in the remote town of Colville, in eastern Washington. These products can sometimes be found in Idaho and Oregon, too. All of them have a good head, a malty start, a clean palate and a hoppy finish. Among the hops used are an Idaho-grown strain of the aroma Hallertau. Hale's **American Pale Ale★★ → ★★★** (1040; 3.9, 4.8) has a lush, straw colour; a malty dryness; and some light, hoppy acidity in the finish. The tasty **Special Bitter★★ → ★★★** (1045; 4.3, 5.4) has a deeper colour, a subtle amber; a warm aroma; a bigger body; and a depth of hop bitterness. The **Celebration Porter**★★ → ★★★ (1050) is lightly chewy, with a hint of wild cherry, and a roasty dryness in the finish.

Kemper

Boutique producing what it describes as a Munich style of lager, but with a distinctively fruity palate. The fruitiness is so emphatic as to hint at blueberries. **Thomas Kemper Lager** is so eccentric as to be hard to rate. The brewery is on Bainbridge Island, near Seattle.

Kessler

A most interesting and well-made range of bottom-fermenting beers from a boutique in an unlikely location: near Last Chance Gulch, in Helena, Montana, in the wilds of the Rockies. This new boutique revives the name of a long-defunct local brewery. Its beers in general have a complexity of hop aroma and flavour, but are malt accented. The regular, Pilsener-style **Kessler Beer**★★ is aromatic and soft, big-bodied, with a clean sweetness. **Kessler Wheat Beer** ★★ → ★★★ is broadly a *Dunkelweizen*, with a tawny-red colour, some iron-like tones in the nose, and a dry, malty palate; it needs a slice of lemon. The brewery's **Oktoberfest** ★★★, at 13 to 14 Plato, has a fine reddish colour and plenty of malt in the aroma and palate, with a gentle dryness of hop in the finish; an outstanding example of its style. A dry-hopped **Holiday Beer**★★★, for Christmas, has a medium amber colour; a rich, fruity aroma; a malty palate; and a lovely, lingering bitterness in the finish. A **Bock**★★★, marketed in March and April, has a subtle, tawny colour; a firm, malty body; and again plenty of hop, both in aroma and finish.

Küfnerbräu

The only bottle-conditioned, bottom-fermenting beer in the United States, from a brewery that is not so much boutique as back-room. After its bottle-conditioning, the beer is pasteurized. The result is too eccentric to rate. The brewery is in Monroe, not far from Seattle, and is run by an American German. With its yeasty fruitiness – almost cidery – **Küfnerbräu Gemütlichkeit Old Bavarian Style** could just have been made in a Franconian farmhouse.

Olympia

Once chic for their classically western lightness, **Olympia**★ beers were overtaken in the mass market by more sure-footed local rivals, and among more demanding drinkers by the billowing of boutiques. The brewery, in Tumwater, Olympia, is now owned by Pabst.

Palo Alto

English-style naturally conditioned draught ales, the first to be served in the United States by a hand-pumped beer "engine". Brewed not only for expatriates but also for cosmopolitan tastes, in Silicon Valley. The brewery is at Mountain View, near Palo Alto, on San Francisco Bay. It was founded by a computer entrepreneur, who sold out to his employees in 1985. Initial products were modelled on the ales of Brakspear, in England. Palo Alto uses malt extract from Edme, Hereford Fuggles and East Kent Goldings, with dry-hopping. Early brews were a 1035 **Drake's Golden**

Ale★★ → ★★★ and a 1042 **London Real Ale**★★ → ★★★, both with a hoppy, yeasty, fruitiness, and with hints of oak, though an interesting Bourbon-wood character no doubt came from an odd barrel.

Portland Brewing Co

New boutique and brewpub in Portland, Oregon, with its own ale, and licensed versions of the Grant's products. Too early to rate.

Pyramid

Definitively New Western ales from the small Hart boutique in Kalama – in Washington State but not far from Portland, Oregon. The combination of a clean, soft but dry fullness with an intense hop character – notably in aroma as well as bitterness – renders **Pyramid Pale Ale**★★★ such a good example. Various seasonal specialities have included a summer wheat beer. With the curious name **Wheaten Ale**★★ → ★★★, this combines a surprisingly full hop character with citric tones – almost grapefruit, though without the bitterness; acceptable, perhaps, in a wheat beer.

Rainier

Before the boutiques, Rainier was famous among brew-lovers throughout the West for its ale. Perhaps the north-west's new enthusiasm for the brewing of ales was en-couraged by the example of Rainier. Even among today's colourful contemporaries, the copper-coloured **Rainier Ale**★★★ in its full-strength version (around 5.8 by weight; 7.25 by volume, where state laws permit; popularly known, after its potency and label colour, as "The Green Death") remains a force with which to be reckoned. It is bottom-fermented but with its own yeast and at high temperatures. The boutique ales are more authentic, but Rainier has a far greater character than its mass-market counterparts in Canada, whence it originated. There is also a firm-bodied lager called **Rainier Beer**★. The brewery is in Seattle, with Mount Rainier as a backdrop. It is owned by Heileman.

Red Hook

Well-established boutique in Seattle, founded by people with backgrounds in the wine and coffee businesses. **Red Hook Ale**★★★, although less rampant than it once was, remains the fruitiest in America. Initially, its fruitiness (notably from banana esters) was a *cause célèbre* in Seattle, winning admirers and critics of equal ferocity. It would probably have been more widely appreciated in Belgium. **Black Hook Porter**★★ → ★★★ is very dry but soft and soothing. **Ballard Bitter**★★ → ★★★ is, contrary to its name, on the sweet side, lightly malty and nutty.

Saxon

Home-brewer gone legal, in the Sierra Nevada foothills at Chico, California. Too early to rate.

Sierra Nevada

Classic boutique. Established in the early days of the movement, it has grown quickly, not only in size but also in the esteem of knowledgeable beer-lovers far beyond its little home-town of Chico (in northern California, close to the

Sierra Nevada range). The brewery's **Pale Ale**★★★ has both the floweriness of Cascade hops and the citric fruitiness of the yeast in its bouquet, and is beautifully balanced, with a clean, fresh character. Its **Porter**★★★ is among the best brewed anywhere; firmly dry, but with a gently coffee-ish finish. Its **Stout**★★★ is well-balanced and full of flavour. Its **Big Foot Barley Wine**★★★ → ★★★★, with a huge hoppiness in its earthy aroma and chewy palate, is the strongest beer in the United States (1095; 24.5 Plato; 8.48 percent alcohol by weight; 10.6 by volume).

Smith and Riley

"Honest beer", its creators call it. **Smith and Riley**★ → ★★ is a firm-bodied, Pilsener-style beer, with some hop flavour in the finish. Devised by a couple of beer-lovers in Vancouver (the US town in Washington State, not the one nearby in Canada). Produced for them by a commercial brewery.

Snake River

A hop-farming family owns this small boutique, in Caldwell, west of Boise, Idaho. A hop field surrounds the brewery, and the family also grow their own malting barley. Surprisingly, there is only a light – albeit very fresh – hop character in **Snake River Premium Lager**★ → ★★, which is on the sweet side. There is also an emphatically sweet and malty **Amber Lager**★★. Yet more surprisingly for a boutique, and especially one that grows its own barley, this brewery uses a proportion of adjunct: rice in this case.

Stanislaus

The *Altbier* launched in 1984 by Stanislaus was the first to be produced in the United States since at least the time of Prohibition. This boutique takes its name from its location east of San Francisco, in Stanislaus County, at Modesto, a major winery town of the Central Valley of California. In launching a style unfamiliar to the United States, "St Stan's" further complicated matters by having two versions, **Amber**★★★ and **Dark**★★★. Although these are more than creditable, most *Altbier* is made in just one colour somewhere between the two. Perhaps St Stan could not decide whether to be inspired, among the Düsseldorf originals, by Schumacher or Zum Uerige.

Thousand Oaks

A home brewery gone commercial, in Berkeley, California. A wide range of rather yeasty products, somewhat eccentric, but with a local following.

Widmer

Second *Altbier* brewery in the US, in 1985. Brewer Kurt Widmer, a second-generation American based in Portland, Oregon, has family connections in Düsseldorf, and was freely advised by a (perhaps incredulous) Zum Uerige. His **Widmer Alt**★★★ is brewed from four malts, with step infusion, and hopped twice, with American-grown Perle and Tettnang blossoms. It is a fine example of the style, with a dense head; a deep, burnished-copper colour; both malt and hops in the nose; and a very hoppy palate. Widmer has also turned its attention to other German-style specialities, including a very hoppy **Weizenbier**★★ → ★★★.

THE SOUTH

Social geography is not always what might be expected of it. In the United States the drinker had best go to San Francisco or Seattle, perhaps Chicago or New York, to find a really good selection of Kentucky whiskeys. Gastronomic interest in drink has yet to make much impression on the South, certainly in relation to whiskey – its native tradition – and scarcely more in respect of beer.

Serious interest in beer in the United States began in the West, took three or four years to vault to the East, and is still in its early stages in Middle America. As for the South, some of the more cosmopolitan cities are beginning to take an interest, but even a bustling place like Atlanta has little to offer. In some states, notably Alabama and the Carolinas, the number of dry counties means that the drinker is grateful for whatever can be provided.

Where to drink

The one gastronomically famous city of the South, New Orleans, has probably the best-known spot for devotees of beer: Cooter Brown's (509 S Carrollton). New Orleans also has its own independent brewery, Dixie, which shows signs of revival under a new ownership.

Gastronomically inclined visitors to the "Third Coast" might also discover something to enjoy in Houston – and at 2425 Alabama they will find the Ale House. One of the best retail selections of beer in the South is in Dallas, at the Bluebonnet grocery store (2106 Lower Greenville Avenue). Dallas also has its own boutique, with the unlikely (but justifiable) name of Reinheitsgebot Brewing. Even more incongruously, the state capital of Texas – Austin – has a Belgian speciality beer bar, called Gambrinus, in its main street. There are also good selections of beer in several of the bars along Austin's nightlife strip of 6th Street, notably Maggie Mae's.

The Arkansas Brewing Company (originally Riley Lyon), in Little Rock, is also a boutique, if such an effete term may be used there. Boutiques are planned elsewhere in the south, and no doubt selections of beers are growing in several cities, but too often the message is: "Coldest beer in town". Or: "Last beer before dry county". In either case, what is on offer is probably a popsicle made from Schlitz.

Arkansas Brewing Co

This boutique was originally called Riley-Lyon, after its founders. The first product was **Riley's Red Lion**★★★, a well-made, copper-coloured pale ale, with a fresh, fruity acidity in the finish. This proved too challenging for some local palates, and emphasis has subsequently been given to the more orthodox **White Tail Lager**★ ➔★★, which is only lightly hopped, quite full in body, with a rather quick finish.

Dixie

The beer called simply **Dixie**★ is very light and sweetish. However southern, the name hardly captures the spirit of New Orleans, Louisiana, where the brewery resides. Perhaps a Cajun beer will emerge in due course.

When this old-established brewery was rescued by a distributor called Coy, a "super-premium" product was added.

This is called **Coy International Private Reserve**★→★★, and is markedly full in body, with slightly more colour and a hint of hop.

Duncan

This former supermarket brewery in Auburndale, Florida, has recently been producing an all-malt, bronze lager, **Hatuey**★★, on behalf of Bacardi, for the Hispanic market.

Lone Star

Chauvinistic Texans swear by the crisp, dry **Lone Star** ★→★★. It is a pleasant enough beer, but in no way exceptional. The brewery, in San Antonio, is owned by Heileman.

Pearl

Also in San Antonio, this brewery is owned by the same group as Pabst. **Pearl**★ is a light, sweetish beer.

Reinheitsgebot Brewing Co

The name is an allusion to the German Beer Purity Law, the inspiration and credo of this boutique, which is in the community of Plano, in Collin County, on the edge of Dallas. Its principal product is **Collin County Pure Gold**★★★, a full-bodied, all-malt, Pilsener-style beer, with a hearty, dry-hopped, bouquet. More products are planned.

Shiner

A "Spanish mission" building in a tiny town in the middle of nowhere, about 70 miles (112km) south of Austin, and slightly farther from San Antonio. It is a wonderfully romantic brewery, serving a scatter of old and seemingly incongruous Bohemian and Bavarian settlements, but its principal product, **Shiner Premium**★, is an undistinguished product. **Shiner Bock**★→★★ has something of a following among young drinkers in Austin. This is a dark beer, but sadly a *Bock* is not allowed to be of high strength under Texas law.

THE CARIBBEAN

Emigrants from the Caribbean have helped spread the popularity of several beers from the region. The best-known internationally is **Red Stripe**★, a light-tasting, soft-bodied lager from Jamaica. Other examples include the maltier and fruitier **Banks Lager**★, from Barbados; and the malty, but drier, **Carib Lager**★→★★, from Trinidad. Gravities are typically in the classical Pilsener range of 11.5–12 Plato (1046–48); units of bitterness low (15–19); and lagering times short (two weeks is common).

Several Caribbean breweries also have sweet or medium-dry stouts, often bottom-fermented, and usually at "tropical" gravities: in the range of 15–20 Plato (1060–1080), with alcohol contents of between 4.5 and 6 percent by weight; 5.75–7.5 by volume.

Colonists introduced beer-brewing to the Caribbean, and many European links remain, though there are also companies under local control. At least ten islands currently have their own breweries (sometimes more than one), as do most countries on the Central American mainland.

LATIN AMERICA

From Mexico through Central and South America, the Latin countries of the New World all have breweries, and most are excitably proud of their beers: from **Cerveza Panama★** (dry, spritzy, quenching) to **Colombian Gold★→★★** (which tastes noticeably of hops, rather than their cousin cannabis), the beer trail stretches to Chile (where drinkers order beer by the square metre, to fill a table) and Brazil (the biggest brewing nation in Latin America, boasting even the odd top-fermenting beer, like **Brahma Porter★★★**, at 17.5 Plato; 1070; 6.7; 8.6).

Mexico is also a major brewing nation in volume, and the biggest exporter from Latin America, with its industry in the hands of three large companies: Cuauhtemoc and Moctezuma are separate enterprises under one holding company; Modelo is family-owned. These three companies own 17 breweries, subject to current rationalization. Although all of the beers are bottom-fermenting, they are more varied, and interesting, than is commonly appreciated.

Cuauhtemoc

Second-largest of the Mexican brewing companies. Also owns Cruz Blanca. The products of Cuauhtemoc are lightened by a high proportion of corn, and tend to have a dry, slightly tannic, finish. A typically Mexican range includes a *bière ordinaire*, perilously bottled in clear glass, **Chihuahua★**; a dry, crisp quencher, **Tecate★**, customarily served with a pinch of salt and a slice of lime or lemon; a mainstream beer, **Carta Blanca★** (which in the US market has a notably smooth **Dark★★** version); a pleasantly hoppy, Pilsener-type, **Bohemia★→★★**, which has a higher than normal gravity (13; 1052; 4.2; 5.4); Vienna-type beer, **Indio Oscura★**, rather thin and dry for the style; and a dark, strong Christmas beer, **Commemorativa★★** (14.3; 1057; 4.3; 5.6). There is also a low-cal beer, **Brisa★**.

Moctezuma

Biggest exporter, but smallest in the Mexican market. Uses a lower proportion of adjuncts and makes a point that they include rice. Its beers tend to be relatively smooth, with a spritzy finish: kräusening is another point of policy. **Sol★** is its clear-glass beer; a very dry, light brew called **Hussong's★** is a newcomer to the range; **Superior★→★★** is a lightly fragrant, spritzy, Pilsener-type (11.5; 1046; 3.6; 4.5). Then comes the rather confusing Equis range. **Tres Equis★→★★** is a marginally fuller Pilsener-type. **Dos Equis Lager Especial ★→★★** is fractionally fuller again (12; 1048; 3.7; 4.6). The best-known version, simply called **Dos Equis★★★**, is amber-red in colour, and is the closest example among such Mexican beers to the traditional Vienna style. It, too, has a gravity of 12 Plato, and its palate achieves a teasing balance of malt and hop. **Tres Equis Oscura★★** is slightly darker in colour, and fuller-bodied (with a lovely malty finish) despite being brewed from a slightly lower gravity. The dark brown **Noche Buena**★★★ Christmas Beer (15; 1060; 4.2; 5.4) is very full-bodied, with both malt and hop in its long finish.

Modelo

Biggest of the Mexican brewing companies, also owning Yucatan. Its most noteworthy product is the **Negra Modelo**★★, on the dark side for a Vienna-style beer, creamy in body, with a hint of chocolate (just the thing with chicken molé). The Yucatan brands include a similar beer, the tasty, hoppier, **Negra Leon**★★. The group's other products embrace the clear-glass **Corona**★, dry, firm and fruity; and the carbonic **Victoria**★, a favourite with the working man in Mexico. Some kräusening is done.

ASIA

When the United States sent Commodore Perry to "open up" Japan in 1853, the idea of beer-brewing was seeded, and soon grew. Outside the United States, the biggest brewing company in a domestic market is Kirin, of Japan. The basic **Kirin Lager Beer**★→★★ has the fullest body among the Japanese Pilseners, with Hallertau and Saaz hops in both aroma and flavour. Among several excellent specialities, **Kirin Stout**★★★ (18 Plato; 1072; 6.4; 8) is especially notable. It is bottom-fermenting, but full of "burnt treacle toffee" flavour.

Sapporo Black Beer★★★ represents a Japanese speciality (which seems originally to have been based on the Kulmbach beers). This dry, dark lager, with licorice tones, can best be tasted in the beer garden in the Victorian part of the brewery in Sapporo. This company also has an unpasteurized (micro-filtered), all-malt premium Pilsener called **Yebisu**★★, very fruity, with some hop bitterness in the finish. Asahi's beers tend to be dry and fruity, but with a weak finish. Suntory produces unpasteurized beers that are notably clean and mild, though dry. This company's speciality is the all-malt **Suntory Märzenbier**★★★, slightly paler than those of Bavaria, with a drier, firmer palate and a wonderfully fresh Saaz hoppiness in both its bouquet and finish.

When Germany enjoyed a colonial "concession" in Shantung, China, a brewery was established in the resort town of Tsingtao. This is now one of China's major exporters, and **Tsingtao Beer**★→★★, a hoppy Pilsener, is a popular accompaniment to its national cuisine in New York and San Francisco. The very sweet **Tsingtao Porter**★ is harder to find in the West.

Brews from other towns, such as **Tientan★**, a smooth, malty Pilsener from Beijing, are exported in a small way, but China's economic growth means that demand for beer cannot be met, despite every major town already having at least one brewery (several have two). More are planned, with technical help from Western and Japanese brewers, and from at least one British boutique-owner.

German technical help was used in 1934 to set up the Boon Rawd Brewery, which produces the outstandingly hoppy **Singha Lager★★★** (13.8 Plato; 1055; 4.8; 6; and a hearty 40 units of bitterness) in Thailand. The local rival **Amarit★→★★** is milder.

While the Singha is a mythical creature resembling a lion, Tiger Beer is a legend in its own lunchtime, perhaps because it entered literature through the pen of Anthony Burgess. **Tiger Lager Beer★→★★** is a hoppier cousin to Heineken. The same brewery has in its range the creamy, roasty, medium-dry **ABC Extra Stout★★→★★★** (18.2; 1073; 6.5; 8.1). These products are made in Singapore and Malaysia.

India had 14 breweries in Colonial days, four by Independence, and now has no fewer than 32. United Breweries, of Bangalore, is active in export markets with its dry, well-balanced **Kingfisher★** lager and a slightly hoppier, and smoother, premium Pilsener variously called **Jubilee** and **Flying Horse★→★★**. The company also makes a roasty, bottom-fermenting **London Stout★★** (1046). In Sri Lanka, McCallum makes an all-malt **Three Coins Pilsener★★** and a smooth, chocolatey, bottom-fermenting **Sando Stout★★→★★★** (15; 1060). The rival Ceylon Breweries has the fruitier, top-fermenting (in wood) **Lion Stout ★★★**, also all-malt, at a similar gravity, producing 5 percent alcohol by weight; 6.3 by volume. Astonishingly, Ceylon Breweries' lager and stout are available, unpasteurized, from wooden casks, drawn by hand-pump, at The Beer Shop, in the brewery's home town of Nuwara Eliya, and at U.K.D. Silva, in the holy city of Kandy.

Except in fundamentalist Muslim countries, almost every corner of Asia has breweries. In a reversal of Colonial roles, Spain's San Miguel breweries have their parent company in The Philippines. In addition to the light, smooth, dry **San Miguel★→★★**, a pale Pilsener, the Filipinos also enjoy **Gold Eagle★→★★**, lower in gravity but fuller in colour, and the stronger (14; 1056; 5.5; 6.8) **Red Horse★★**, soft-bodied, with some fruity notes. **San Miguel Dark Beer★★** also has an above-average gravity (13.5; 1054; 4.1; 5.2) and a good toasted-malt character. The new rival Asia Brewery is notable for its all-malt **Max ★→★★** (11.2; 1045; 4.5; 5.6).

AUSTRALASIA

For the lover of distinctive beers, the establishment of boutique breweries in Western Australia (Anchor and Matilda Bay) and on the South Island of New Zealand (Mac's) during the early 1980s represented a tiny hope of better things to come. So did the glimmerings of a greater appreciation for Cooper's ales and stouts, once widely regarded with puzzlement even in their native South Australia.

The provincialism of the Australian beer-drinker has long rung as hollow as an empty schooner. Even in the days when breweries like Carlton (in Victoria) emphasized the scope of their range, the differences between most of the beers was not great. Nor were there huge distinctions between the beers of one state and another, contrary to the chauvinistic insistence of their respective drinkers.

Such sensibilities were flouted when Carlton began to promote one of its products, Foster's, as a national brand, on the way acquiring Tooth's Brewery (of New South Wales), the two companies then being subsumed into the agricultural group Elders IXL, which then turned its attention to international markets. While this grouping was soon claiming almost 50 percent of the Australian market, a further 40 percent was coalescing into a rival power bloc, embracing Swan (of Western Australia), Castlemaine (of Queensland) and Toohey's (of New South Wales).

All of these mergers took place between 1983 and 1985. These were breathless years in the Australian brewing industry, but the excitement dwelt little on its heritage, or the individuality of any products involved (such as the dark ale **Toohey's Old★★★** or the characterful **Sheaf Stout★★★**). Beer had become a commodity for the financial pages, with attention focused on the swashbuckling entrepreneurs: for Elders, chairman and chief executive John Elliott; for the rival group, Alan Bond, the British-born Australian who was at the same time helping his country seize the America's Cup.

Meanwhile, in New Zealand, Lion swallowed Leopard. This feline act left the country with only two major brewing companies, the other being Dominion.

If there is a national character to the brews of either country, it might be argued that Australia's lagers have traditionally been quite full-bodied, firm and on the sweet side (sometimes using cane sugar as an adjunct); New Zealand has some extremely sweet beers (often copper in colour, an inherited memory of British ales, though bottom-fermenting), as well as a number of Pilseners in a more international style.

Anchor

First revivalist pub brewery in Australia, at the "Sail and Anchor" (locally known by its previous name "The Freemason"; ☎335 8433), in Fremantle. In a beautifully restored 1850s pub, hand-pumps are used to serve a selection of very traditional, top-fermenting ales. Early examples have included a sweetish pale **Mild**★★★ (1035) similar to those found in the West Midlands of England; a Burton-style, cask-conditioned **Traditional Bitter**★★★ (1050), also available in chilled draught form as "Best", bottle-conditioned as "Anchor Real Ale" and in a more carbonated variation as "Steam Beer"; a dark, strong ale called **Dogbolter**★★★ (1080); and a sweet **Milk Stout**★★★ (1065). All merit attention, not least for their rarity. The same company's Matilda Bay boutique specializes in bottom-fermentation. Initial products have all been all-malt (for which praise is deserved) lagers of 1055. They include a fairly hoppy, "Czech-style" **Pilsener**★★ ➜★★★; a slightly milder, "Danish-style" **Light**★★ (the name refers to colour rather than body) and a "Bavarian-style" **Dark**★★ ➜★★★.

Carlton

The basic **Carlton Draught**★ ➜★★ is a firm-bodied lager with a medium bitterness and full, golden colour. **Melbourne Bitter**★ ➜★★ is a little drier; **Victoria Bitter**★ lighter in flavour, darker in colour; **Foster's**★ full-bodied and sweetish.

Cascade

Tasmanian brewery. Its **Cascade Draught**★ ➜★★ has a slightly lower gravity and alcohol content (10.2; 1041; 3.7; 4.6), but a fuller colour and more flavour, than its **Special Lager**★ ➜★★ (10.8; 1043; 3.8; 4.8). While these typically Australian products have bitterness units in the range of 20, a bottom-fermenting **Sparkling Pale Ale**★★ (11.7; 1047; 4.1; 5.2) has 25 B.U. **Cascade Export Stout**★ (15; 1060; 4.9; 6.1) has 29 B.U. Cascade, in Hobart, and Boag's, of Launceston, are under the same ownership. Boag's Export Stout is marginally lower in gravity and alcohol content, and less bitter, but fuller in colour. Boag's range includes a fairly full-bodied and dry **Lager**★★ (11.5; 1046; 4.3; 5.4).

Castlemaine

Known for its "Fourex" probably since the days when the mark XXXX was branded on to wooden barrels to identify a premium product. **Castlemaine XXXX**★★ is the most characterful of Australia's mass-market lagers, firm-bodied, sweetish but with a definite hop flavour. Blossoms are used. **Gold Lager**★★ is slightly higher in gravity, drier, clean and smooth. The company still makes its full-bodied, tangy **Carbine Stout**★★ ➜★★★ (13–14; 1055; 4.03; 5.10).

Cooper

Classic brewery that must seem wildly incongruous in Australia. Cooper's is the only established Australian brewery to retain top-fermenting ales and stouts as its principle products. As if that were not enough to distinguish it, Cooper's also uses wooden tuns for maturation. Better still, it bottle-conditions. It is hard to say whether this devotion to tradition resulted originally from principle or sleepiness. Now that Cooper's products are beginning to be appreciated, it is to be hoped that tradition is not diluted. The characteristically cloudy, "real" **Ale★★★ → ★★★★** (ironically, labelled in some markets as "sparkling") is already paler than it once was. It is nonetheless a characterful brew (with an alcohol content of 4.6; 5.75), full of fruitiness and hop bitterness. Likewise the earthy, dryish **Extra Stout ★★★★** (5.4; 6.8).

Dominion

The dubious achievement of having developed the continuous-fermentation method is accorded to this New Zealand brewing company. **Dominion Bitter★** is its main product.

Leopard

Despite its having been taken over by Lion, this New Zealand company still operates its Hastings brewery, producing **Leopard DeLuxe★ → ★★**, a premium Pilsener using yeast from Heineken (former part-owners). It is a lightly fruity beer with some hop character.

Lion

Formerly known as New Zealand Breweries. Its **Lion Red★ → ★★** has a pale copper colour, a gravity of 9 Plato (1036; 2.95; 3.7), and is malty, sweet and bottom-fermenting. A pale lager called **Rheineck★** is marginally stronger (9.8; 1039; 3.05; 3.85), again very sweet, but with some fruitiness. **Steinlager★★** is a mildly dry premium Pilsener produced at slightly different gravities depending upon the market.

Mac's

Boutique brewery in New Zealand, near Nelson, at Stoke. Founder Terry McCashin buys hops and barley grown in the locality, and has his own maltings. His products, though, suggest caution either on his part or that of the consumer. **Mac's Real Ale★★** is actually produced with a lager yeast and, in its bottled form, pasteurized. It is intended to have ale characteristics but is really a malty, full-flavoured, bronze lager. **Black Mac★★** is a dark (deeply copper-coloured) lager. **Mac's Gold★★ → ★★★** is a pale lager, well-hopped and smooth. **Southop★ → ★★** is a sweet lager in the style typical of New Zealand.

South Australian

Adelaide brewery whose products include the dryish **West End Draught★ → ★★** (9.9; 1040; 3.6; 4.5); the perfumy, but maltier, **Southwark Premium★ → ★★** (12; 1048; 4.4; 5.5); and the sweetish **Old Southwark Stout★★ → ★★★** (16.3; 1065; 5.9; 7.4). An export lager recalling the old **Broken Hill★ → ★★** brewery has earthy hoppiness in the nose and a spritzy body.

South Pacific

The well-made **South Pacific Export Lager★ → ★★** is a lightly fruity and dry, refreshing beer with a family resemblance to its parent Heineken. The brewery is in Papua New Guinea.

Swan

West Australian giant, producing beers that are, by national standards, dryish and fairly light-bodied. Recently successful with a low-alcohol **Swan Special Light★**.

AFRICA

The continent of Africa might claim to have had some of the first brewers, as the ancient Egyptians produced beer in at least 3000BC. These beers were brewed from barley that was "malted" by a process of being germinated and then baked into a bread-like condition. This was then fermented, and must have produced something like the *kvass* that is still widely consumed in Russia. The unfiltered beer may have resembled the turbid, porridge-like traditional brews that are still made in Africa, from millet, cassava flour, plantains, or whatever is locally available.

However, all except the most fundamentalist Muslim countries of Africa have their own breweries producing modern beers. Most of these beers are of the Pilsener type, though the odd Bock can occasionally be found – and there are one or two ales (in South Africa) and stouts (in several countries, notably Nigeria). The stouts are usually dry, and sometimes of considerable strength (the tropical version of Guinness, at more than 18 Plato and 1070; around 8 percent alcohol by volume is typical).

Household names in most western European nations have established breweries in Africa, or contracted or licensed their products to be made there. Or they have acted as consultants or partners to local breweries, often with participation from national governments. In all, there are about 175 breweries in Africa, in at least 45 countries. By far the most heavily-breweried country is Nigeria, with more than 50, most of them built in the last two decades. Zaire and South Africa are also significant brewing nations in terms of volume. However, some very well-made beers are brewed in very small countries, like Gambia, Togo and the Seychelles.

Africa's first boutique brewery went into operation in 1984, in Knysna, Cape Province. The brewery began with an all-malt draught lager, then began to experiment with seasonal ales and stouts, cask-conditioned. Knysna is on the south coast, between Cape Town and Port Elizabeth. The owner of this remarkable enterprise, Lex Mitchell, formerly worked for South African Breweries, who otherwise enjoy a monopoly.

Having imported a taste for European beer, Africa is now flexing its muscles in export markets. Two early contenders are the slightly woody-tasting Ngoma Castel, from Kinshasa, and the smooth, sweetish Mamba, from Ivory Coast. Both are full-bodied and robust – lusty, emergent beers.